# Laidlaw
# English

# Reviewer•Consultants

**Sherryl Daniels Broyles**
Specialist, Secondary Reading
Los Angeles Unified School District
Los Angeles, California

**Veronica R. Garcia**
Language Arts Coordinator
Rudder Middle School
Northside Independent School District
San Antonio, Texas

**Gerald R. Hartzell**
Reading Consultant
Allentown School District
Allentown, Pennsylvania

**Adrian W. McClaren**
Supervisor of English
Memphis City Schools
Memphis, Tennessee

**Kevin C. McHugh**
Chairperson, English Department
Finneytown Junior and Senior High School
Cincinnati, Ohio

**Marlene V. Schroeder**
Curriculum Coordinator
North Marion Middle School
Ocala, Florida

**JoAnn B. Smith**
Teacher
Mill Street School
Naperville, Illinois

**Connie Vilott**
Principal
Center Elementary School
Kansas City, Missouri

# Laidlaw
# English

**Laidlaw Brothers•Publishers**

**River Forest, Illinois**

**Sacramento, California • Chamblee, Georgia
Dallas, Texas**

# Acknowledgments

Developed by Intentional Educations, Inc., under the direction of Laidlaw Brothers, Publishers.

**Laidlaw Editorial Staff**
Editorial Manager: Raymond B. Walters/Senior Editor: Ursula Szwast/Editor: JoAnn S. Martin/Manager of Production: Kathleen Kasper/Production Editors: Mary Greeley, Brenda B. Tropinski/Manager, Art and Design: Gloria J. Muczynski

Cover Design: Miller & Seper Inc.

**Illustrators**

Robert J. Blake, pages 6, 7, 14–15, 31, 38–39, 45, 56, 58, 59, 63, 69, 77, 89, 99, 106–107, 111, 123, 126–127, 132, 136, 140, 141, 143, 149, 159, 176, 179, 193, 207, 219, 228, 230–231, 244, 252–253, 254–255, 265, 270, 278–279, 288, 297, 309, 325, 335, 343, 359.
Robert Brooks, pages xvi–1, 48–49, 126–127, 182–183, 234–235, 282–283, 312–313.
Daniel Clifford, pages 150–151, 169, 171, 247, 248, 250–251, 260, 263, 268, 273, 274–275, 276, 292, 350–351, 354–355.
Brian Cody, pages 8, 9, 12, 37, 40, 43, 61, 67, 84, 85, 86, 102, 104, 121, 154, 166, 210, 216, 317, 332, 348, 352–353.
Ruth Ferrara, pages 236–237, 238.
Ruth J. Flanigan, pages 4 (top and bottom), 18–19, 20–21, 26, 53, 72, 80, 81, 82, 96–97, 108, 118–119, 130, 147, 152, 153, 156, 175, 224–225, 226, 241, 286, 294–295, 304, 318, 328.
Penny Jackim, page 5.
Robert Spellman, pages 22–23, 24, 34–35, 70, 75, 92, 103, 116, 135, 138–139, 167, 172, 188–189, 190–191, 200, 215, 242, 290–291, 300, 331.

Clarissa P. Erving, pages 17, 101.
Jim Roberts, pages 28, 95, 198, 199.
David Berry, page 33.
Travel Bureau, Michigan Department of Commerce, pages 51, 161.
Katie Clay, pages 52, 65, 337.
Gail Oskin, page 54.
Chris Kehoe, pages 66, 299.
Kathy Madden, page 67.
J. Gaffney, page 79.
James Daly, pages 91, 186 (right), 222, 336, 346 (right).
Richard Howard, page 94.
J. Austin Freeman, page 113.
Association of American Railroads, page 114.
Boy Scouts of America, page 129.
Peter Dublin, page 131 (top).
Rosemary Fortin, page 131 (bottom).
Sara Dowse, page 145.
Arden Danekas, page 146.
UPI/Bettman Archives, page 163.
Mark Tetrault, page 185.
Dwight R. Kuhn, page 186 (left), 186 (middle right), 202.
Audrey W. Jones, page 186 (middle left).
U.S. Parachute Association, page 195.
C.V. Rice, pages 196, 239.

**Photographers**

Cover photograph, Peter Fronk/Click/Chicago
David Lancaster, pages 3, 10.
Joseph Van Wormer/Bruce Coleman, Inc., page 13.

ISBN 0-8445-2805-6
Copyright © 1987 by Laidlaw Brothers, Publishers

Ralph Morang, page 205.
Paula Stack, page 209, 285.
Sheila Taft, page 212.
ITT Corporation, page 221.
Julie O'Neil, page 257.
Media Action, page 267.
National Park Service, page 315.
Kathy Madden/Arthur Ingalls, page 320.
Kansas Department of Economic Development, page 322.
Jorge Garcia Crasto, page 327.
Bill Gillette/EPA-Documerica, page 345.
Margorie Siegel, page 346 (left and middle).
Wide World Photos, page 357.

## Acknowledgments

"A-Ha!" from ALL TOGETHER by Dorothy Aldis. Copyright 1952 by Dorothy Aldis; renewed 1980 by Roy E. Porter. Reprinted by permission of G.P. Putnam's Sons.
"A Horse Is a Horse" from I WOULD LIKE TO BE A PONY by Dorothy W. Baruch. Copyright © 1959 by Harper Brothers. Reprinted by permission of Bertha Klausner International Literary Agency, Inc.
"Abraham Lincoln 1809–1865" by Rosemary and Stephen Vincent Benét. From A BOOK OF AMERICANS by Stephen Vincent and Rosemary Benét. Copyright 1933 by Rosemary and Stephen Vincent Benét. Copyright renewed © 1961 by Rosemary and Stephen Vincent Benét. Reprinted by permission of Brandt & Brandt Literary Agents, Inc.
Excerpt from THE DOOR IN THE WALL by Marguerite De Angeli. Copyright 1949 by Marguerite De Angeli. Reprinted by permission of Doubleday & Company, Inc.
"The Snowflake" by Walter de la Mare. Reprinted by permission of the Literary Trustees of Walter de la Mare and the Society of Authors as their representative.
"City Rain" from TAXIS AND TOADSTOOLS by Rachel Field. Copyright 1926 by Doubleday & Company, Inc. Reprinted by permission of the publisher.
"Mice" from FIFTY-ONE NEW NURSERY RHYMES by Rose Fyleman. Copyright 1931, 1932 by Doubleday & Company, Inc. Reprinted by permission of the publisher.
"Raccoon" from A LITTLE BOOK OF LITTLE BEASTS by Mary Ann Hoberman. Copyright © 1973 by Simon & Schuster, Inc. Reprinted by permission of Russell & Volkening, Inc., as agents for the author.
"Brontosaurus" from WRITE IT RIGHT by Gail Kredenser. Copyright © 1968 by Sterling Publishing Co., Inc. Reprinted by permission of Sterling Publishing Co., Inc., Two Park Avenue, New York, NY 10016.

"The Horses" from UP COUNTRY by Maxine Kumin. Copyright © 1972 by Maxine Kumin. Reprinted by permission of Curtis Brown, Ltd., Ten Astor Place, New York, NY 10003.
Excerpt from A WRINKLE IN TIME by Madeleine L'Engle. Copyright © 1962 by Madeleine L'Engle Franklin. Reprinted by permission of Farrar, Straus and Giroux, Inc.
"Calendar" from WIDE AWAKE AND OTHER POEMS by Myra Cohn Livingston. Copyright © 1959 by Myra Cohn Livingston. Reprinted by permission of Marian Reiner for the author.
"How to Eat a Poem" from IT DOESN'T ALWAYS HAVE TO RHYME by Eve Merriam. Copyright © 1964 by Eve Merriam. Reprinted by permission of the author. All rights reserved.
"Afternoon on a Hill" by Edna St. Vincent Millay. From COLLECTED POEMS, Harper & Row. Copyright © 1917, 1945 by Edna St. Vincent Millay. Reprinted by permission.
Excerpt from THE YOSEMITE by John Muir. Copyright 1912 by The Century Co., renewed 1940 by Wanda Muir Hanna. A Hawthorn book. Reprinted by permission of E.P. Dutton, Inc.
"Oh Yeah" by Richard Power.
"Loneliness" by Harlane Radler. Copyright © 1985 by Harlane Radler.
Excerpts from NATE THE GREAT AND THE MISSING KEY by Marjorie Weinman Sharmat. Text copyright © 1981 by Marjorie Weinman Sharmat. Illustration copyright © 1981 by Marc Simont. Reprinted by permission of Coward, McCann & Geoghegan.
"The Fourth" from WHERE THE SIDEWALK ENDS: THE POEMS AND DRAWINGS OF SHEL SILVERSTEIN. Copyright © 1974 by Snake Eye Music Inc. Reprinted by permission of Harper & Row, Publishers, Inc. and Jonathan Cape Ltd.
Excerpt from index from WRITE TO THE POINT by Bill Stott. Copyright © 1984 by Bill Stott. Reprinted by permission of Doubleday & Company, Inc.
Excerpt from ROLL OF THUNDER, HEAR MY CRY by Mildred Taylor. Copyright © 1976 by Mildred D. Taylor. Reprinted by permission of the publisher, Dial Books for Young Readers, a Division of E.P. Dutton, Inc.
Entries for *abide, atrocious, loud, fell, figure,* and *cultivation* from SCOTT, FORESMAN INTERMEDIATE DICTIONARY by E.L. Thorndike and Clarence L. Barnhart. Copyright © 1979 by Scott, Foresman and Company. Reprinted by permission.
"Sleet Storm" from A WORLD TO KNOW by James S. Tippett. Copyright 1933 by Harper & Row, Publishers, Inc.; renewed 1961 by Martha K. Tippett. Reprinted by permission of Harper & Row, Publishers, Inc.

# Contents

A Walk-Through: A Student Introduction to the Text     xiv

## Unit One    Communication Skills

Sharing a Poem    *A Horse Is a Horse*   Dorothy Baruch
LITERARY APPRECIATION/READING    2

### Chapter 1    Ways of Communicating    3

Lesson 1    Sharing Ideas   SPEAKING/LISTENING    4
Lesson 2    Looking and Listening   SPEAKING/LISTENING    6
Lesson 3    Discussing Your Ideas   SPEAKING/LISTENING    8
Lesson 4    Giving a Talk   SPEAKING/LISTENING    10
Lesson 5    Taking Notes   RESEARCH/STUDY    12
   Chapter Review   SPEAKING/LISTENING/COMPOSITION    14
   Word Study: Pronunciations   VOCABULARY/DICTIONARY    16

### Chapter 2    Expressing Your Ideas    17

Lesson 1    Writing Sentences   GRAMMAR    18
Lesson 2    Writing Paragraphs   COMPOSITION    20
Lesson 3    Writing Stories   LITERARY APPRECIATION/READING    22
Lesson 4    Writing Dialogue   MECHANICS    24
Lesson 5    The Writing Process   COMPOSITION    26
Lesson 6    Sharing Your Writing   COMPOSITION    28
   Chapter Review   GRAMMAR/COMPOSITION    30
   Word Study: Denotation and Connotation
VOCABULARY/DICTIONARY    32

### Chapter 3    Exchanging Information    33

Lesson 1    Using Language as a Tool   COMPOSITION    34
Lesson 2    Giving and Following Directions   COMPOSITION    36
Sharing a Poem    *Mice*   Rose Fyleman   LITERARY APPRECIATION/READING    38
Lesson 3    Telling Facts From Opinions   COMPOSITION    40
Lesson 4    Persuading Others   COMPOSITION    42

Chapter Review   COMPOSITION                                          44
Word Study: Diction   COMPOSITION                                     46
Unit Test                                                            47

## Unit Two   Parts of Speech

Sharing a Poem   *Afternoon on a Hill*  Edna St. Vincent Millay
                 LITERARY APPRECIATION/READING                       50
**Chapter 4**    **Nouns**                                           **51**

Lesson 1   Understanding Nouns   GRAMMAR                              52
Lesson 2   Common and Proper Nouns   GRAMMAR                         54
Lesson 3   Singular and Plural Nouns   GRAMMAR                       56
Lesson 4   More Ways of Forming Plurals   GRAMMAR/USAGE              58
Lesson 5   Possessive Forms of Nouns   GRAMMAR                       60
           Chapter Review   GRAMMAR/COMPOSITION                      62
           Word Study: Word Origins   VOCABULARY/DICTIONARY          64

**Chapter 5**    **Verbs**                                           **65**

Lesson 1   Understanding Verbs   GRAMMAR                             66
Lesson 2   Verb Tenses   GRAMMAR                                     68
Lesson 3   Irregular Verbs   GRAMMAR/USAGE                           70
Lesson 4   Other Forms of Regular Verbs   GRAMMAR                    72
Lesson 5   Other Forms of Irregular Verbs   GRAMMAR/USAGE            74
           Chapter Review   GRAMMAR/USAGE/COMPOSITION                76
           Word Study: Inflected Forms   VOCABULARY/DICTIONARY       78

**Chapter 6**    **Pronouns**                                        **79**

Lesson 1   Understanding Pronouns   GRAMMAR                          80
Lesson 2   Personal Pronouns   GRAMMAR/USAGE                         82
Lesson 3   Possessive Forms of Pronouns   GRAMMAR/USAGE              84
Lesson 4   Demonstrative Pronouns   GRAMMAR                          86
           Chapter Review   GRAMMAR/USAGE/COMPOSITION                88
           Word Study: Word Origins   VOCABULARY/DICTIONARY          90

| | | |
|---|---|---|
| **Chapter 7** | **Adjectives** | **91** |
| Lesson 1 | Understanding Adjectives  GRAMMAR | 92 |
| Lesson 2 | Comparing with Adjectives  GRAMMAR/USAGE | 94 |
| Lesson 3 | Demonstrative Adjectives  GRAMMAR | 96 |
| | Chapter Review  GRAMMAR/USAGE/COMPOSITION | 98 |
| | Word Study: Sensory Appeal  COMPOSITION | 100 |
| **Chapter 8** | **Adverbs** | **101** |
| Lesson 1 | Understanding Adverbs  GRAMMAR | 102 |
| Lesson 2 | Comparing with Adverbs  GRAMMAR | 104 |
| Sharing a Poem | *A Narrow Fellow in the Grass* Emily Dickinson  LITERARY APPRECIATION/READING | 106 |
| Lesson 3 | More About Adverbs  GRAMMAR | 108 |
| | Chapter Review  GRAMMAR/COMPOSITION | 110 |
| | Word Study: Sensory Appeal  COMPOSITION | 112 |
| **Chapter 9** | **Other Parts of Speech** | **113** |
| Lesson 1 | Understanding Prepositions  GRAMMAR | 114 |
| Lesson 2 | Using Prepositional Phrases  GRAMMAR | 116 |
| Lesson 3 | Understanding Conjunctions  GRAMMAR | 118 |
| Lesson 4 | Understanding Interjections  GRAMMAR | 120 |
| | Chapter Review  GRAMMAR/COMPOSITION | 122 |
| | Word Study: Parts of Speech  VOCABULARY/DICTIONARY | 124 |
| | Unit Test | 125 |

## Unit Three   Sentences

| | | |
|---|---|---|
| Sharing a Poem | *Calendar* Mary Cohn Livingston  LITERARY APPRECIATION/READING | 128 |
| **Chapter 10** | **Parts of Sentences** | **129** |
| Lesson 1 | Four Kinds of Sentences  GRAMMAR | 130 |
| Lesson 2 | Subjects and Predicates  GRAMMAR | 132 |
| Lesson 3 | Objects in Sentences  GRAMMAR | 134 |

| | | |
|---|---|---:|
| Lesson 4 | Subject-Verb Agreement   USAGE | 136 |
| Lesson 5 | Compound Sentence Parts   GRAMMAR | 138 |
| Lesson 6 | Statements and Questions   GRAMMAR | 140 |
| | Chapter Review   GRAMMAR/COMPOSITION | 142 |
| | Word Study: Guide Words   VOCABULARY/DICTIONARY | 144 |

**Chapter 11**   **Writing Sentences**   **145**

| | | |
|---|---|---:|
| Lesson 1 | Adding Words to Sentences   COMPOSITION | 146 |
| Lesson 2 | Combining Sentences   GRAMMAR | 148 |
| Sharing a Poem | *A-Ha!* Dorothy Aldis   LITERARY APPRECIATION/READING | 150 |
| Lesson 3 | Avoiding Sentence Fragments   GRAMMAR/USAGE | 152 |
| Lesson 4 | Avoiding Run-On Sentences   GRAMMAR/USAGE | 154 |
| Lesson 5 | Avoiding Wordiness in Sentences   COMPOSITION | 156 |
| | Chapter Review   GRAMMAR/USAGE/COMPOSITION | 158 |
| | Word Study: Finding Words in a Dictionary   VOCABULARY/DICTIONARY | 160 |

**Chapter 12**   **Capitalization and Punctuation**   **161**

| | | |
|---|---|---:|
| Lesson 1 | Capitalization   MECHANICS | 162 |
| Lesson 2 | Capitalization in Letter Writing   MECHANICS | 164 |
| Lesson 3 | Using Quotation Marks   MECHANICS | 166 |
| Lesson 4 | More About Writing Quotations   MECHANICS | 168 |
| Lesson 5 | Commas in Sentences   MECHANICS | 170 |
| Lesson 6 | Using Apostrophes   MECHANICS | 172 |
| Lesson 7 | Using Colons   MECHANICS | 174 |
| Lesson 8 | Proofreading Sentences   COMPOSITION | 176 |
| | Chapter Review   MECHANICS/COMPOSITION | 178 |
| | Word Study: Word Divisions   VOCABULARY/DICTIONARY | 180 |
| | Unit Test | 181 |

**Unit Four**   **Paragraphs**

| | | |
|---|---|---:|
| Sharing a Poem | *Brontosaurus* Gail Kredenser   LITERARY APPRECIATION/READING | 184 |

**Chapter 13    Elements of Paragraphs**                                    **185**

Lesson 1    The Paragraph    COMPOSITION                                     186
Lesson 2    Main Ideas in Paragraphs    COMPOSITION                         188
Lesson 3    Adding Details to Paragraphs    COMPOSITION                     190
            Chapter Review    COMPOSITION                                    192
            Word Study: Alphabetical Order    VOCABULARY/DICTIONARY          194

**Chapter 14    Descriptive Paragraphs**                                    **195**

Lesson 1    Writing Descriptive Paragraphs    COMPOSITION                   196
Lesson 2    Describing Persons and Places    COMPOSITION                    198
Lesson 3    Describing Events    COMPOSITION                                200
Lesson 4    Revising Descriptive Paragraphs    COMPOSITION                  202
Sharing a Poem    *Sleet Storm* James S. Tippett    LITERARY APPRECIATION/READING    204
            Chapter Review    COMPOSITION                                    206
            Word Study: Idioms    VOCABULARY/DICTIONARY                      208

**Chapter 15    Factual Paragraphs**                                        **209**

Lesson 1    Writing Factual Paragraphs    COMPOSITION                       210
Lesson 2    Limiting a Topic    COMPOSITION                                 212
Lesson 3    Order in Factual Paragraphs    COMPOSITION                      214
Lesson 4    Revising Factual Paragraphs    COMPOSITION                      216
            Chapter Review    COMPOSITION                                    218
            Word Study: Definitions    VOCABULARY/DICTIONARY                 220

**Chapter 16    Building Paragraphs**                                       **221**

Lesson 1    Choosing a Topic    COMPOSITION                                 222
Lesson 2    Developing a Topic    COMPOSITION                               224
Lesson 3    Revising What You Write    COMPOSITION                          226
Lesson 4    Proofreading What You Write    COMPOSITION                      228
            Chapter Review    COMPOSITION                                    230
            Word Study: Compound Words    VOCABULARY/DICTIONARY             232
            Unit Test                                                        233

## Unit Five  Becoming a Writer

|  | The Process of Writing  COMPOSITION | 236 |
| **Chapter 17** | **Narrative Writing** | **239** |
| Lesson 1 | The Nature of Stories  COMPOSITION | 240 |
| Lesson 2 | Prewriting a Story  COMPOSITION | 242 |
| Lesson 3 | More About Prewriting  COMPOSITION | 244 |
| Lesson 4 | Organizing a Story  COMPOSITION | 246 |
| Lesson 5 | Writing the First Draft of a Story  COMPOSITION | 248 |
| Lesson 6 | Revising a Story  COMPOSITION | 250 |
| Sharing a Poem | *Abraham Lincoln*  Stephen Vincent Benét  LITERARY APPRECIATION/READING | 252 |
|  | Chapter Review  COMPOSITION | 254 |
|  | Word Study: Word Origins  VOCABULARY/DICTIONARY | 256 |
| **Chapter 18** | **Writing a Mystery** | **257** |
| Lesson 1 | Prewriting a Mystery Story  COMPOSITION | 258 |
| Lesson 2 | Organizing a Mystery Story  COMPOSITION | 260 |
| Lesson 3 | Writing a Mystery Story  COMPOSITION | 262 |
|  | Chapter Review  COMPOSITION | 264 |
|  | Word Study: Context Clues  VOCABULARY/DICTIONARY | 266 |
| **Chapter 19** | **More About Mysteries** | **267** |
| Lesson 1 | Revising the Beginning  COMPOSITION | 268 |
| Lesson 2 | Revising for Clarity  COMPOSITION | 270 |
| Lesson 3 | Revising for Errors  COMPOSITION | 272 |
| Sharing a Poem | *Raccoon*  Mary Ann Hoberman  LITERARY APPRECIATION/READING | 274 |
| Lesson 4 | Revising for Publication  COMPOSITION | 276 |
|  | Chapter Review  COMPOSITION | 278 |
|  | Word Study: Dictionary Review  VOCABULARY/DICTIONARY | 280 |
|  | Unit Test | 281 |

## Unit Six    Types of Writing

Sharing a Poem    *The Snowflake*  Walter de la Mare
LITERARY APPRECIATION/READING    284

**Chapter 20    Descriptive Writing    285**

Lesson 1    Using Details in Writing
LITERARY APPRECIATION/READING/COMPOSITION    286
Lesson 2    Using Similes and Metaphors    VOCABULARY/DICTIONARY    288
Lesson 3    Knowing About Poetry    LITERARY APPRECIATION/READING    290
Lesson 4    Writing Lyric Poetry    COMPOSITION    292
Lesson 5    Revising Poetry    COMPOSITION    294
            Chapter Review    LITERARY APPRECIATION/READING/COMPOSITION    296
            Word Study: Prefixes    VOCABULARY/DICTIONARY    298

**Chapter 21    Writing for Special Purposes    299**

Lesson 1    Writing a Book Report    COMPOSITION    300
Lesson 2    Writing a Friendly Letter    COMPOSITION    302
Lesson 3    Writing a Business Letter    COMPOSITION    304
Lesson 4    Writing Telephone Messages    COMPOSITION    306
            Chapter Review    COMPOSITION    308
            Word Study: Word Origins    VOCABULARY/DICTIONARY    310
            Unit Test    311

## Unit Seven    Study Skills

Sharing a Poem    *Oh Yeah*  Richard Power    LITERARY APPRECIATION/READING    314
**Chapter 22    More About Words    315**

Lesson 1    Using Wrods That Are Related    VOCABULARY/DICTIONARY    316
Lesson 2    Using Contractions    MECHANICS    318
Lesson 3    Using Prefixes    VOCABULARY/DICTIONARY    320
Lesson 4    Using Suffixes    VOCABULARY/DICTIONARY    322
            Chapter Review    VOCABULARY/DICTIONARY/COMPOSITION    324
            Word Study: Prefixes    VOCABULARY/DICTIONARY    326

| | | |
|---|---|---:|
| **Chapter 23** | **Gathering Facts** | **327** |
| Lesson 1 | Finding Sources of Information RESEARCH/STUDY SKILLS | 328 |
| Lesson 2 | Using a Dictionary VOCABULARY/DICTIONARY | 330 |
| Lesson 3 | Using an Encyclopedia RESEARCH/STUDY SKILLS | 332 |
| Lesson 4 | Using Other Reference Books RESEARCH/STUDY SKILLS | 334 |
| Sharing a Poem | *The Horses* Maxine Kumin LITERARY APPRECIATION/READING | 336 |
| Lesson 5 | Using Library Card Catalogs RESEARCH/STUDY SKILLS | 338 |
| Lesson 6 | Finding Facts in Books RESEARCH/STUDY SKILLS | 340 |
| | Chapter Review RESEARCH/STUDY SKILLS/COMPOSITION | 342 |
| | Word Study: Definitions VOCABULARY/DICTIONARY | 344 |
| | | |
| **Chapter 24** | **Writing a Report** | **345** |
| Lesson 1 | Planning a Report RESEARCH/STUDY SKILLS/COMPOSITION | 346 |
| Lesson 2 | Recording Information RESEARCH/STUDY SKILLS/COMPOSITION | 348 |
| Lesson 3 | Organizing Information COMPOSITION | 350 |
| Lesson 4 | Outlining Information RESEARCH/STUDY SKILLS/COMPOSITION | 352 |
| Lesson 5 | Writing from an Outline COMPOSITION | 354 |
| Lesson 6 | Revising a Report COMPOSITION | 356 |
| | Chaper Review RESEARCH/STUDY SKILLS/COMPOSITION | 358 |
| | Word Study: Technical Terms VOCABULARY/DICTIONARY | 360 |
| | Unit Test | 361 |
| | | |
| | More Chapter Practice | 362 |
| | More Lesson Practice | 386 |
| | Handbook | 396 |
| | Capital Letters | 396 |
| | Punctuation | 397 |
| | Usage | 401 |
| | Glossary | 415 |
| | Index | 425 |

**Lesson Number and Title**

## INSTRUCTION

The **Introduction** tells you about the lesson. The important words are in heavy print. These words are also in the glossary.

Some lessons have a **Rule.** The Rule tells you what you should do.

The **Example** shows more about what you learned in the Introduction.

LESSON 3 **Singular and Plural Nouns**

Nouns like *boy, beach, tree,* and *hope* are **singular** nouns. A singular noun names one person, place, thing, or idea. Nouns that name more than one person, place, thing, or idea are **plural** nouns. The words *boys, beaches, trees,* and *hopes* are plural nouns.

Adding *-s* to most singular nouns makes them plural: *spoon, spoons.* If a singular noun ends in *s, x, ch, sh,* or *z,* adding *-es* makes the noun plural: *dish, dishes.*

■ **Add an *-s* to most singular nouns to make them plural. Add the ending *-es* to nouns that end in *s, x, ch,* or *sh* to make them plural.**

**Example**

Read this paragraph. The underlined words are plural nouns.

Rusty thought she spotted two <u>fins</u> cutting through the water. Could they be <u>sharks</u>? She squinted her <u>eyes</u> and wiped her <u>goggles</u>. The <u>fins</u> made two <u>passes</u> by Rusty as she held her breath. Then with two enormous <u>splashes</u>, Willie burst up from below. She had rubber <u>paddles</u> strapped to her <u>hands</u> and <u>feet</u>. The sun danced in her hair like <u>patches</u> of pure light. Soon the laughter of both <u>girls</u> was rippling with the <u>waves</u>.

What is the singular form of each plural noun?
Which nouns add *-s* to form the plural and which add *-es?*

*Parts of Speech*

**Unit Title**

**PRACTICE 1** Write the plural noun in each sentence. Beside each plural noun, write its singular form.
1. Patches of white foam appeared on the rough sea.
2. There were several flashes of bright lightning.
3. The gulls soared inward toward the land.
4. The ship tossed on the surges of the tide.
5. Sailors called to each other above the storm.

**PRACTICE 2** Write the plural forms of the first ten nouns. Write the singular forms of the last ten nouns.

| | | | |
|---|---|---|---|
| 1. tax | 6. dress | 11. flashes | 16. lunches |
| 2. wish | 7. bench | 12. axes | 17. grasses |
| 3. inch | 8. brush | 13. bosses | 18. churches |
| 4. moss | 9. branch | 14. bushes | 19. crashes |
| 5. box | 10. glass | 15. foxes | 20. beaches |

**WRITE** Plan and write a brief story about two or more friends playing tricks on each other. Tell what happened. Your story can be a true one or one that you make up. Use at least five plural nouns in your story.

■ **Check your work. Make sure you followed the rules for forming plurals.**

**GO BEYOND** Do this activity with the whole class or in several groups. Imagine that you are going on a trip and have to pack a suitcase. One person begins by saying, "In my suitcase I put _____ ." He or she adds a plural noun that begins with the letter *a*. The next person repeats what the first person has said and adds a plural noun that begins with the next letter of the alphabet. A player who cannot repeat the named items is out of the game. Continue until all the letters of the alphabet have been used.

*Nouns*                                                                57

**Chapter Title**

# APPLICATION

**Practice 1** helps make sure you understand the lesson.

**Practice 2** lets you review what you have learned.

**Write** lets you explore and apply what you have learned.

The **Checkup** reminds you to use the Rule you have learned in this lesson.

**Go Beyond** is an activity you often do with other classmates.

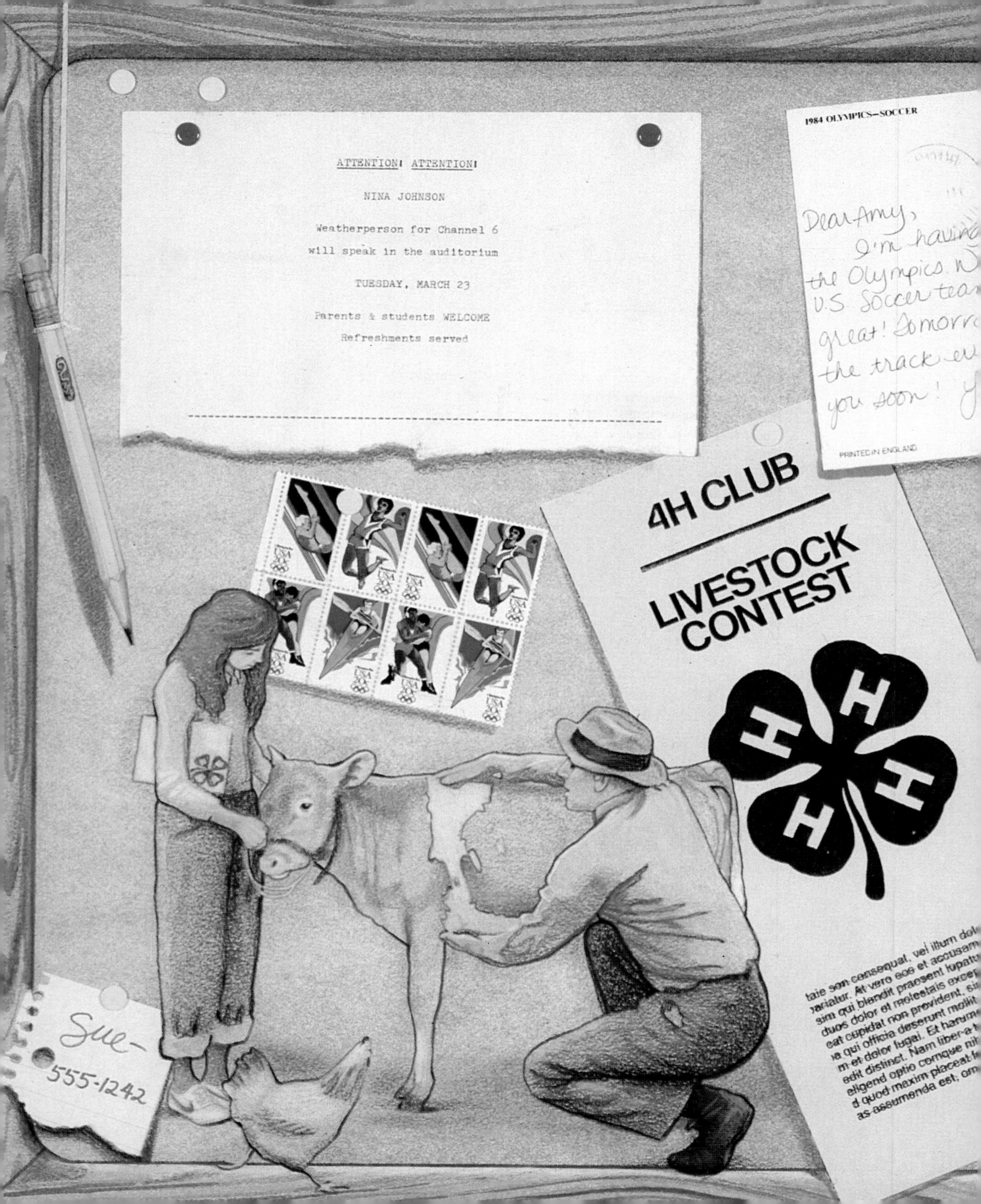

ATTENTION! ATTENTION!
NINA JOHNSON
Weatherperson for Channel 6
will speak in the auditorium
TUESDAY, MARCH 23
Parents & students WELCOME
Refreshments served
1984 OLYMPICS—SOCCER
Dear Amy,
I'm having
the Olympics.
U.S. Soccer
great!
the track
you soon!
PRINTED IN ENGLAND
USA 20c
4H CLUB
LIVESTOCK CONTEST
Sue-
555-1242

# Unit One
# Communication Skills

Chapter 1
**Ways of Communicating**

Chapter 2
**Expressing Your Ideas**

Chapter 3
**Exchanging Information**

## Sharing a Poem

**A Horse Is a Horse**

I would like to be
A horse wild and free
Galloping with flying mane
Over miles of wide field,
Leaping fences and walls,
With the whistle of wind-sound
So strong in my ears
  That I
  Can simply not
  Certainly
  Not possibly
  Hear
    When anyone
      Calls

*Dorothy W. Baruch*

What idea is the poet expressing?
What other ways can be used to communicate this?

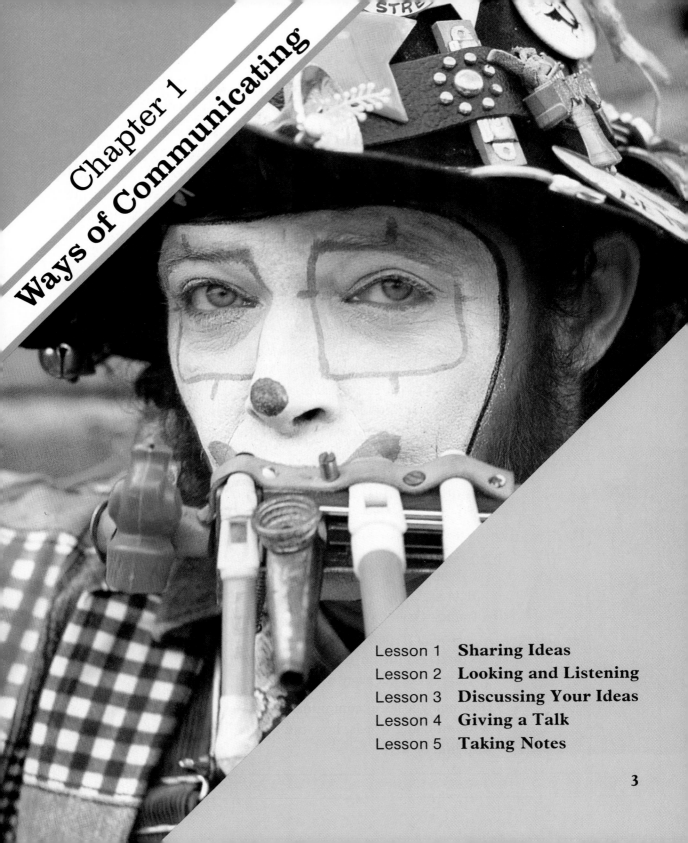

Lesson 1  **Sharing Ideas**
Lesson 2  **Looking and Listening**
Lesson 3  **Discussing Your Ideas**
Lesson 4  **Giving a Talk**
Lesson 5  **Taking Notes**

3

# Sharing Ideas

*Finger Spelling: Some letters of the alphabet.*

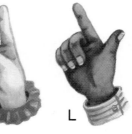

H  V  L

When people send messages that are received by others, they **communicate**. Speaking, writing, drawing, and signaling are four ways to communicate. Choose the way of communicating that is best for the ideas you want to share.

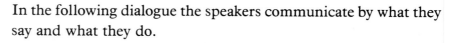

## Example

In the following dialogue the speakers communicate by what they say and what they do.

POLICE OFFICER: (*Pacing back and forth.*) Could Dr. Knowzit possibly be away on a trip, Mrs. Knowzit?

MRS. KNOWZIT: (*Shaking her head.*) Someone must have gone through his room while my daughter and I were out. Clothes were pulled out of the drawers, furniture was tipped over . . . .

BELLA: (*Handing a piece of paper to the police officer.*) My mother and I found this note.

POLICE OFFICER: (*Reading the note aloud.*) "It will cost $100,000 in unmarked bills to get Dr. Knowzit released. Leave the money tomorrow at 10:17 P.M. at the old boarded-up gas station on Ferris Drive."

BELLA: Ferris Drive. Where is that?

POLICE OFFICER: (*Drawing a map in his notebook.*) That's the strangest part of the request. Ferris Drive is just about here—right on the edge of the desert. How can someone expect to get away with the money?

How many ways of communicating does the dialogue show? Without using words, how can you tell someone that you agree with him or her?

*Communication Skills*

**PRACTICE 1**   Write these four column headings: Speaking, Writing, Drawing, and Signaling. Write each word under the correct heading.

1. map
2. wave
3. grin
4. laugh
5. print

6. scream
7. whisper
8. type
9. smile
10. sketch

**PRACTICE 2**   Beside the number of each activity, tell how you would communicate. Write *by speaking, by writing, by drawing,* or *by signaling.* For some activities you can write more than one correct answer.

1. telephoning a friend
2. telling someone who cannot hear to stop
3. telling someone who has not seen you to wait for you
4. telling a story to the class
5. sharing with a friend the sound of popping corn

**WRITE**   Introduce yourself in writing. Describe your personality by telling your likes and dislikes. Be sure to tell what is important to you. Read your introduction to a classmate.

**GO BEYOND**   Think of a well known place that you like to visit. Perhaps it is a park, a building, an amusement area, or a shopping mall that is near your home. See if your classmates can guess the place you have in mind. Give them clues by speaking, by writing, by drawing, or by signaling.

# Looking and Listening

Before you can share information with others, you must collect it by using your senses. Seeing and hearing are two of the most important ways of gathering information.

Get in the habit of looking closely at the world around you. See and remember important details. Listen carefully to the sounds that surround you. Remember what you have heard.

## Example

In the following passage the writer communicates important details.

I was nervously crossing the marsh—about halfway home, I judged. There were no sidewalks, no streetlights, no cars along that empty stretch of road—only a vast expanse of grayish-white ice, barely visible beneath a moonless sky. I could hear the ice creak and groan and occasionally split apart with a crack like a pistol shot as the tidewater beneath it rose or fell. The soft shuffling of my feet and the crunch of snow along the unplowed road was lost in the immensity of the landscape.

Was that the sound of another person behind me? I turned my head without breaking my stride, and saw nothing but white. Or was it, I thought, the sound of some nameless creature sliding across the ice in my direction?

Why was the writer nervous?
What similar situation have you ever been in?

**PRACTICE 1**   Show how the writer described each item in the Example. Write the words under these headings: Looking, Listening. A word may belong in both columns.

1. sky        2. ice        3. road        4. snow        5. feet

**PRACTICE 2**   Write at least two words to tell how each object might look. Then write at least one word to tell how it might sound.

1. rain        2. truck        3. hail        4. car        5. bicycle

**WRITE**   Listen to and take notes on the sounds around you during a five-minute period. The sounds may come from your classroom, from other classrooms, or from outside. Write an account of each sound. Then describe each in terms of what it might look like (you may have to use your imagination).

**GO BEYOND**   Write a paragraph about one of the topics listed below. Fill it with good details of sight and sound. Read your paragraph to the class. What did you like about each paragraph? How could it have been improved?

1. a walk in the woods        3. a family reunion
2. a day at the lake          4. a shopping trip

# Discussing Your Ideas

In a **discussion** people talk about different sides of a question or topic. Discussions let each person give a point of view and learn what others think. Discussions often lead to good decisions.

To have a good discussion, discuss only one topic at a time. Make sure each comment is about that topic. Listen carefully. Allow only one person at a time to speak. Respect the opinions of others.

## Example

Here is part of a discussion about vacation plans.

MOM:   Where shall we go for our vacation this year? Let's try to do something we all enjoy.

DAD:   I've always wanted to visit San Francisco. It's not too far away.

JOHN:   How about camping? We could go to Lassen Volcanic National Park.

BETTY:   I loved the zoo last summer.

JIMMY:   So did I. Remember the monkeys?

MOM:   We are talking about this year's vacation, children, not last year's. Any suggestions?

DAD:   San Francisco has many things to do outdoors.

JOHN:   We never do what I suggest. I want to camp. How about going to the beach?

Where do you think this family will decide to go on vacation?
Did everyone follow the rules for a good discussion? Explain.

*Communication Skills*

**PRACTICE 1**   Remember the rules for a good discussion. Write *true* or *false* for each suggestion below.

1. In a discussion try to cover as many topics as possible.
2. Make sure that what you say relates to the topic.
3. Pay attention only to ideas with which you agree.
4. Speak whenever you think of something to say.
5. Do not make fun of the ideas of others.

**PRACTICE 2**   Follow these instructions for making a discussion chart.

1. Place a sheet of paper on your desk. In the middle of the top line, write the title "Discussion Rules."
2. Draw a line down the center of the paper.
3. Skip a line after the title. Then, in the left column, write the first rule for a good discussion. (See the introduction.)
4. Write the last four rules. Skip a line after each rule.
5. Save your paper to use later.

**WRITE**   Write a conversation that a family might have when discussing something they want to do. They might be deciding on a restaurant or a movie. Share your dialogue with a partner.

**GO BEYOND**   Work with four or five classmates. Select one person to be the observer of your discussion. The observer should use the chart made in Practice 2. Discuss one of the following questions for ten minutes: Should homework be assigned? Should students choose school lunch menus? Should school be held for only four longer days each week?

Have the observer put a check mark beside a discussion rule when the rule is followed. If a rule is not followed, have the observer mark an *X* beside it. After the discussion, the observer should report how many times each rule was or was not followed.

**Giving a Talk**

A talk is a speech made to an audience. A good talk begins with a short **introduction** that describes the topic. The **body** of the talk is the part that presents details and facts about the topic in an order that makes sense. The **closing statement** of the talk is a sentence that sums up what has been said.

## Example

Leah is a fifth-grader. Here is the introduction of her talk.

How will people get around in the year 3000? People have many different ideas about this. One opinion is that people will have their own planes. Instead of having garages for cars, people will have hangars for their planes. Police officers will direct traffic in the sky. The speed limit will be different, too. People will not fly over 500 miles an hour. If people flew planes, they could travel from one place to another more quickly.

What would be a good title for this talk?
What forms of transportation do you think may be important in the year 3000?

**PRACTICE 1**  Write answers to the following questions. Use the information in the Example for help.

1. What do you think will be the topic of Leah's talk?
2. What question did Leah ask at the beginning of her introduction?
3. What is the answer to Leah's question?
4. How many details did Leah provide to show what changes ownership of planes would make?
5. What was Leah's final point in her introduction?

**PRACTICE 2**  Here are five sentences from Leah's next paragraph, which ends with the closing statement of the talk. Write the sentences in order.

1. Moving sidewalks will carry large numbers of people from their homes to the train station.
2. By the year 3000 people will be getting around more than they do now, and they will be getting there faster.
3. Airplanes are fine for long-distance travel, but people will need other forms of transportation for shorter trips.
4. Large air tubes will shoot them from the train station to downtown office and shopping areas.
5. High-speed trains, traveling over 200 miles an hour, will carry people from city to city.

**WRITE**  Plan to give a talk explaining what is most important to you about school. Be sure your talk includes an introduction, a body, and a closing statement.

**GO BEYOND**  Work with four or five other students. Give the talk you prepared during the last exercise. Discuss what you liked about each talk. How could it be improved?

**Taking Notes**

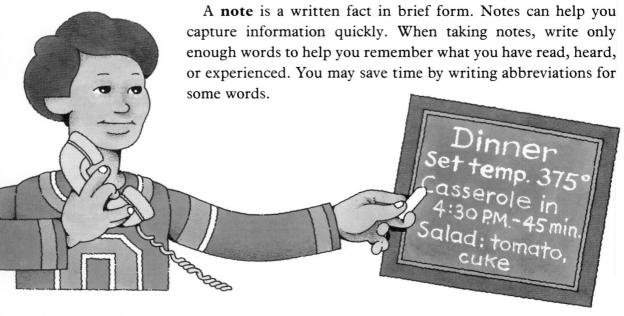

A **note** is a written fact in brief form. Notes can help you capture information quickly. When taking notes, write only enough words to help you remember what you have read, heard, or experienced. You may save time by writing abbreviations for some words.

*Dinner*
*Set temp. 375°*
*Casserole in*
*4:30 P.M. — 45 min.*
*Salad: tomato,*
*cuke*

## Example

Benjamin took these notes on one classmate's talk.

Judy—The Armadillo
mammal
covered with armor
armor—small bony plates—protect arm. from enemies
rolls into armored ball for protection
hunts at night
eats fruit, ants, worms
stays in burrow days
babies—always four at time—look alike, can't tell apart
Amer. animal

What missing words can you add to each note?
What other information would you like about the armadillo?

**PRACTICE 1**   Here are five sentences from the end of Judy's talk. Write them as notes.

1. Armadillos are found mainly in the countries of South America, Central America, and Mexico.
2. In the United States, armadillos can be seen by people in some of our southern states.
3. The kind of armadillo that is found in the United States grows to be about 15 inches or so long.
4. Some kinds of armadillos are longer than the one in this country, but other kinds are shorter.
5. Some armadillos that lived long ago grew as large as rhinoceroses!

**PRACTICE 2**   Jay took notes on how to care for a dog. Write them as sentences in an order that makes sense.

1. brush coat after walk
2. add 2 cups water to food
3. walk after feeding
4. fill water dish before feeding
5. pour dry food in dish

**WRITE**   Take notes to describe an object, but do not name it. Use as many of your senses as possible. How does it look, sound, feel, taste, smell? Save your paper to use with the next exercise.

**GO BEYOND**   Read to the class the notes you wrote during the last exercise. Can your classmates name the object you described? Were your notes easy to understand? How could they be improved?

## Practice

**A.** Is the student described in each numbered sentence doing something that contributes to a good discussion? Write *yes* or *no* beside each sentence number.

1. Jeremy, who is leading a group discussion about a class trip, is calling on each person by name.
2. Perry is talking about a trip his family took last summer.
3. Samantha is answering Perry and saying that her family took the same trip.
4. Carly is telling Jeremy why his idea for the trip is not a good one.
5. Sue keeps interrupting everyone's statements to offer her own opinions.

**B.** Read the part of a talk that follows. Write a sentence or two that you could use to introduce the talk.

I collect stamps from many different countries. Some are valuable and some are merely pretty or are interesting in other ways. Stamps come in all shapes, sizes, and colors. Many stamps are real works of art.

**C.** Choose one of the following experiences. Write notes to describe it fully. Use as many of your senses as possible to recapture the experience: sight, sound, feel, taste, smell.

1. a day at the beach
2. a shopping trip
3. a day at the circus
4. a camping trip
5. a party

## Composition

One fifth-grader took notes about something that happened in her neighborhood. Use her notes to write a story. Turn each note into a sentence and write the sentences in the order that the events took place.

couldn't get down
fire fighters put up ladder
neighbors clap
Mrs. Potter's cat, Gertrude, in tree
1 f. fighter brings down G.
neighbors hear noise, run to Mrs. P's
fire engines leave
G. meows, prances into house
Mrs. P. calls fire department
f. engines scream down our street

## Advanced Challenge

Find five cartoons in magazines, newspapers, or books. At least two of the cartoons should have words explaining what the cartoon is about. That is, there should be a caption—a few words or a sentence under the picture—showing words spoken by a character in that cartoon. The rest of the cartoons should have no captions. If you wish, you may create your own cartoons, rather than finding some.

Analyze why some cartoons need words to explain them and some do not. Show a classmate the cartoons that have words, but cover up the words. Ask your classmate to tell what each cartoon means. Ask a second person to do the same. Did the answers differ? If so, how?

Now write captions for each cartoon that does not have one. Show the cartoons with your captions to the same two classmates. Did the classmates feel the cartoons were better with the words or without? Why did they feel the way they did?

15

## DICTIONARY

As you probably know, you can use a dictionary to learn how to pronounce, or say, words correctly. When you look up a word, you will find the pronunciation next to the entry word. It is usually in parentheses.

An example from one dictionary is the word **a bom i na ble** (a bom′ ə nə bəl). Notice the accent mark after the second syllable—the syllable you should stress, or say more loudly. Some words have more than one stressed syllable. The syllable that should be stressed more has the darker accent mark.

Some words have more than one correct pronunciation. In most dictionaries the first pronunciation given is the preferred one. This is the pronunciation that is used by the majority of American people.

Different dictionaries use different letters and marks to show how to pronounce words. Look at the pronunciation key or guide in your own dictionary to learn how it can help you.

EXAMPLE
**ca nal** (kə nal′)
**can a pe** (kan′ ə pā *or* kan′ ə pē)

Which syllable is stressed in *canal?*
Which is the preferred pronunciation for *canape?*

PRACTICE   Look up these words in your dictionary and write their pronunciations. Then, taking turns with a friend, practice saying the words aloud.

1. catastrophe
2. grandiloquent
3. negotiate
4. naive
5. anemone

16

# Chapter 2
# Expressing Your Ideas

Lesson 1   **Writing Sentences**

Lesson 2   **Writing Paragraphs**

Lesson 3   **Writing Stories**

Lesson 4   **Writing Dialogue**

Lesson 5   **The Writing Process**

Lesson 6   **Sharing Your Writing**

## LESSON 1   Writing Sentences

A **sentence** is a group of words that contains a complete thought. A sentence tells what a person, place, thing, or idea does or is.

## Example

Look at the following groups of words. Notice the difference between the groups in the two columns.

| NOT SENTENCES | SENTENCES |
|---|---|
| the small red flower | The flower finally bloomed. |
| an anteater | An anteater has a long tongue. |
| after the long winter | After winter the spring arrives. |
| on a chair by the window | She sat on a chair. |
| Dallas, a city in Texas, | Dallas is a large city in Texas. |
| my father in the garden | The garden is dry. |

Is a sentence always longer than a group of words that is not a sentence?

How can you make each group of words in the first column into a sentence?

**PRACTICE 1**   Write five sentences by adding a word group from the right column to each word or word group in the left column. Your sentence will tell a story.

1. Peter's shirt
2. Peter
3. Then he
4. After that he
5. The wind

a. hung it outside.
b. rinsed the shirt out.
c. had grease spots on the sleeves.
d. blew it dry.
e. washed it with detergent.

**PRACTICE 2**   The following word groups refer to a puppet show. Use your own words to complete each word group. Write the sentence.

1. Mario and his friends _____ .
2. _____ built a wooden puppet stage.
3. _____ invited the neighbors to the show.
4. The children _____ the show.
5. Everyone who came to the show _____ .

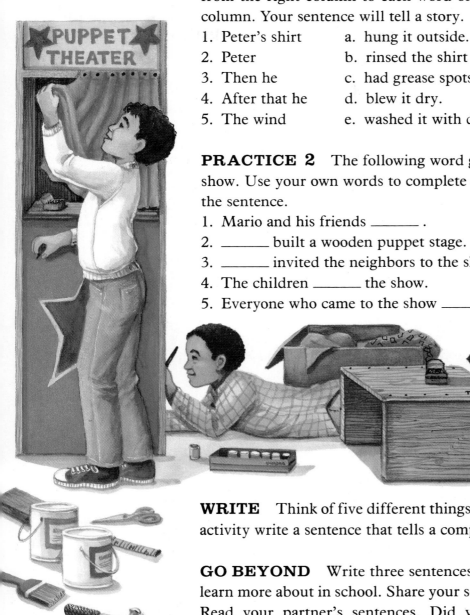

**WRITE**   Think of five different things you like to do. For each activity write a sentence that tells a complete thought.

**GO BEYOND**   Write three sentences. Tell what you hope to learn more about in school. Share your sentences with a partner. Read your partner's sentences. Did you both use complete sentences? Did you both write about any of the same things?

# Writing Paragraphs

A **paragraph** is a group of sentences about one main idea, or topic. The first sentence usually states the topic. The others add details and facts about the topic. The last sentence often sums up what has been said.

## Example

Here is the first paragraph of a letter the Jamison family wrote to a newspaper editor.

We have heard of the town council's plan to sell the Maple Street Playground to make way for a shopping center. Since we live near the playground, we feel that our opinions on the town council's plan should be heard. We think the plan to build a shopping center is a terrible idea. In the first place, our neighborhood doesn't need a shopping center. The downtown area is very close and has plenty of stores. Also, a shopping center would increase traffic on our busy street. Most important, our children will have no place to play. For these three reasons, we feel the town council should change its plans.

Why is the playground important to the Jamisons?
What other reasons might convince the town council to change its plans?

**PRACTICE 1** Answer these questions about the paragraph in the Example. Write a complete sentence for each answer.

1. What is the topic of the paragraph?
2. What is one reason for thinking the sale is a bad idea?
3. What is another reason for that opinion?
4. What is a third reason for that opinion?
5. What does the Jamison family want the town council to do?

**PRACTICE 2** The Jamisons gathered information by talking with people in their neighborhood. These sentences are part of a letter to the town council. Write them in correct order.

1. We do not approve of the idea of selling the Maple Street Playground.
2. We hope you will think about those facts and stop the sale of the playground.
3. There are nearly twenty houses and apartments in the Maple Street Playground area.
4. Twenty-five children live in these homes and use the playground.
5. The only other playground is two miles from this neighborhood.

**WRITE** Think of a place in your community that is important to you. What does it look and smell and sound like? What can you do there? Write a paragraph describing the place. Help a reader imagine it and understand why it is special to you.

**GO BEYOND** When something in your community is important to you, you should explain why to others. Perhaps the same thing will be important to them. In a group of six students, talk about your community. Could something be changed to make it a better place? Write a paragraph explaining what should be changed. Share your paragraph with the other groups in the class.

# Writing Stories

A person must plan a story in order to write it well. Every story needs a **setting** (a time and a place), **characters** (the people in the story), and a **plot** (what happens). A story also needs a beginning that will interest readers and details that will help them picture the setting, the characters, and the actions. The ending should satisfy the readers and seem "right" for the story.

## Example

This is the way "The Fisherman and His Wife" begins.

Once there was a fisherman who lived with his wife in a tiny cottage by the sea. One day when he was fishing, his line suddenly went down in the clear water, and he brought out a large flounder. The flounder said, "Fisherman, let me live. I am no flounder but an enchanted prince. Let me go." The fisherman put him back in the clear water and went home.

When he told his wife what had happened, she said, "Did you not wish for anything first?"

"No," said the man. "What should I wish for?"

"Husband, this cottage is too small for us. Go to the flounder and tell him to give us a great stone castle."

The man's heart grew heavy. He thought, "It is not right," and yet he went. When he came to the sea, it was purple and dark blue but still quiet. And he stood and said,

"Flounder, flounder in the sea, come, I pray thee, here to me;

For my wife, good Isabel, wills not as I'd have her will."

"Well, what does she want, then?" said the flounder.

"Alas," said the man, half scared, "she wants to live in a great stone castle."

"Go, she is standing before the door," said the fish.

The next morning the wife said, "Go to the flounder. I wish to be queen." So the man went and was quite unhappy. And when he got to the sea, it was dark gray, and the water heaved up from below. He summoned the fish as he had before.

Where does the story take place?
Who are the characters in the story?

**PRACTICE 1**   Each of these sentences is about the story on page 22. For each sentence choose the right word in parentheses.
1. The wife seems (generous, greedy) because she makes such a large demand.
2. The husband seems (strong, weak) because he asks the fish for a favor he thinks is wrong.
3. The water turns different colors because (the fish is growing angrier, the wind is blowing harder).
4. The second time the wife asks for a (larger, smaller) gift.
5. The wife will probably be (rewarded, punished) by the flounder.

**PRACTICE 2**   Think about something you want to do or see happen. Plan a story about the thing you choose. List your ideas for these parts of the story. Think of an ending that seems "right."
1. setting   2. characters   3. plot   4. beginning   5. details

**WRITE**   Use the story ideas you listed in Practice 2. Tell the events in your story in an order that makes sense.

**GO BEYOND**   Work with a partner. Ask your partner to suggest ways to make your story better. Did you introduce the setting and characters clearly? Did your plot make sense? Were there enough details? Think about the suggestions your partner makes. If you want to make changes, rewrite the story.

*Expressing Your Ideas*

# Writing Dialogue

FISHERMAN, LET ME LIVE.

A conversation between two or more people is a **dialogue.** Writers show the exact words of each speaker in one of two ways. One way is to put quotation marks around the speaker's words. *"Fisherman, let me live. I am no flounder but an enchanted prince. Let me go."* The other way is to use play form. MOM: *Where shall we go for our vacation this year?*

You can use the play form of dialogue to show conversation in plays and discussions. Because that form can be written quickly, you can use it to take notes about speakers. You can even use that form when planning stories. Later, when you write your first draft, you can use quotation marks.

## Example

CHARACTERS:  WALLACE, twelve years old, confident
               ALAN, eight-year-old brother, nervous
SCENE:  *Late Friday night. All lights in the neighborhood are out. The two boys are in a tent in their backyard.*

ALAN:  (*Excitedly.*) Wally, Wally. Wake up!
WALLACE:  (*Sleepily.*) What's the matter?
ALAN:  (*Frightened.*) I heard a noise.
WALLACE:  Go back to sleep. You were probably just dreaming.
ALAN:  No, I wasn't—honest. Listen. There it is again!
WALLACE:  Shh.
(*They listen for a few seconds, hear the muffled rattle of metal.*)
ALAN:  (*Whispering.*) What is it, Wally? I'm scared!

How can the reader tell how the characters feel?
What do you think Wallace will do next?

**PRACTICE 1**   Here are five more lines of the play in scrambled order. Write them in an order that makes sense. Add the speaker's name to each line. Write words in the parentheses to show what the speaker feels or does. Underline these words.

1. _____ : (*Finds the flashlight.*) Ah, here it is. It was under your sleeping bag.

2. _____ : (            ) I don't <u>care</u> where the light is. I'm scared!

3. _____ : (            ) We'll have to take that chance. We've got to find out who—or what—is out there!

4. _____ : (            ) Please don't turn that flashlight on. He'll see us!

5. _____ : (            ) Where's the flashlight? (*Searches around the floor of the tent.*) I need that light.

**PRACTICE 2**   Turn the following dialogue into play form. Combine sentences if you wish. Show a speaker's feeling or action with words in parentheses. Underline these words.

1. "Don't move!" the police officer shouted. "You're under arrest."

2. "Whatever for?" the man in the black outfit asked in surprise.

3. "For robbery," the officer snapped. "I know you robbed that bank."

4. The officer moved toward the man, and the suspect laughed.

5. "This is my bank," the man told the officer. "And I'm out for my usual morning run—in my black jogging suit."

**WRITE**   Finish the play continued in Practice 1. If you prefer, you may write your own short play instead.

**GO BEYOND**   Share your play with a partner. Can your partner suggest ways to improve the play? Based on those suggestions and your own ideas, you may want to rewrite your play.

# The Writing Process

You share your thoughts with others through writing. You should pay close attention to what you write so that those who read it will know exactly what you mean. Think of writing as a process, a series of steps taken to reach a particular goal.

Here are the steps of the writing process.

1. Choose a topic and gather information about it. This step is called **prewriting**.

2. Arrange the information you have gathered in order. The order you choose will depend on what you are writing. This step is called **organizing**.

3. Put your ideas on paper. When you express your ideas in writing for the first time, don't stop to correct errors in spelling or punctuation. Don't even pause too long to choose the best possible words. Get the main ideas down. This step is called **writing**.

4. Make improvements in what you have written. Add to it, take parts out, rearrange material, or rewrite it. Then correct any errors in spelling, punctuation, or usage. This step is called **revising**.

Alicia wanted to write about the Fourth of July. She started by writing down everything she could think of about the holiday. Here is part of what she wrote.

| | | |
|---|---|---|
| picnic | baseball game | Aunt Jane's homemade root beer |
| parade | marching band | Declaration of Independence |
| speech | pesty flies | flags in windows |
| fireworks | floats | grilling hamburgers |

After Alicia finishes her prewriting, what is the next step she should take?
Which of Alicia's ideas could be grouped together?

**PRACTICE 1**   After Alicia studied the ideas she had written, she chose to limit her topic. Which of the following limited topics would include most of the details she listed?
1. Why Americans celebrate the Fourth of July
2. Summer picnics
3. How our town celebrates the Fourth of July

**PRACTICE 2**   Under each of the following headings, list the details from the Example.
A. Fourth of July morning
B. Fourth of July afternoon
C. Fourth of July evening

**WRITE**   Use the plan in Practice 2 to write the first draft of a composition on the Fourth of July. Use the details in the Example, or use other details that you have thought of yourself.

**GO BEYOND**   Read the first draft you have written. Make any improvements that you think are necessary.

**Sharing Your Writing**

Readers and writers need each other. Writers express every message with a certain reader in mind. If the reader does not understand the message, the writer has failed to communicate.

You are both a reader and a writer. As a reader, you can help your classmates improve their writing. As a writer, you can depend on your classmates to help you improve your writing. They may notice mistakes you overlooked. They can let you know whether your message is clear.

## Example

Jonah and Sue discussed Jonah's paragraph called "My Tree."

Mostly, the maple tree looks bright-colored. That's because the sun shines on it. One side still has some green. That side looks more like the other trees. The orange and yellow leaves look brighter when the sun is out.

SUE: Do you mean that the tree's colors seem to change?
JONAH: Well, some of the leaves do.
SUE: That's not really clear to me until the end.
JONAH: I really like watching my tree. Can you tell that?
SUE: Yes, because you tell good details. I think the information about the changing colors should come earlier in the paragraph.

How did Sue show respect for Jonah's work?
What question would you have asked Jonah?

**PRACTICE 1**   Imagine that you are helping Jonah. Write the better question in each pair.

1. a. Whose tree are you describing?
   b. Has anybody else noticed this tree?
2. a. Do you like this tree?
   b. What is special about this tree?
3. a. Could you explain some of the words in your paragraph?
   b. What do you mean by "bright-colored?"
4. a. Why do the leaves have different colors?
   b. Do the leaves change color?
5. a. Is this tree near other trees?
   b. Where is this tree?

**PRACTICE 2**   Here is Jonah's new paragraph. Answer the questions by comparing this paragraph with the earlier one.

The leaves on the maple tree in my backyard are different colors. This tree is a beautiful mixture of green, orange, and yellow. The leaves on its south side receive sunlight almost all day. The orange and yellow leaves look brighter when the sun is out. On the other side some leaves are still green.

1. How did Jonah explain which tree he was describing?
2. How did he rewrite "bright-colored"?
3. How did he tell what was special about his tree?
4. Which question in Practice 1 has Jonah not answered?
5. What questions would you ask Jonah?

**WRITE**   Think of something you like or admire, and write a paragraph about it. Save your paragraph.

**GO BEYOND**   Work with a partner. Read the paragraph your partner wrote, and ask questions about anything that is unclear. Point out what you like, and offer suggestions for improvement.

## Practice

**A.** Change these word groups to sentences. Write the sentences.
1. the man in the circus ring
2. the large one-wheel bicycle
3. then climbed the ladder to the swing
4. the bandleader signaled, and the band
5. clapped at the end of the performance

**B.** Each of these sentences offers a main idea for a paragraph. Write two supporting sentences for each main idea.
1. Ned is the best player on the team.
2. These books are a very good buy.
3. Orange Lake is a great town to live in.
4. Everyone always asks me for advice.
5. Sandy should make the soccer team.

**C.** Look at "The Fisherman and His Wife" on page 22 for help in answering these questions.
1. Why did the fisherman decide to let the flounder go?
2. Who decided that the flounder should be asked for a favor?
3. Was the fisherman greedy?
4. How did the fisherman feel about asking the flounder for favors?

**D.** Write this dialogue in play form.
1. "How much is this birthday card?" Jill asked the clerk.
2. "One dollar," he told her.
3. "Oh dear," Jill sighed, "I only have eighty-five cents with me."
4. "Don't worry," Phoebe said. "I'll loan you the rest."
5. "Thanks, Phoebe," Jill grinned. "I'll pay you back as soon as we get home."

**E.** Write the numbered word groups. Next to each, write the step of the writing process it describes.
1. putting ideas on paper
2. arranging information in order
3. improving what you have written
4. choosing a topic and arranging the information

**F.** Imagine that you are making suggestions to help improve a classmate's writing. What suggestions would you make for this paragraph?

The garden in front of our apartment building has many kinds. We worked all summer to keep it healthy and growing and were well rewarded by a splendid crop.

## Composition

Each of the following sentences is the main idea for a paragraph. Choose the main idea that you know the most about or with which you agree most strongly. Develop the idea you select. Write five or six supporting sentences.

1. Kindness has great power.
2. Everyone can improve gradually through practice.
3. Having a pet teaches you a great deal.
4. Patience is something you cannot do without.
5. Becoming a good shopper takes time.

## Advanced Challenge

Think of a short story you know well. Then tape-record yourself reading the story. Before you begin taping, however, practice reading the story aloud. Think about how you will change your voice to suit the mood of various parts of the story. Make your recording.

Next, listen to the tape you made. Take notes as you listen. What things would you change? Does each character stand out as an individual? Do you speak slowly enough to be understood? Do you put the appropriate expression in your voice?

## DENOTATION AND CONNOTATION

Have you ever heard anyone talk about making a house into a home? You can sense what this means—that a house is a building where people can live, but a home is one in which they feel comfortable and safe.

The word *home*, then, can be understood in two somewhat different ways. It has a **denotation,** or exact meaning, which is "a building in which people live." Its **connotation** is its more emotional meaning. The connotation of a word is the feelings, pleasant or unpleasant, that the word suggests. When you write, you want to use words that have certain connotations. You want to suggest certain feelings to your reader.

EXAMPLE

Maybe you want to write that someone is pleasantly round. Which would you say the person is, fat or plump? *Fat* usually has an unpleasant connotation. *Plump* would be the better word. It has a pleasant connotation.

PRACTICE   Choose the word with the connotation that better fits the meaning of each sentence.
1. We provided hot dogs and soda for the hungry (crowd, mob).
2. They are the kind of people who will (tell, betray) secrets.
3. He gets his work done by being (stubborn, determined).
4. They must meet our (request, demand) by tomorrow.
5. Anita succeeds because she is so honest and (tricky, clever).

# Chapter 3
# Exchanging Information

Lesson 1   **Using Language as a Tool**
Lesson 2   **Giving and Following Directions**
Lesson 3   **Telling Facts from Opinions**
Lesson 4   **Persuading Others**

# Using Language as a Tool

Language is a valuable tool. With it you can shape information to fit your goals and your readers' interests. Language lets you tell, describe, and explain.

You **tell** when you write about something that happened to you or to other real or imaginary people. You **describe** when you write about the way a person or thing looks or acts. You **explain** when you write directions or reasons.

## Example

Notice the purpose of each sentence that follows. A writer may tell, describe, and explain all in one story.

TELL    When Randolph Twit returned home from the club Friday night, he found his wall safe open and a half-million-dollars' worth of jewelry missing.

DESCRIBE    Bollivar Bland, with his round, innocent face, dull beady eyes, and wooden expression, did not look like a detective.

EXPLAIN    "I knew you were guilty," the detective told the startled parrot. "You left a trail of cracker crumbs."

What differences can you find among the three types of writing? What subjects can you think of to tell? Describe? Explain?

**PRACTICE 1** Here are some other sentences from the mystery story in the Example. Write whether each tells, describes, or explains.

1. The detective called us all into the dining room and made us sit around the table.
2. "The cook couldn't have taken the jewels," Bollivar Bland explained. "She'd have left flour fingerprints."
3. Then Detective Bland picked up a table knife and sliced the cake in half.
4. Out of the steaming center of the cake tumbled a colorful mass of gleaming jewels, sparkling under the soft glow of the dining room light.
5. "Just as I suspected," the detective said. "Hot ice."

**PRACTICE 2** Would you write something that *tells about*, *describes*, or *explains* each of the following? There may be more than one correct answer.

1. a scientific experiment
2. a funny story
3. a lost pet
4. a strange sound
5. a recipe for your favorite dessert

**WRITE** Choose a subject to tell about, to describe, or to explain. Write two or three sentences about that subject.

**GO BEYOND** Read to the class the writing you did for the previous exercise. Could your classmates tell whether you were telling, describing, or explaining? How could you improve your writing?

# Giving and Following Directions

Good directions are simple and complete. Keep your readers or listeners in mind when you give directions. Directions for second-graders, for example, should have easier words than directions for fifth-graders.

Pay close attention when you must follow directions. Listen carefully to oral directions. Read written directions from beginning to end before you do what they say. Ask questions about any directions you do not understand. Follow all directions in the order that they are given.

## Example

Harry did the following trick for his part in the class show. These are his secret directions.

Before going onstage, fill two large glasses about three-quarters full with water. In one glass dissolve eight tablespoons of sugar. Onstage follow these steps.

1. Hand two hard-boiled eggs and a pencil or crayon to someone in the audience. Ask the person to write *sink* on one egg and *float* on the other. Put the egg marked *sink* in the glass of water that has no sugar.

2. In the glass with the sugar put the egg marked *float*. This egg will float, and the other one will sink to the bottom of the glass.

3. Then crack the shells of both eggs to show the audience that both eggs were hard-boiled.

What makes Harry's directions clear enough for you to do his trick?

What magic tricks could you teach someone?

**PRACTICE 1**   Here are directions for making dried-flower place mats. Write the steps in order.

1. In about two weeks paste the dried blossom on a mat made of colored construction paper.
2. Put a heavy book on top of the blotting paper. The book should be large enough to entirely cover all the blossoms.
3. Pick fresh blossoms from plants.
4. Cover both sides of the mat with acetate.
5. Put the blossoms between blotting paper.

**PRACTICE 2**   These directions for painting walls are out of order, and two steps are not mentioned. Write the directions correctly, adding the missing steps.

1. Open the can of paint.
2. Wipe extra paint off the tip of the brush.
3. Start by covering the floor and furniture with drop cloths.
4. Wipe up any paint spills or drips.
5. Stir the paint with a paint paddle.

**WRITE**   Write directions telling how to go from your classroom to the school library, cafeteria, gym, office, or playground. Provide helpful details, like when to turn right or left and when to go up or down to another floor. Share your directions with several classmates. Do they agree with your directions?

**GO BEYOND**   Work in a group of four. Each player thinks of three tasks that someone can learn by following directions. Use tasks that you are completely sure about, such as making a bed or fixing a bicycle tire. Write the name of each task on a separate card. Take turns picking a card. Write the directions you think are important for doing the task named on the card you drew. Then read your directions aloud. Have other members in the group tell whether they think your directions are easy to follow.

### Mice

I think mice
Are rather nice.
   Their tails are long,
   Their faces small,
   They haven't any
   Chins at all.
   Their ears are pink,
   Their teeth are white,
   They run about
   The house at night.
   They nibble things
   They shouldn't touch
   And no one seems
   To like them much.

But *I* think mice
Are nice.

*Rose Fyleman*

How do these facts make you feel about mice?

# Telling Facts from Opinions

A **fact** is something that is true. A fact can be proved. (Mount Everest is the highest mountain in the world.) That statement can be proved because all the high peaks in the world have been measured. An **opinion** is something someone thinks or believes. (I think Mount Everest is the most magnificent mountain in the world.) The words *I think, I feel,* or *I believe* are often used when an opinion is given.

You must accept a fact when it is given, but you can choose to agree or disagree with an opinion. If a person offers convincing reasons for holding a certain opinion, you are more likely to agree with that person.

## Example

The following explanation of a skateboard accident includes facts and opinions.

Bobby's accident was his own fault. He was riding down the hill on his skateboard. He was crossing Elm Street when he hit a wide crack in the road. The skateboard overturned, and Bobby landed on the pavement, hurting his leg. He shouldn't have been skateboarding on that hill. It's much too steep for a boy his age.

Which statements are facts and which are opinions?
What other examples of facts and opinions can you think of?

**PRACTICE 1**   After the number of each sentence, write either *fact* or *opinion*.

1. Bobby is always careless.
2. Last month he was doing "wheelies" on his bicycle.
3. He ran right into Mrs. Pouter's pansy patch.
4. Bobby took a beautiful swan dive over the handlebars.
5. He landed in Mrs. Pouter's pond.

**PRACTICE 2**   Here are five facts. Each fact is followed by one opinion. Make up and write a second opinion.

1. A Chinese priest had the longest fingernails on record. They were 22¾ inches long.
   OPINION:  He didn't type.
2. The now-extinct elephant bird was 10 feet tall and weighed up to 1,000 pounds.
   OPINION:  It must have laid a big egg.
3. The largest inland body of water is the Caspian Sea, which is 760 miles long.
   OPINION:  It would take a month to swim it.
4. James Cantrell once threw a brick more than 135 feet.
   OPINION:  Few people challenge him to a snowball fight.
5. The world's largest carpet is 88,000 square feet.
   OPINION:  They don't put that down in a telephone booth.

**WRITE**   Your class is holding an election. You are running for president. Write a campaign speech. Tell why you think you are the best candidate for class president. Include facts and opinions.

**GO BEYOND**   Exchange with a partner the papers you wrote for the Write exercise. Underline the facts on your partner's paper. Circle the opinions. Now return the papers and note what your partner decided were facts and opinions. Do you agree? Discuss any statements about which you do not agree.

# Persuading Others

Everything in an advertisement is there to persuade people to buy something. Understanding advertising methods will help you decide what to believe.

Ads use **statistics,** facts stated in terms of numbers. Statistics can be very convincing.

Ads may use the opinion of a famous person. They hint that you, too, may become famous if you buy the product. Other ads show someone dressed as an expert, such as a doctor or dentist. This suggests that well-educated people use the product. Some ads use a symbol, such as a cartoon figure. The advertisers think you will buy the product if you remember the symbol. All ads try to give you a good general impression, or image, of their product.

## Example

Here are some statements for Munchies cereal ads.

USE OF STATISTICS    Eat Munchies for breakfast. Nine out of ten students eat them.

USE OF FAMOUS PERSON    Julia Smithers, the fastest woman sprinter, eats Munchies every morning.

USE OF SYMBOL    Munchie Mouse says, "Start your day with sunshine! Eat Munchies!"

USE OF EXPERT    My doctor says that Munchies give you a good start in the morning.

USE OF IMAGE    Munchies—the crunchy way to start a successful day.

What is your impression of Munchies?
Tell about another ad that you think is very persuasive.

**PRACTICE 1**   According to each advertisement below, what will happen if you eat Munchies? Write your answers.

1. Eat Munchies. All smart people do!
2. Christina Slavers, champion long-distance swimmer, eats Munchies.
3. Molly Moose says, "Put some sunshine in your day! Eat Munchies!"
4. My dentist says Munchies are good for your smile.
5. Munchies let you crunch your way to success!

**PRACTICE 2**   Each statement uses an advertising method to sell Jolly Jeans. Write the name of the method used in each statement.

1. Fashion designers say our jeans are the best-fitting jeans you can buy.
2. Jolly Jeans—the perfect pants for every occasion!
3. Ellie Pipes, lead singer of Decibelles, wears our jeans.
4. Two out of every three men and women who try Jolly Jeans buy Jolly Jeans.
5. Look for the smiling bear on the back pocket of each pair.

**WRITE**   Choose a product you think is terrific. It could be something that you already use or would like to buy. Perhaps you have a favorite brand of frozen food that is delicious. Maybe you want to get a special kind of sneaker. Write a script for a television commercial to advertise the product. Decide what image you want to give. Decide what methods you want to use.

**GO BEYOND**   Design a magazine or newspaper ad for your product. Write one or more paragraphs to persuade your readers that they need the product. Use pictures to emphasize its best-looking features.

## Practice

**A.** Decide whether you would write a paragraph that tells about, describes, or explains each of the following. There may be more than one correct answer. Choose the one you think is best.

1. a movie
2. a new shirt
3. an embarrassing experience
4. why airplanes fly
5. directions to the park
6. an overnight camping trip
7. a little brother
8. a homework assignment
9. a band's uniforms
10. an exciting softball game

**B.** Explain in two different ways, for children and for adults, how to make toast and how to make a peanut butter sandwich. Write the directions you would give.

**C.** Write *F* after the number of each sentence that states a fact. Write *O* after the number of each sentence that gives an opinion.

1. *The Umbrella Man* is a delightful film.
2. The film lasts more than one hour and forty-seven minutes.
3. It stars Claudia Monteverde and Rico Elan.
4. The funniest part is when the children hide from the Umbrella Man.
5. In the film they buy the Umbrella Man a dog.

**D.** What method of advertising does each of these statements represent? Beside the number of each item, write *statistics, famous person, expert, symbol,* or *image.*

1. William Cott, the world's greatest tenor, listens to records on his Sounz stereo.
2. Snappy the Whale says, "Eat more Forster's Seafoods!"
3. Dentists often recommend Nosuga to their patients.
4. Channel 9 is really fine!
5. Nine out of ten people like our soup best!

## Composition

Make up a product, and think about how you can convince other people to buy it. Write an advertisement for your imaginary product. As you write the ad, keep in mind the person who might use the product. Go into detail about the best features of the product. As part of your ad, explain why the product is easy or pleasant to use. Describe how it works. Be sure that your advertisement mentions good things that will happen as people use the product.

## Advanced Challenge

Think of something you might want to teach someone to do. It could be how to make something or get somewhere.

Make three sets of directions, all for the same purpose. One set will be written. That is, you will write the directions on paper in order to get your information across to the other person. In this set of directions you should not use pictures or maps of any kind.

The next set of directions will be drawn. Make a diagram or a map that gives the directions. You may label it with the names of streets, buildings, and places, for example, but do not add any written directions to it. You may use arrows showing directions.

Your third set of directions will be oral. You may plan what you will say, but you should not put this in writing or point or use other gestures.

Give your three sets of directions to three different people. Ask for their comments. Where were your directions not clear? Which set of directions was easiest to understand? Which was most difficult?

## EXACT WORDS

An exact word with the right connotation, or feeling, can make the difference between someone understanding what you write or being confused by it. Exact words make the difference between an exciting story and a dull one, or between a clear report and a muddled one.

PRACTICE   Replace each underlined word with a more exact word from the list. You may use a dictionary for help.

| | | | | |
|---|---|---|---|---|
| leaped | crooned | screamed | waddled | raced |
| alarmed | sauntered | spongy | overjoyed | crept |

Jack was so excited he could hardly sit still. When his mother and he arrived, he <u>got</u> out of the car and <u>went</u> to the pen. There they were, all seven, each more wriggly than the next. "But where is she?" Jack asked, <u>frightened</u>. Then out she <u>walked</u>, cute and floppy and round. She went straight to Jack and gave his nose a wonderful lick with her <u>soft</u> tongue. "There you are," Jack <u>sang</u> softly, "my very own puppy."

**A.** Write the correct meaning of each term.
1. communicate
2. discussion
3. closing statement
4. sentence
5. paragraph

**B.** Write *setting, character,* or *plot* after each number to tell what story part the sentence belongs in.
1. Jean was an excellent swimmer.
2. Foaming waves crashed against the long, sandy beach.
3. Early sun burned across the sand.
4. A lifeguard began blowing loudly on his whistle.
5. Jean was swimming offshore and did not hear him.

**C.** Write *fact* or *opinion* after each number to tell what the statement is.
1. There are thirty-six inches in a yard.
2. I think we should always use the metric system.
3. My dentist is the best dentist in the world!
4. Everyone should learn how to play soccer.
5. I think the squirrels in Colorado are much smaller than the ones in New England.

EDISON ELEMENTARY SCHOOL

FIELD DAY

Friday October 28

WE NEED YOUR SUPPORT! - SHOW UP WITH SCHOOL COLORS!

CHEER US ON TO VICTORY

Sign up for events in the GYM!

---------------------------
Parents Signature

----------------------------------------------------------------------

EDISON ELEMENTARY SCHOOL - NOVEMBER LUNCH MENU

| MONDAY | TUESDAY | WEDNESDAY | THURSDAY | FRIDAY |
|---|---|---|---|---|
| Oct 29 | 30 | 31 | Nov 1 | 2 |
| Hot Dog/Roll | Tacos | Vegetable Soup | Pizza | Fried Clam Roll |
| Baked Beans | Rice/Green Beans | Gr. Cheese Sandwich | Tossed Salad | French Fries |
| Cole Slaw | Jello with Fruit | Raw Veg. Choice | Cheese Sticks | Raw Veg. Choice |
| Fruit | | Halloween Dessert | Fruit | Pudding |
| 5 | 6 | 7 | 8 | 9 |
| Hamburg/Roll | Chicken Nuggets | Juice | Pizza | Tuna Boat |
| French Fries | Sweet Sour Sauce | Cold Cut Grinder | Tossed Salad | Tossed Bread |
| Peas-Carrots | Potato Puffs | Raw Veg. Choice | Cheese Sticks | Cheese Sticks |
| Fruit | Raw Veg. Choice | Potato Chips | Fruit | Jello with Fruit |
| | Fruit | Cake/Salad Bar | | |
| 12 | 13 | 14 | 15 | 16 |
| | Pizza | | | Hot Dog/Roll |
| VETERANS DAY | Tossed Salad | ½ DAY | ½ DAY | Potato Puffs |
| NO SCHOOL | Cheese Sticks | | | Cole Slaw |
| | Fruit | | | Fruit |
| 19 | 20 | 21 | 22 | 23 |
| Juice | Salisbury Steak/Gravy | ½ DAY | | |
| Cheeseburger | Mashed Potato | | THANKSGIVING HOLIDAY | |
| French Fries | Corn | | | |
| Raw Veg. Choice | Dinner Rolls | | | |
| Fruit | Thanksgiving Dessert | | | |
| 26 | 27 | 28 | 29 | 30 |
| Hot Dog/Roll | Chicken Nuggets | Soup/V. | Pizza | Hamburg/Roll |
| French Fries | Sweet Sour Sauce | Tuna Boat | Tossed Salad | French Fries |
| Cole Slaw | Potato Puffs | Cheese Sticks | Cheese Sticks | Raw Veg. Choice |
| Fruit | Raw Veg. Choice | Pudding/Pops | Fruit | Juice/Sauce |
| | Bread/Butter | Salad Bar | | |
| | Fruit | | | |

SALAD BAR EVERY WEDNESDAY—MIDDLE SCHOOL   WHITE, SKIM & CHOCOLATE MILK SERVED DAILY.
ONLY WHITE MILK FOR SNACK.

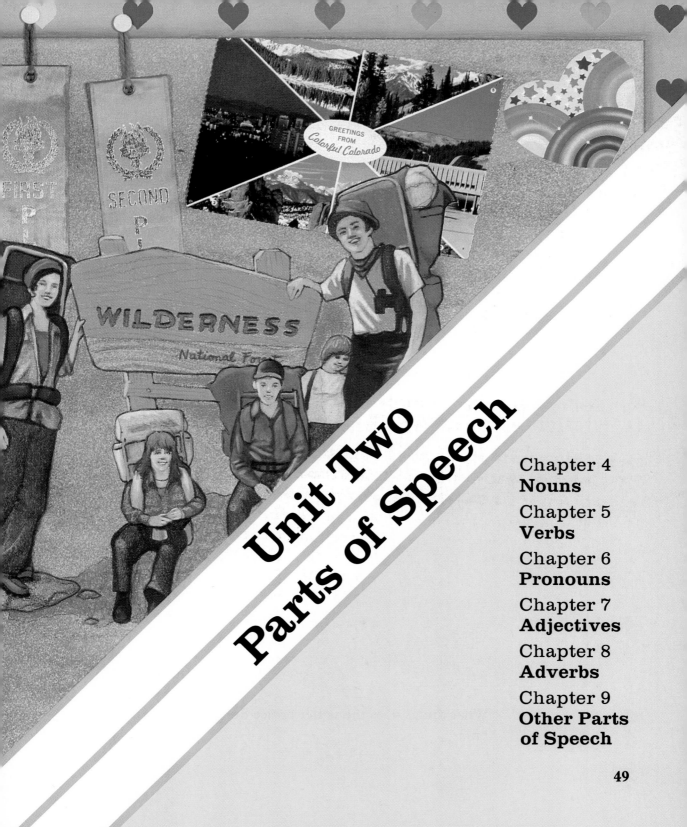

# Unit Two
# Parts of Speech

Chapter 4
**Nouns**

Chapter 5
**Verbs**

Chapter 6
**Pronouns**

Chapter 7
**Adjectives**

Chapter 8
**Adverbs**

Chapter 9
**Other Parts of Speech**

49

**Afternoon on a Hill**

I will be the gladdest thing
    Under the sun!
I will touch a hundred flowers
    And not pick one.
I will look at cliffs and clouds
    With quiet eyes,
Watch the wind bow down the grass,
    And the grass rise.
And when lights begin to show
    Up from the town,
I will mark which must be mine,
    And then start down!

*Edna St. Vincent Millay*

What things does the writer notice during her afternoon on the hill?

Chapter 4
Nouns

Lesson 1  **Understanding Nouns**
Lesson 2  **Common and Proper Nouns**
Lesson 3  **Singular and Plural Nouns**
Lesson 4  **More Ways of Forming Plurals**
Lesson 5  **Possessive Forms of Nouns**

51

# Understanding Nouns

A **noun** is a word that names a person, a place, a thing, or an idea. The words *boy, school, doll,* and *hunger* are all nouns.

The words *a, an,* and *the* are called **articles**. An article is often used to signal that a noun will follow. Not every noun has an article before it, but every article in a sentence is always followed by a noun. The noun may be the first word after the article (*the barn*) or it may come later in a group of words (*the* big red *barn*). Nouns name the things that people write and talk about.

## Example

In this paragraph from Mitchell F. Nayne's *Orphan Pup*, the under-lined words are nouns.

I had just passed the old cedar <u>tree</u> that marks the <u>start</u> of <u>Troublesome</u> <u>Hollow</u>, when I heard a low, odd-sounding <u>whine</u>. I stopped and looked all around, and after a brief <u>search</u>, I found what had made the <u>noise</u>. It was a <u>pup</u> of some <u>sort</u>, with a funny shaped <u>head</u> and dark <u>fur</u>, and the most appealing blue <u>eyes</u> I had ever seen. I tried to pick it up, but the little <u>thing</u> was frightened and ran off a little <u>way</u>. I kept clicking my <u>tongue</u> and whistling and calling, but it would just crouch with its <u>nostrils</u> twitching wildly and run when I approached.

Which nouns follow an article?
Which nouns do not have an article before them?

**PRACTICE 1**  Write each sentence. Underline each noun and circle each article.

1. Almost every young person would like a puppy for a pet.
2. A young dog is a wonderful companion and an eager playmate.
3. Our neighbors recently bought a beagle.
4. The children on the street play with the beagle all the time.
5. The puppy plays constantly and never needs a rest.

**PRACTICE 2**  Complete each sentence by using a noun. Write each sentence.

1. _____ grow under the ground.
2. We went for a nice _____ after dinner.
3. Danny caught the last _____ to Detroit.
4. An _____ is a delicious fruit.
5. I sent the _____ to the wrong address.

**WRITE**  In a letter to a friend, tell about something you would like to do or about somewhere you would like to go. Explain why you would like to do the thing or why you would like to visit the place.

**GO BEYOND**  Exchange with a classmate the letter that you wrote for the Write exercise. Underline each noun on your partner's paper. Circle each article. Return the papers and discuss what you found. Did either of you overlook any nouns or articles?

# Common and Proper Nouns

Ms. Diane Walsh

A noun like *country* is called a **common noun.** A common noun names any person, place, thing, or idea. A noun like *Canada* is called a **proper noun.** A proper noun names a particular person, place, thing, or idea. It always starts with a capital letter. Some proper nouns like *South America* or *Ms. Diane Walsh* are made up of two or more words.

■ **Capitalize proper nouns. Do not capitalize common nouns except at the beginnings of sentences.**

## Example

Read this selection. Both the common nouns and the proper nouns are underlined.

"Where are you going?" George asked.

"I'm taking a bus to Cleveland," the girl answered.

"Why would you ever want to go to that city!" Liz exclaimed.

The usually chalk-white face of the girl turned red as a beet.

"Let me be!" she shouted. "I'm going to visit my Aunt Lilian to help her with my uncle, who has been sick."

"Your friends aren't asking you to stay in Parma, Adelle," said Mr. Hawkins. "They are just interested in you."

"I know," whispered Adelle. Her eyes were moist. "I'm sorry, but I have just had too many upsets this week."

Which nouns are common nouns?

Which nouns are proper nouns?

**PRACTICE 1**   Write each sentence. Underline each common noun once and each proper noun twice.

1. George said, "My mother once visited that city."
2. Cleveland is a wonderful place.
3. Adelle packed her suitcase.
4. "When does the train leave the station?" asked Mr. Hawkins.
5. I hope her uncle will get better soon.

**PRACTICE 2**   Write each sentence. Capitalize each proper noun.

1. Tai asked his teacher, mr. miyamoto, to watch him play tennis.
2. Every tuesday and thursday afternoon they went to the courts at douglas field.
3. Tai's older brother, david, was giving him lessons.
4. David was on a tennis team whose name was sure shots.
5. Tai told his friends nicky and miguel what he had learned by watching the team play.

**WRITE**   Prepare a one-paragraph report on something that you and your classmates did at school this year. If possible, report on something that was a new experience for you. Underline the nouns you used.

■ **Be sure that you capitalize each proper noun.**

**GO BEYOND**   Work with a partner. Describe yourself in writing *without* using any nouns. You might write, for example, "I am strong, female, and adventurous. I am ten and love to skate, swim, and hike." Then describe yourself again, but this time include nouns. Discuss with your partner the differences between the two kinds of writing. Which description was easier to write? Which do you think sounds better?

# Singular and Plural Nouns

Nouns like *boy, beach, tree,* and *hope* are **singular** nouns. A singular noun names one person, place, thing, or idea. Nouns that name more than one person, place, thing, or idea are **plural** nouns. The words *boys, beaches, trees,* and *hopes* are plural nouns.

Adding *-s* to most singular nouns makes them plural: *spoon, spoons.* If a singular noun ends in *s, x, ch, sh,* or *z,* adding *-es* makes the noun plural: *dish, dishes.*

■ **Add an *-s* to most singular nouns to make them plural. Add the ending *-es* to nouns that end in *s, x, ch,* or *sh* to make them plural.**

## Example

Read this paragraph. The underlined words are plural nouns.

Rusty thought she spotted two <u>fins</u> cutting through the water. Could they be <u>sharks</u>? She squinted her <u>eyes</u> and wiped her <u>goggles</u>. The <u>fins</u> made two <u>passes</u> by Rusty as she held her breath. Then with two enormous <u>splashes</u>, Willie burst up from below. She had rubber <u>paddles</u> strapped to her <u>hands</u> and <u>feet</u>. The sun danced in her hair like <u>patches</u> of pure light. Soon the laughter of both <u>girls</u> was rippling with the <u>waves</u>.

What is the singular form of each plural noun?
Which nouns add *-s* to form the plural and which add *-es?*

**PRACTICE 1** Write the plural noun in each sentence. Beside each plural noun, write its singular form.

1. Patches of white foam appeared on the rough sea.
2. There were several flashes of bright lightning.
3. The gulls soared inward toward the land.
4. The ship tossed on the surges of the tide.
5. Sailors called to each other above the storm.

**PRACTICE 2** Write the plural forms of the first ten nouns. Write the singular forms of the last ten nouns.

| | | | |
|---|---|---|---|
| 1. tax | 6. dress | 11. flashes | 16. lunches |
| 2. wish | 7. bench | 12. axes | 17. grasses |
| 3. inch | 8. brush | 13. bosses | 18. churches |
| 4. moss | 9. branch | 14. bushes | 19. crashes |
| 5. box | 10. glass | 15. foxes | 20. beaches |

**WRITE** Plan and write a brief story about two or more friends playing tricks on each other. Tell what happened. Your story can be a true one or one that you make up. Use at least five plural nouns in your story.

■ **Check your work. Make sure you followed the rules for forming plurals.**

**GO BEYOND** Do this activity with the whole class or in several groups. Imagine that you are going on a trip and have to pack a suitcase. One person begins by saying, "In my suitcase I put _____ ." He or she adds a plural noun that begins with the letter *a*. The next person repeats what the first person has said and adds a plural noun that begins with the next letter of the alphabet. A player who cannot repeat the named items is out of the game. Continue until all the letters of the alphabet have been used.

# More Ways of Forming Plurals

You know that adding -*s* to most singular nouns makes them plural. When a singular noun ends in *y* following a vowel, adding -*s* makes that noun plural. The plural form of the noun *boy* is *boys*.

If a singular noun ends in *y* following a consonant, form the plural by changing the *y* to *i* and adding -*es*. The plural of the noun *company* is *companies*.

Some singular nouns that end in *f* or *fe* are made plural by changing the *f* or *fe* to *v* and adding -*es*. The plural form of the noun *elf* is *elves*; the plural of *wife* is *wives*.

Some nouns, such as *woman, child,* and *mouse,* have special plurals. The nouns *women, children,* and *mice* are called irregular plurals because they are not formed according to a rule. Other irregular plurals, such as *deer* and *sheep*, have singular and plural forms that are the same.

## Example

The underlined words in this selection are plural forms of nouns.

Mr. Hale was a favorite of all the <u>families</u> in the neighborhood. He used to be a special guest at Halloween <u>parties</u>. He always told scary <u>stories</u> about <u>ghosts</u>, <u>monsters</u>, <u>monkeys</u>, <u>elves</u>, and <u>bats</u>. The <u>stories</u> made the <u>children</u> shiver and shriek, but they loved them. You might think that he liked to scare the <u>boys</u> and <u>girls</u>. The opposite was true. Of all the <u>men</u> I have ever met, Mr. Hale was the kindest. He understood how wonderful it is to let your imagination travel on the wildest <u>adventures</u> when you are safe among <u>friends</u> and family.

How was each underlined plural formed?
Why do most people like scary stories?

**PRACTICE 1**   Find the plural nouns in the following sentences. Write the plural noun and its singular form.
1. Mr. Hale was a favorite guest of all the families.
2. He came to all our Halloween parties.
3. He was an important person in our lives.
4. Do you think he liked to scare children?
5. I wish there were more men like Mr. Hale.

**PRACTICE 2**   Write each sentence. Use the correct plural form of the noun in parentheses.
1. My (buddy) Peg and Greg belong to a science club.
2. The club is making a guidebook for (child) who visit the zoo.
3. The first section describes common animals like (mouse).
4. The second part tells about wild animals like (deer).
5. The third part tells about unusual animals like (kangaroo).

**WRITE**   In a paragraph, tell what is happening in the picture. Use plural nouns to name as many of the animals and things as you can.

**GO BEYOND**   As you grow older, you learn more nouns. Once your world included only your family, your crib, and your playthings. Then you learned about your house, street, and neighborhood. Make a chart for at least three ages, for example, six months, three years, and six years. Use plural nouns to name people, places, and things that became part of your growing world at each age.

# Possessive Forms of Nouns

The word *possess* means "to have or own." A **possessive noun** is one that shows ownership. Adding an apostrophe and -*s* (-'s) to a singular noun makes that noun possessive. You can write about *Jim's* horse, the *horse's* tail, an *animal's* ears, or Ms. *Jones's* cars.

The possessive of a plural noun that already ends with the letter *s* is formed by using an apostrophe after the *s* (-s'). You can write about *horses'* hooves, the *players'* mistakes, or the *Joneses'* cars.

If a plural noun does not end in *s*, adding an apostrophe and -*s* (-'s) shows possession or ownership. You can write about the *women's* jobs, the *children's* games, or the *deer's* antlers.

■ **To make a singular noun show ownership, add -'s. To make a plural noun that ends in s show ownership, add an apostrophe ('). To make a plural noun that does not end in s show ownership, add 's.**

## Example

Here are some nouns that show ownership.

| NOUN | POSSESSIVE FORM | |
|---|---|---|
| dog | dog's | The dog's collar is red. |
| dogs | dogs' | The dogs' collars are leather. |
| child | child's | The child's toy is broken. |
| children | children's | The children's toys are in the box. |
| actress | actress' | The actress' costume did not fit properly. |
| actresses | actresses' | The actresses' costumes were new. |

**PRACTICE 1**   Write each sentence. Use the possessive form of the noun in parentheses.

1. The (twins) afternoon was very long.
2. Olin and Julio worked in their (grandparents) garden.
3. That night the (children) backs ached.
4. They could hardly laugh at (Uncle Victor) jokes.
5. When they snuggled into (Dad) old bed, it felt great.

**PRACTICE 2**   Make three columns. Head the first column *Word,* the second column *Singular,* and the third, *Plural.* In the first column, write the nouns listed below. Then write the singular and plural possessive forms for each noun. Add another noun to each possessive to show what belongs to the owner or owners.

| EXAMPLE | WORD | SINGULAR | PLURAL |
|---|---|---|---|
| | dog | dog's dish | dogs' dishes |

1. winner          6. man
2. family          7. teacher
3. woman          8. girl
4. friend          9. coach
5. farmer         10. baby

**WRITE**   Using possessive nouns, write a question and an answer. You can write a riddle and its answer if you wish.

EXAMPLE     If Tim's father is Bob's son, how is Bob related to Tim? *Bob is Tim's grandfather.*

■ **Check to be sure that you wrote singular and plural possessive nouns correctly.**

**GO BEYOND**   Work in groups of three or four. Make a list of at least ten items that could belong to certain people or animals. Then add a possessive noun to each item to show ownership.

## Practice

**A.** Write each sentence and underline every noun. Write *C* above each common noun and *P* above each proper noun.

1. Merryl and Julian and their family moved to Austin from San Antonio.
2. The pen on the table belongs to Bob.
3. Did Nicky see the picture of the Simpsons in our hall?
4. Carrie saw a rainbow after it rained in Carson City on Tuesday.
5. Marla bought the chair for Dad at the Quint Furniture Market.

**B.** Choose a proper noun to replace each underlined word or group of words in the sentences. Rewrite each sentence.

1. Did <u>the girl</u> read that book?
2. <u>The man</u> went to <u>the city</u> on business.
3. I'm going to visit a <u>friend</u> in his new home over the <u>holiday</u> weekend.
4. We took <u>my cat</u> to the veterinarian.

5. Could <u>the team member</u> charge some sports equipment at <u>a store</u>?

**C.** Write each sentence. Make each noun in parentheses plural.

1. Jill packed the (dish) in the (box).
2. Pedro carefully placed the (glass) in the cabinet.
3. There are three (company) in the area that make clothing for (baby).
4. These (knife) need sharpening.
5. Janet put a dozen (guppy) in the tank.
6. The (sheep) are grazing in both fields.
7. These (mouse) love to eat sausage.
8. The (deer) come to the lake for water.
9. Young (child) love to sing.
10. My little brother has four new (tooth).

**D.** Rewrite each of the following sentences. Use a possessive and a noun to take the place of the underlined words.

1. George untied <u>the shoes of his brother</u>.
2. Fred borrowed <u>the book of James</u>.
3. The <u>problems of the cities</u> were the same.
4. The <u>mothers of the children</u> watched them carefully.
5. All pilots check <u>the instruments of their planes</u>.

## Composition

Whenever something new is invented or discovered, people have to name it so that they can talk about it. Otherwise, it would be difficult or impossible to refer exactly to the new thing.

Imagine that you have invented or discovered something. Perhaps you have invented a machine that can weed a garden. Or perhaps you have discovered an animal that no one knew about before. Think of a name for your invention or discovery. Then write a paragraph that tells how it works or what it is like. Make sure that your paragraph tells your reader why the name you selected for it is a good one.

## Advanced Challenge

The nouns that name places in the United States are very interesting. Some come from other languages. Vermont, for example, comes from the French words for "green mountains" and Las Vegas comes from the Spanish word for "the city of the plains." Some places, such as Illinois and Utah, are named after the native Americans who first lived there. Other places, such as Houston and Denver, are named after people. Still other places are named after features that the places have, such as Rocky Ridge and Mountain View.

As a class project, do a study of the place names in your state or area. Each student may be given five or six place names to find out about. Decide how long you will need to gather information about the names. Then choose a time when reports are due. Each member of the class can then report his or her findings to the entire class. You might want to share your findings with the rest of the class in the form of a written report. The title of the report could be "Names in Our Land."

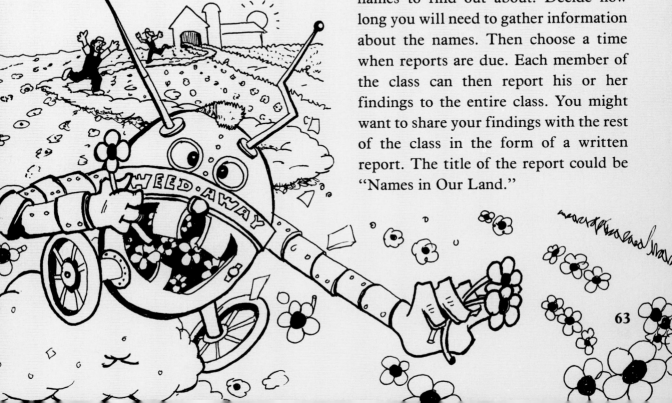

## WHERE DO WORDS COME FROM?

Do you know that the bologna in your sandwich got its name from Bologna, a city in Italy, where it was first made? Many foods that we eat, objects that we use, or games that we play are named after the places where they were first made or started.

PRACTICE  Find out what places gave their names to the following things. Use your dictionary, a big dictionary in your school or public library, or an encyclopedia for help.
1. frankfurter
2. hamburger
3. jeans
4. marathon
5. bayonet

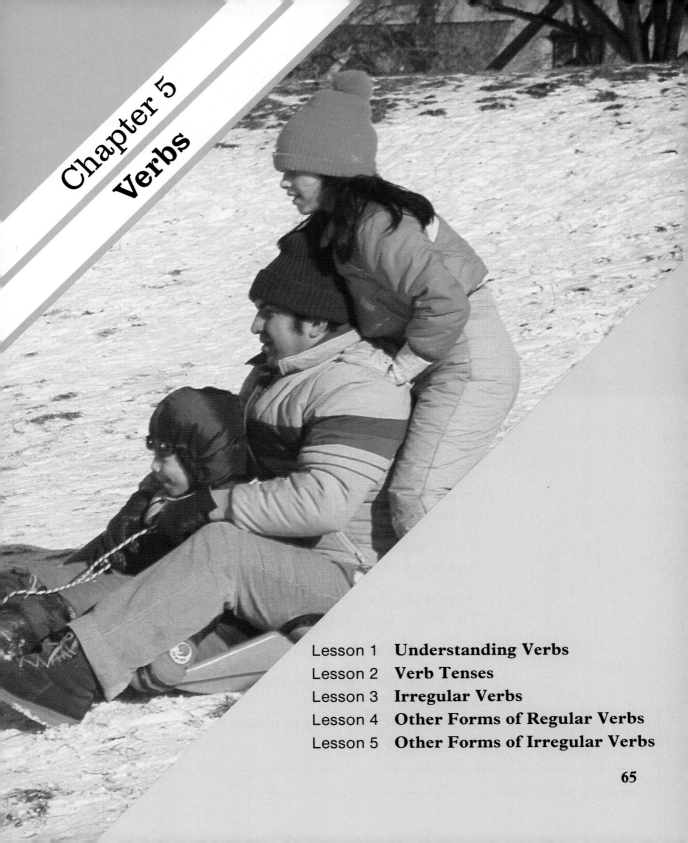

# Chapter 5
# Verbs

Lesson 1    **Understanding Verbs**
Lesson 2    **Verb Tenses**
Lesson 3    **Irregular Verbs**
Lesson 4    **Other Forms of Regular Verbs**
Lesson 5    **Other Forms of Irregular Verbs**

65

# Understanding Verbs

There are two general types of verbs—**action verbs** and **linking verbs**.

Action verbs tell what the subject of a sentence does: The kitten purrs. The verb *purrs* in this sentence explains what the kitten does.

Linking verbs link, or connect, the subject of a sentence with a word that follows the verb. The word that follows a linking verb names or describes the subject: That kitten is Hugo. The word *Hugo* provides another name for *kitten.* Look at this sentence: Hugo seems frisky. The word *frisky* describes *Hugo.* The verb *is* and *seem* are linking verbs.

Linking verbs may be some form of *be,* such as *am, is, are, was,* or *were.* Some other linking verbs are *seem, taste, look, smell, and become.*

## Example

Here are some sentences. The action verbs and linking verbs are underlined.

Those students <u>play</u> well. (*Play* is an action verb.)
Sara <u>knows</u> the anwer. (*Knows* is an action verb.)

Some students <u>are</u> players. (*Are* is a linking verb.)
The answer <u>seems</u> easy. (*Seems* is a linking verb.)

Some verbs can be either action verbs or linking verbs.

My grandparents <u>grow</u> tomatoes every summer. (*Grow* is an action verb.)
Every day the children <u>grow</u> restless before lunch. (*Grow* is a linking verb.)

**PRACTICE 1** Write each sentence. Draw one line under each action verb and two lines under each linking verb.

1. Jackie and Eva buy cat food at the store.
2. Their cat is always hungry.
3. Eva carries the heavy bag inside.
4. Jackie opens the bag with scissors.
5. The food smells awful.
6. The cat gallops into the kitchen.
7. He rubs against the girls' legs.
8. He meows loudly.
9. He seems very hungry.
10. Jackie puts some food into the cat's bowl.

**PRACTICE 2** Write each sentence. Add an action verb or a linking verb. Use these verbs: <u>seem</u>, <u>smells</u>, <u>brings</u>, <u>love</u>, <u>plays</u>. After each sentence write *A* if the verb is an action verb and *L* if the verb is a linking verb.

1. This rose _____ wonderful!
2. I _____ the taste of picnic foods.
3. Alice always _____ homemade pickles.
4. Our team _____ volleyball at 3 o'clock.
5. These parties always _____ too short.

**WRITE** Write three sentences about one of your favorite places. Use linking verbs. Then write three sentences about what you do there. Use action verbs.

**GO BEYOND** Trade the sentences that you wrote for the Write exercise with a partner. Check each other's work. Do the action verbs tell what the subjects of the sentences are doing? Do the words that follow the linking verbs name or describe the subjects?

# Verb Tenses

Verbs tell when things happen. Verbs can tell that something is happening now, that it happened in the past, or that it will happen in the future.

A verb in the **present tense** tells that something is happening now, at the present time. Verbs in the present tense end in -*s* when the subject is singular: The cat *cleans* her kittens every day. She *washes* them carefully. When the subject is *I, you,* or plural, present tense verbs do not end in *s*: Cats *keep* themselves clean. I *like* them.

A verb in the **past tense** tells that something happened at some point in time before the present. Most verbs in the past tense end in *d* or *ed:* The cat *cleaned* her kittens yesterday. She *washed* them carefully.

A verb in the **future tense** tells that something will happen at some time after the present. The word *will* is used with the verb in the future tense: The cat *will clean* her kittens tomorrow. She *will wash* them carefully.

## Example

Verbs in the present tense are underlined in these sentences.

Delores <u>walks</u> two miles every day.
My brothers <u>weed</u> the garden every Saturday.

Verbs in the past tense are underlined in these sentences.

Brad <u>laughed</u> at the joke.
The plane <u>landed</u> a moment ago.

Verbs in the future tense are underlined in these sentences.

I <u>will listen</u> to the instructions carefully.
My aunt and uncle <u>will arrive</u> tomorrow.

**PRACTICE 1**  Write each sentence and underline the verb. After each sentence write present, past, or future to tell the tense of the verb.

1. Juanita looked at the unusual coin.
2. Emily really enjoys the pool.
3. I will remember her telephone number.
4. The painters washed their brushes.
5. The farmer waters the crops every day.

**PRACTICE 2**  Rewrite each sentence. Change the tense of the verb to the tense given in parentheses.

1. Mel and Sandy worked together on their model cars. (future)
2. They discuss the features of different cars. (past)
3. Mel liked Sandy's suggestions. (present)
4. Mel thanks Sandy for her ideas. (past)
5. He suggested some ideas to Sandy. (future)

**WRITE**  Write five sentences that tell about things that you have seen in the last hour. Use past tense verbs in all your sentences.

**GO BEYOND**  Rewrite each of the sentences you wrote for the Write exercise twice. Use present tense verbs in your first rewrite and future tense verbs in your second rewrite.

# Irregular Verbs

The past tense of most verbs is formed by adding *-d* or *-ed* to the present tense form of the verb. Verbs that form the past tense in this way are called **regular verbs**. Verbs that do not form the past tense in this way are called **irregular verbs**.

The past tense forms of irregular verbs follow no set pattern. You have to remember these forms. But you do know most of these forms already because you use irregular verbs all the time when you speak and write.

## Example

Here is a listing of some irregular verbs. Notice the past tense forms.

| PRESENT | PAST |
|---------|------|
| bring | brought |
| buy | bought |
| catch | caught |
| choose | chose |
| come | came |
| draw | drew |
| drink | drank |
| fall | fell |
| fight | fought |
| go | went |
| have | had |
| run | ran |
| ring | rang |
| sing | sang |
| say | said |
| think | thought |
| write | wrote |

**PRACTICE 1**   Write each sentence. Use the correct past tense form of each verb in parentheses. If you are not sure about the spelling, look at the list in the Example.

1. We (go) on a picnic last Saturday.
2. I (bring) the fruit.
3. Walter and Agnes (choose) sides for a game of softball.
4. Samantha (catch) a little toad in center field.
5. Todd (say) something to the pitcher.

**PRACTICE 2**   Rewrite each sentence. Change the present tense form of the irregular verb to the past tense form.

1. Chad draws people very well.
2. My mother sings in our church choir.
3. The alarm bell rings very loud.
4. Many of my classmates run every day.
5. The rain falls constantly.
6. The members come from all over the state.
7. People think about the next election.
8. These boats catch a lot of fish.
9. The swimmers bring towels with them.
10. The best shoppers choose the freshest vegetables.

**WRITE**   In two paragraphs tell about a time when a friend was careless and broke something of yours. The story can be a true one or one you make up. In the first paragraph tell how you felt about what happened. In the second paragraph tell what you said and did. Underline the irregular verbs in your paragraphs. Circle the past tense forms of any irregular verbs that you used.

**GO BEYOND**   Discuss with the class the paragraphs you wrote for the Write exercise. Did others handle the problem the way you did? Have you learned other or better ways to handle the same problem?

# Other Forms of Regular Verbs

In addition to the present and past forms, all verbs have two other forms—the **present participle** and the **past participle**.

The present participle of regular verbs is formed by adding *-ing* to the present form: rest, resting; jump, jumping. The past participle of regular verbs is exactly the same as the past tense: rested, jumped.

The present and past participles of regular verbs combine with **helping verbs** to form two-word verbs. Forms of the verb *be* (*am, is, are, was, were*) act as helping verbs with the present participle: *am enjoying, is resting, was walking.* Forms of the verb *have* (*has, had*) act as helping verbs with the past participle: *have enjoyed, has rested, had jumped.*

## Example

Here are some sentences with two-word verbs. Notice that the verbs include a helping verb and the present or past participle.

Jennifer is polishing her shoes.
I am studying for a test.
Many companies are moving to this area.
Larry was watching television.
The men were working on the bridge.
Sheila has ordered her lunch.
Our neighbors had watered their lawns.

*Parts of Speech*

**PRACTICE 1**  Write these sentences. Underline each two-word verb. Circle the helping verb.

1. We have hiked all the way from camp.
2. Leon is practicing on the piano.
3. I was talking to my grandmother yesterday.
4. Gretchen had walked all the way home.
5. The judges were counting the votes.
6. The principal has locked the school.
7. I am dreaming about the summer.
8. Fred has finished his homework.
9. The visitors were enjoying our park.
10. Those people are waiting for the bus.

**PRACTICE 2**  Use a helping verb or a present or past participle to complete each sentence. Write each sentence.

1. Henry is _____ his vacation.
2. Several people _____ arrived late.
3. I _____ checking the windows and doors.
4. Lea has _____ her room from top to bottom.
5. The police were _____ for the child.
6. Ben has _____ California twice.
7. Our class _____ prepared a good meal.
8. The boys _____ arranged the chairs.
9. The rain has _____ .
10. Peter _____ cutting the lawn.

**WRITE**  Write ten sentences with two-word verbs. Underline the present or past participle in each and circle the helping verbs.

**GO BEYOND**  Form groups of three. Each person gets a list of five regular verbs in the present tense. Each player must use the present and past participle of each verb in a sentence. The sentence must have a helping verb formed from *be* or *have*.

---

*Verbs*                                                                 73

# Other Forms of Irregular Verbs

The present participle of irregular verbs is formed in the same way as the present participle of regular verbs. The ending *ing* is added to the present tense form: *come, coming; draw, drawing; bring, bringing.* A form of the helping verb *be* combines with the present participle to form two-word verbs in sentences: My aunt and uncle *are coming* from California today.

The past participle of irregular verbs is formed in different ways and must be remembered. It is used in sentences with a form of the helping verb *have.* The past participle of an irregular verb is always the form that makes sense with *have: (have) come; (have) drawn; (have) brought.* In sentences a form of *have* combines with the past participle to form a two-word verb: She *has brought* a new game to play.

## Example

Here is a list of the past participles of some irregular verbs. The present tense form is also given.

| | | | | | |
|------|---------|--------|---------|-------|----------|
| see | seen | choose | chosen | run | run |
| be | been | come | come | ring | rung |
| give | given | draw | drawn | sing | sung |
| bring | brought | fall | fallen | say | said |
| catch | caught | go | gone | think | thought |

Here are some present and past participles of irregular verbs used in sentences with helping verbs.

She <u>was</u> <u>singing</u> in the morning.
Karen <u>is</u> <u>bringing</u> a friend to the party.
Ben <u>has</u> <u>caught</u> a tremendous fish.
Claudia <u>had</u> <u>gone</u> home early.
A judge <u>has</u> <u>chosen</u> the winners.

**PRACTICE 1**  Write each of the following sentences. Underline the two-word verb that is made up of the present or past participle of an irregular verb and a helping verb. Circle the helping verb.

1. The kite was falling rapidly.
2. I have seen that man before.
3. My mother had been a teacher.
4. James has thought of some good stories.
5. Ms. Smalley has given an assignment.
6. This car has run for hours.
7. The circus is coming to town.
8. She has sung that song before.
9. The storms had come from the west.
10. All of the church bells have rung.

**PRACTICE 2**  Complete each sentence with the past participle of the verb in parentheses. Write each sentence.

1. Tim has _____ a new shirt. (buy)
2. A tree had _____ across our lawn. (fall)
3. The storms have _____ cooler temperatures. (bring)
4. My uncles have _____ in the army. (be)
5. Louise has _____ me a ticket. (give)

**WRITE**  Write five sentences that contain a helping verb and the past participle of an irregular verb.

**GO BEYOND**  Study the list of past participles in the Example. Answer these questions. Which past participles are formed by adding -*n* or -*en* to the present tense form? Which are the same as the present tense form? Which are the same as the past tense form?

---

**B.** Write each sentence. Underline every present and past participle and circle every helping verb.

1. We are beginning a new year.
2. The plate had fallen from the table.
3. I have worked here for two years.
4. John has been to Europe.
5. I am thinking about dinner.
6. The bell was ringing.
7. I have drawn a new set of plans.
8. Carol has seen this movie before.
9. Shirley is being foolish.
10. I have run all the way from Maple Street.

## Practice

**A.** Write each sentence. Underline the verb in each. Write *AV* above each action verb and *LV* above each linking verb. After each sentence, write the tense of the verb—present, past, or future.

1. Carol and Wendy are dancers.
2. The ship docked at noon.
3. The drivers will rest for a half hour.
4. This peach tastes delicious.
5. My brother will be a pilot in two years.
6. Tim and Andy painted the fence.
7. That dog seems lazy.
8. The government agreed to the plan.
9. Those trees look sturdy.
10. The members of the team practice every Saturday morning.

**C.** Write each sentence. Use the correct form of the verb in parentheses.

1. Linda _____ her breath. (catch)
2. I have _____ to large groups before. (talk)
3. The papers _____ out of my hand. (fall)
4. This book _____ me now. (interest)
5. Maple trees will _____ very tall. (grow)
6. Miguel _____ this picture yesterday. (draw)
7. She has _____ a lot about the problem (say)
8. The game had _____ very well until the seventh inning. (go)
9. The horses were _____ around the pasture. (gallop)
10. I am _____ more every day. (learn)

## Composition

Verbs tell what happens. Writers try to use verbs that tell exactly the kind of action taking place. Instead of writing The kite stayed above the tree, a good writer may write The kite hung above the tree.

Each of the following groups of words has a noun that names an animal. Add a verb and other words to each group to form a sentence. Try to find a verb that tells exactly how the animal acts.

1. The playful kittens
2. A large elephant
3. A swift antelope
4. A long snake
5. The slow turtle
6. The tall giraffe
7. The baby fox
8. A clever raccoon
9. The speedy horse
10. A tiny piglet

## Advanced Challenge

In English a number of verbs can be formed from nouns by adding a suffix to some part of the noun. Look at the following list of nouns. What verb can you make out of each? After you have formed a verb from each noun, write a rule that explains how verbs are formed from some nouns.

1. memory
2. organ
3. colony
4. criticism
5. alphabet
6. fantasy
7. revolution
8. reality
9. character
10. crystal

## DICTIONARY

A dictionary can help you spell and remember difficult words. If you are looking up an unfamiliar verb, a dictionary can show you its various forms.

EXAMPLE

**a bide** (əˊbīd). 1. put up with; endure: *I can't abide their always being late.* 2. stay; remain: *Abide with me for a time.* 3. dwell; reside. 4. wait for. v., **a-bode** or **a-bid-ed, a-bid-ing. - a-bid-er,** n.

The first two words in dark type at the end of the entry tell you that the past tense of *abide* is either *abode* or *abided.* The third word in dark type is the present participle, *abiding,* the form used in an expression such as "I am *abiding.*"

PRACTICE Use a dictionary to answer the following questions.
1. How do you spell the present participle of *ski?*
2. What is the past tense of *entice?*
3. What is the past tense of *creep?*
4. Is *shaven* a correct form?
5. How many *e's* are in the present participle of *pulverize?*

Lesson 1   **Understanding Pronouns**
Lesson 2   **Personal Pronouns**
Lesson 3   **Possessive Forms of Pronouns**
Lesson 4   **Demonstrative Pronouns**

79

**Understanding Pronouns**

A **pronoun** is a word that can take the place of a noun. Notice how the pronouns printed in dark type take the place of nouns in the following sentences: Lenny liked Marilyn. **He** knew that **he** could always count on **her**. When a difficult thing had to be done, **she** told **him** about **it**. **Her** energy was great, and **her** ideas were better than **his**. **He** needed **her** advice. In these sentences, the pronouns *he, his,* and *him* take the place of *Lenny.* The pronouns *she* and *her* take the place of *Marilyn.* The pronoun *it* takes the place of *thing.*

You can improve your writing by learning how to use pronouns correctly.

The following selection is adapted from James Street's "Weep No More, My Lady." The underlined words are pronouns.

The dog turned <u>her</u> head from one side to the other and watched Skeeter. <u>She</u> was trembling, but <u>she</u> didn't run. When Skeeter knelt by <u>her</u>, <u>she</u> stopped trembling.

<u>He</u> petted <u>her</u>. <u>She</u> looked up at <u>him</u> and blinked <u>her</u> big eyes. Then <u>she</u> turned over, and Skeeter scratched <u>her</u>. <u>She</u> closed <u>her</u> eyes, stretched, and chuckled. Jesse walked up. The dog leaped to <u>her</u> feet and sprang between the boy and the man.

What word does each underlined pronoun stand for?
How can you tell that the dog likes the boy?

**PRACTICE 1**  Write each sentence. Underline the pronouns. Draw a line from each pronoun to the noun it takes the place of.

1. John took off his jacket and handed it to his aunt.
2. Diane bought an old bowl and polished it.
3. Maria lost her keys, but Claire found them.
4. The farmer plowed his field and planted seed in it.
5. The searchers found the lost children, and they took them home.

**PRACTICE 2**  Each sentence sounds strange because one or more nouns are repeated. Replace each underlined word or group of words with the correct pronoun. Rewrite the sentence.

1. My friend Dave was interested in spiders, so <u>Dave</u> read about <u>spiders</u>.
2. Dave told me what <u>Dave</u> had learned.
3. Spiders do not see well even though <u>spiders</u> have six eyes.
4. After Dave had looked at a picture of a spider's web, <u>Dave</u> looked for a real one.
5. In the attic Dave found a web, and <u>Dave</u> thought <u>the web</u> was beautiful.

**WRITE**  In a paragraph, tell about a place where you enjoy being with other people. It can be a room in your house or a place you have visited. Use at least four pronouns in your paragraph. Underline each pronoun you use.

**GO BEYOND**  Find a picture that shows people or objects. Paste the picture on paper. Below the picture write several pairs of sentences. Have the first sentence in each pair name a person or object in the picture. In the second sentence, use a pronoun to refer to that person or object.

EXAMPLE      <u>A small girl</u> is swinging. <u>She</u> is wearing a blue dress.

---

*Pronouns*                                                              **81**

**Personal Pronouns**

She broke my rope-jumping record!

A **personal pronoun** stands for or refers to one or more persons or things. What pronoun you choose depends on its use in the sentence.

The personal pronouns *I, you, he, she, it, we,* and *they* are often subjects of verbs. They name the doers of actions expressed by verbs.

Most personal pronouns have a different form when they follow an action verb. The pronouns *me, him, her, us,* and *them* tell who or what receives the action of an action verb. They are the objects of verbs. The pronouns *you* and *it* use the same form whether they are subjects or objects.

Pronouns can be singular or plural.

The pronouns *he* and *him* replace the names of males. The pronouns *she* and *her* replace the names of females.

**Example**

This list will help you remember the personal pronouns.

| SUBJECT PRONOUNS | | OBJECT PRONOUNS | |
|---|---|---|---|
| SINGULAR | PLURAL | SINGULAR | PLURAL |
| I | we | me | us |
| you | you | you | you |
| he, she, it | they | him, her, it | them |

*Parts of Speech*

**PRACTICE 1**   Write each sentence. Underline the subject pronoun once and the object pronoun twice.

1. He had helped her often.
2. I never asked you any questions.
3. You can make rolls and bring them to the picnic.
4. We found Jed's keys and phoned him.
5. She asked him for directions.

**PRACTICE 2**   In each sentence replace the group of underlined words with a pronoun.

1. Silvana and I decided to read about Elizabeth Blackwell.
2. Elizabeth Blackwell was the first woman to receive a medical degree in the United States.
3. Elizabeth and her sister started a medical school for women in New York City.
4. Many authors have written about Elizabeth Blackwell.
5. The books gave Silvana and me much information.

**WRITE**   What was the nicest gift you ever received? Did you like it because it was a thoughtful gift? Or did you like it because it was something you had always wanted? Write a paragraph. Tell who gave you the gift and why. Tell how you felt. Use subject pronouns and object pronouns. Underline the subject pronouns once and the object pronouns twice.

**GO BEYOND**   Write a paragraph that explains how two people you know are very alike or very different. One of the people must be a woman or girl and the other a man or boy. Begin your paragraph with one of these sentences: _____ and _____ are very much alike, or _____ and _____ are very different. Underline the subject pronouns that you used once and the object pronouns twice.

**Possessive Forms of Pronouns**

Like a possessive noun, a **possessive pronoun** shows owner-ship or possession. Unlike a possessive noun, a possessive pronoun has no apostrophe.

*My, your, his, her, its, our,* and *their* are the forms of the posses-sive pronoun that are used before nouns: *My* book is at home. Kim and Anna have *their* books.

*Mine, yours, his, hers, its, ours,* and *theirs* are the forms of the possessive pronouns that can be used alone in place of a noun either before or after a verb: *Mine* is at home. Kim and Anna have *theirs.*

## Example

This list will help you remember the possessive pronouns.

| SINGULAR | PLURAL |
|---|---|
| USED WITH NOUN | USED WITH NOUN |
| my   your   his, her, its | our   your   their |
| USED ALONE | USED ALONE |
| mine   yours   his, her, its | ours   yours   theirs |

## Exercises

**PRACTICE 1**   Write each sentence and underline the posses-sive pronoun or pronouns. Draw two lines under the verb that the pronoun comes before or follows.

1. Your shirt and her skirt are the same color.
2. The dog wagged its tail.
3. Tears were coming into his eyes.
4. When Julie and Greg smiled, their faces glowed.
5. That book belongs on my desk.

**PRACTICE 2** Write each sentence and underline the posessive pronoun. Draw two lines under the verb that the pronoun comes before or follows.

1. Theirs was the best float in the parade.
2. The Johnson's oak is small, but ours towers over the house.
3. I bought mine in New York City five years ago.
4. You borrow Mike's jacket, and I will borrow hers.
5. The coat on the hanger is yours.

**WRITE** The electricity has gone off in your home. It is a very cold day, and three friends are coming for dinner. Write a paragraph telling the problems you will have if the power is not turned on soon. Use at least four possessive pronouns.

**GO BEYOND** Work with a friend and plan a playroom. Decide which areas each of you will plan alone and which you will plan together. When you are through planning, each of you will write about the room. Explain which areas of the room will show your own ideas. Tell which will show your friend's ideas. Use at least five possessive pronouns in your paragraph.

# Demonstrative Pronouns

The words *this, that, these,* and *those* are **demonstrative pronouns**. The word *demonstrate* means "to point out or to show." Demonstrative pronouns point to one or more persons or things.

The demonstrative pronouns *this* and *that* are singular. The pronouns *these* and *those* are plural. The pronouns *this* and *these* point to things that are close: *This* is old. *These* need painting. The pronouns *that* and *those* point to things that are further away: Please wrap *that*. She will take *those*.

In sentences demonstrative pronouns serve as subjects and also appear after action and linking verbs.

## Example

In the following sentences, the demonstrative pronouns are underlined.

| | |
|---|---|
| <u>This</u> will do nicely. | <u>These</u> seem new. |
| I will use <u>this</u>. | We sell <u>these</u>. |
| <u>That</u> is a good idea. | <u>Those</u> are difficult. |
| He fixed <u>that</u>. | Karen bought <u>those</u>. |

**PRACTICE 1**   Write each sentence. Underline the demonstrative pronoun. Write an s above the demonstrative pronoun if it is singular and p if it is plural.

1. These seem harder.
2. We counted those yesterday.
3. Sandra bought that three weeks ago.
4. The police will investigate this very carefully.
5. Those are the most beautiful bushes in the garden.

**PRACTICE 2**   Complete the second sentence in each pair with a demonstrative pronoun. Write each sentence that you complete.

1. Mary's kite flies well. _____ doesn't fly at all.
2. Fred's marbles are brand new. _____ are ancient.
3. My uncle's car runs well. _____ doesn't run at all.
4. Laura's dog barks all the time. _____ is a very quiet dog.
5. John's camp has a lot of activities. _____ has hardly any at all.

**WRITE**   Write five sentences of your own that contain a demonstrative pronoun. The pronoun can be the subject or it can come immediately after the verb.

**GO BEYOND**   Work in a small group. Have each person prepare four cards. On two of the cards, the person writes the names of two objects that can be seen from where the group is sitting. On the other two cards, the names of two objects that are out of sight should be written. The cards should include two singular and two plural nouns. Collect all the cards and put them into a single stack. Each person picks a card and uses a demonstrative pronoun to refer to one of the nouns in a sentence. Each member of the group examines all sentences to be sure that the demonstrative pronouns appear either before or directly after the verb.

**Chapter 6 Review**

## Practice

**A.** Choose the correct pronoun in parentheses. Write each sentence.

1. (He, Him) is afraid the cup will break.
2. (We, Us) want to go to that park.
3. We saw (they, them) several times last week.
4. I met (she, her) at a club meeting.
5. Did you tell (he, him) about that movie?
6. (She, Her) needs a little more practice.
7. They told (we, us) the truth about the weather.
8. (They, Them) practice every day.
9. Mr. Garcia told (I, me) where her son went.
10. Vincent described (he, him) very accurately.

**B.** Use the possessive form of the pronoun in parentheses.

1. I want the sun to shine on (I) _____ garden.
2. Jennifer wants (she) _____ father to come to the game.
3. Fernando left (he) _____ hat home.
4. That dog wags (it) _____ tail all the time.
5. Please take (you) _____ place in line.
6. (You) _____ is the package on the top shelf.
7. You can borrow (we) _____ map.
8. Jennifer won (she) _____ race easily.
9. (I) _____ is the room at the end of the hall.
10. The Cougars won (they) _____ game.

**C.** Write each sentence. Underline the demonstrative pronouns.

1. That is Andrew's canoe.
2. This comes first.
3. These are the books you asked for.
4. Give those to Cristina.
5. This is Louise's sweater.
6. Sandra asked me to give you these.
7. Don't touch that!
8. Those are mine.
9. Please mail this at once.
10. This is interesting.

## Composition

Think of an event that you have witnessed when someone acted bravely or did something very well. For example, perhaps you have seen fire fighters performing a rescue. Perhaps you have seen a thrilling sports play. In a single paragraph describe the event. Underline all of the pronouns that you use. You may use an imaginary event if you wish or one that you recall from a book or movie.

## Advanced Challenge

Find a passage from a book, a magazine, or from your own writing that contains at least ten pronouns. Replace each of the pronouns with the noun that it substitutes for. Study and compare the original passage with the one without pronouns. What does your comparison tell you about the role that pronouns play in language? Prepare a brief written report on the usefulness of pronouns.

## WHERE DO WORDS COME FROM?

In some countries a person's last name shows how he or she is related to someone else. The Scandinavian names Oleson and Hansen originally meant "son of Ole" and "son of Hans." The Russian name Petrovna means "daughter of Peter."

In many Spanish-speaking countries last names are formed by joining the father's last name with the mother's. Juan López y Rodríguez is the son of a man whose family name is López and a woman whose family name is Rodríguez. If Juan married María García y Gonzáles, their children would have the last name López y García.

In the United States, women sometimes use joined names. A woman whose last name is Anders might use the name Anders-Holton after she marries a man whose last name is Holton.

PRACTICE Work with your own last name. Make a list of imaginary children and grandchildren for yourself. Make up names and have them show family relationships. You can link the last names in any way you want. Use hyphens, *y,* and *son,* or any parts of names that you happen to know mean *"son of"* or *"daughter of."*

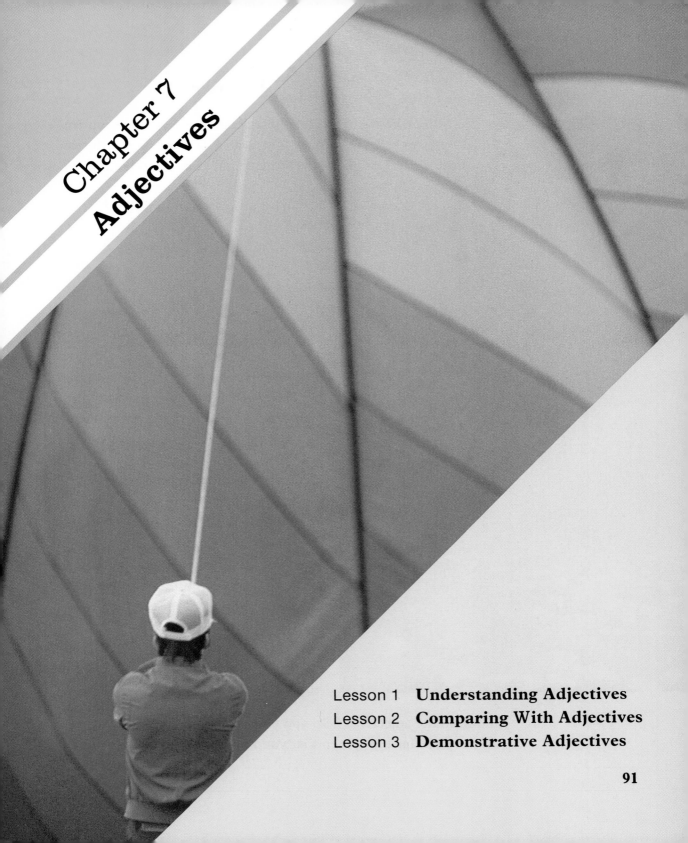

# Chapter 7
# Adjectives

Lesson 1    **Understanding Adjectives**
Lesson 2    **Comparing With Adjectives**
Lesson 3    **Demonstrative Adjectives**

# Understanding Adjectives

An **adjective** is a word that describes a noun or pronoun. An adjective can tell which one, how many, or what kind. Notice what the adjectives do in this sentence: The *new* club has *several* members with *strong* opinions.

Most adjectives come before nouns (*happy* child) or after linking verbs. (The child is *happy*.) Sometimes adjectives follow the nouns they describe (the child, *happy* and *eager*).

## Example

In this passage from John Muir's *The Yosemite*, the author describes a beautiful valley. The adjectives are underlined.

I looked eastward from the summit of Pacheco Pass. The day was <u>shiny</u> and <u>bright</u>. In spite of all my wanderings throughout this <u>magnificent</u> world, the landscape that I saw that day still seems to me the most <u>beautiful</u> that I ever saw. At my feet lay the <u>great</u> <u>central</u> valley of California, <u>level</u> and <u>flowery</u>, like a lake of <u>pure</u> sunshine. From the <u>eastern</u> boundary of this <u>vast</u> <u>golden</u> bed of flowers rose the <u>mighty</u> Sierra, miles in height. It was so <u>colorful</u> and <u>glorious</u> that it seemed not clothed with light but made of light itself, like the wall of some <u>heavenly</u> city.

How do the adjectives help you to see and feel this scene?
What place have you seen that you thought was very beautiful?

**PRACTICE 1**   Write each of the following sentences. Underline each adjective. Draw two lines under the noun that the adjective describes.

1. The unusual house faced a beautiful park.
2. Elaine has a happy smile and a spunky personality.
3. A gigantic rock rolled down the steep hill.
4. Roman seemed angry and upset about the decision.
5. Dusty sheets covered the old furniture.

**PRACTICE 2**   Change the underlined adjective in each sentence to one that is more interesting and exact. Instead of *big*, for example, you might use *large*, *huge*, or *gigantic*.

1. The weather was <u>bad</u> today.
2. However, I had a <u>nice</u> day.
3. I saw <u>many</u> friends.
4. As usual, Jennifer told me some <u>good</u> jokes.
5. Kim showed me a <u>big</u> map of Washington, D.C.

**WRITE**   With what group do you spend a lot of time? Think of a group you know well—your family, a few close friends from your neighborhood, or a club. Write a paragraph describing one of the people in the group. Use adjectives to make your sentences more interesting and exact.

**GO BEYOND**   Tell a group story in class. Ask one person in the group to record the story as it develops. The first person starts by saying a sentence that has at least one adjective. For example, the first sentence might be, "It was a stormy night when strange things began happening." Each of the other persons adds to the story a sentence with one or more adjectives. If the group develops a good story, one or more students might tell it to a younger class.

**Comparing With Adjectives**

An adjective has three different forms, which are used when comparing people, places, and things. The **positive form** is the adjective itself, such as *small*. The **comparative form** compares two things and usually ends in *-er* (*smaller*). The **superlative form** compares more than two things and usually ends in *-est* (*smallest*).

The endings *-er* and *-est* are not added to some longer adjectives, such as *interesting*. Add *more* and *most* to those adjectives for the comparative and superlative forms—*more interesting* and *most interesting*. The words *less* and *least* are also used for comparative and superlative forms—*less weak* and *least weak*.

Some adjectives—such as *good*, *bad*, and *many*—have irregular comparative and superlative forms.

## Example

Here are the three forms of some common adjectives.

| POSITIVE | COMPARATIVE | SUPERLATIVE |
| --- | --- | --- |
| young | younger | youngest |
| ripe | riper | ripest |
| big | bigger | biggest |
| wonderful | more wonderful | most wonderful |
| good | better | best |
| bad | worse | worst |

**PRACTICE 1**  Write each sentence. Use the correct form of the adjective in parentheses.

1. This is the (odd) story I have ever read.
2. It is about Vern, the (unusual) man in the world.
3. He lived in a cave that was (dark) than midnight.
4. Vern was (tall) than a giraffe.
5. He was (talkative) than a parrot.
6. He could run (fast) than the wind.
7. Vern could swim down to the (deep) parts of the ocean.
8. He was (brave) than anyone else in the kingdom.
9. Vern fought the (horrible) dragon that ever lived.
10. The story was (enjoyable) than the one I read last week.

**PRACTICE 2**  Find and write the adjective in each sentence. Write *comparative* or *superlative* to tell what kind of adjective each one is.

1. Paula knows more riddles than I do.
2. Our brother Greg knows the most riddles.
3. The answer to one of Paula's riddles is the best joke I ever heard.
4. Paula said, "I've got one that's even better."
5. After that Greg and Paula told the worst riddles they knew.

**WRITE**  Look at both pictures of the 72nd Street Playground. What is different about them? What is the same? Write at least five sentences about the two scenes. Use adjectives that compare.

**GO BEYOND**  Work with a partner. Exchange the sentences you wrote for the Write exercise. Make suggestions about improving each other's work. Do the comparisons need better adjectives, more explanation, or clearer details? Was anything important left out? Take the best of your partner's suggestions and rewrite your own sentences.

## LESSON 3    Demonstrative Adjectives

A **demonstrative adjective** points out a particular person, place, or thing. The words *this, that, these,* and *those* are used as demonstrative adjectives.

*This* describes one nearby person or object. *That* describes one person or object that is farther away. *These* describes more than one person or object that is nearby. *Those* describes more than one person or object that is farther away.

A demonstrative adjective always comes before the noun that it points out. A demonstrative that is not followed by a noun is called a demonstrative pronoun. We will use *this* magnet now. *That* magnet is broken. Let's not buy *these* peaches. *Those* plums look better.

## Example

The underlined words are demonstrative adjectives.

<u>This</u> team has blue shorts and striped socks.
<u>That</u> team has green shorts and white socks.
<u>These</u> children belong to the blue team.
<u>Those</u> children belong to the green team.

**PRACTICE 1**   Write each sentence. Use the correct word in parentheses.

1. (This, These) pictures show my sister Ingrid and me.
2. (That, Those) picture shows our soccer team, the Blue Eagles.
3. We wear (this, these) blue uniforms with the red stripes.
4. (That, Those) players, Matta and Carla, are the best.
5. (That, Those) man is Coach McGovern.

**PRACTICE 2**   Use the demonstrative adjectives *this, that, these,* or *those* to complete each sentence. Write each sentence.

1. I would like to live in _____ city.
2. _____ soccer balls in the locker room need inflating.
3. I think _____ idea is better.
4. _____ red circle on my sweater means I'm a member of the band.
5. Let me give you one of _____ posters.

**WRITE**   Demonstrative adjectives can help you make clear to someone else which of two things you are talking about: *this* cat or *that* cat; *these* cats or *those* cats. Write five sentences that contain demonstrative adjectives. Use *this* or *that* to point out singular nouns and *these* or *those* to point out plural nouns.

EXAMPLE      This pencil is shorter than <u>that</u> pencil.
             <u>These</u> pencils are sharper than <u>those</u> pencils.

**GO BEYOND**   Prepare a drawing that could accompany one of the sentences you wrote for the Write exercise. The drawing should clearly show the difference between *this* and *that* or *these* and *those*. Share your drawing with your classmates.

---

*Adjectives*                                                      **97**

## Practice

**A.** Write each sentence. Underline the adjectives.

1. The creaky old boards let everyone know we had arrived.
2. The telephone gave a loud, shrill ring.
3. The little children liked the colorful magazines.
4. Sam blinked his big blue eyes as if he couldn't believe what he saw in the stuffy room.
5. The pot of hot soup overturned and made an ugly mess on the clean floor.

**B.** Complete each sentence by adding an adjective. Write the sentence.

1. Marisol has three _____ dogs.
2. Can you bring me the _____ umbrella?
3. Poppy is my _____ cat.
4. Two horses live in the _____ stable near the Cluett house.
5. Do those flowers have _____ leaves?

**C.** Write each sentence, using the correct form of the adjective in parentheses.

1. This sidewalk is (hot) than a stove. The sun is the (hot) star in our solar system.
2. Bobby is (young) than Bert. Carlos is the (young) boy in our class.
3. This pond has the (clear) water in the state. I can't believe it has (clear) water than Lake Osseenee.
4. Last night we saw the (beautiful) sunset we have ever seen. It was even (beautiful) than the sunset over the Pacific Ocean in Hawaii.
5. Ken is (tall) than Lars. Do you think Ken is the (tall) boy in the room?

**D.** Choose the correct demonstrative adjective for each sentence. Write the sentence.

1. (These, Those) packages are getting heavy in my arms.
2. Do you see (this, that) book on the table at the end of the room?
3. (This, That) table we are sitting at is very old and should be repaired.
4. Look at (these, those) cars directly in front of us.
5. (These, Those) three stories in this book are my favorites.

## Composition

Writers use adjectives to add color and detail to writing. Think of an object that you often notice because there is something unusual about it. The object could be a house that is badly run down. The object might be a car that is old but well kept, or it might be a tree with a strange shape. Describe what you always notice. Write a single paragraph and use precise adjectives.

## Advanced Challenge

You will need a partner for this exercise. Think of a familiar object. You may limit yourself to something in the room if you wish. Think of words that describe the object. That is, think of adjectives. Choose the most descriptive and specific adjective you can to describe the object. Tell your partner the adjective. Use one that will make him or her guess the object right away. For example, if what you describe is water, you can use the adjective *wet*. Give a second adjective if necessary, but try to identify your object with no more than two adjectives.

Now play the second round of this game. Give an adjective that is *not* very specific. For example, for the noun *water* you might give the adjective *cool*. Many things are cool, so your partner is not likely to guess on the first try what you had in mind. Try to give as many adjectives as possible before your partner guesses correctly. Remember, you must not mislead your partner by giving inappropriate adjectives.

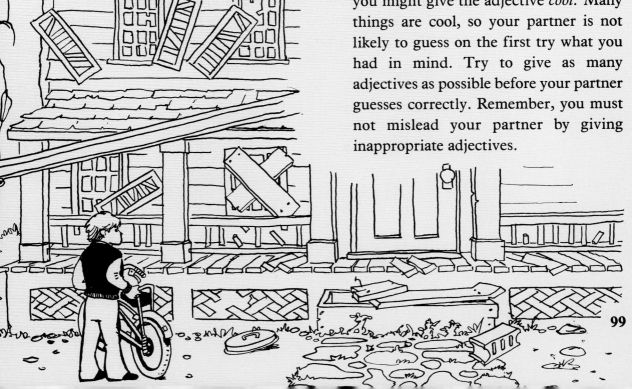

## WORDS THAT DESCRIBE

There are many words you can use to describe the world around you. There are words that tell how things look, feel, sound, taste, or smell. When you use these words effectively in your writing, it becomes more vivid and alive.

EXAMPLE

Here is a list of words describing how things feel.

| | | | |
|---|---|---|---|
| rough | soft | warm | cool |
| scratchy | fluffy | tepid | icy |
| slimy | gritty | hot | chilly |

PRACTICE   List as many words as you can that describe each of the five topics below. Then choose one topic and write a paragraph about it, using the words you listed for that topic.

1. City Sounds
2. Beach Sounds
3. Smells of Cooking
4. Smells of Summer
5. Yummy Tastes

# Chapter 8
# Adverbs

Lesson 1  **Understanding Adverbs**
Lesson 2  **Comparing With Adverbs**
Lesson 3  **More About Adverbs**

**101**

# Understanding Adverbs

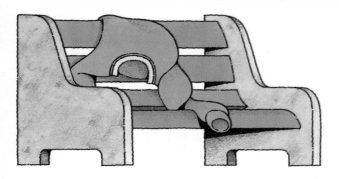

An **adverb** is a word that tells more about the meaning of a verb. Adverbs can tell how, when, or where the action takes place. Someone might say, for example, "*Yesterday* I *carelessly* left my sweater *outdoors*." In a sentence, an adverb often comes immediately before or after the verb it tells about.

## Example

Here are some adverbs that are frequently used.

| HOW | WHEN | WHERE |
|-----|------|-------|
| quickly | soon | outdoors |
| well | always | everywhere |
| carefully | never | inside |
| powerfully | often | there |
| suddenly | tomorrow | here |
| cheerfully | now | nowhere |
| silently | later | anyplace |

## Exercises

**PRACTICE 1**   Write the adverb used in each sentence. Next to each adverb, write the verb that the adverb tells about.

1. Our class is going to the zoo tomorrow.
2. We often go to the movies on Saturday afternoon.
3. Jake walked slowly down the hallway to his room.
4. On Monday, Wednesday, and Thursday the class went outside for recess.
5. Please stack the books neatly on the table.

**PRACTICE 2** Complete each sentence by adding an adverb from the lists on page 102. Write the sentence and underline the adverb. Next to each sentence write whether the adverb tells how, when, or where.

1. Nino ran _____ along the beach.
2. He looked _____ for the missing coin.
3. He stopped _____ to dig in the sand.
4. His fingers searched the tiny grains _____ .
5. He must find the coin _____ !

**WRITE** Think of something that you have learned to do well and that you are proud of. It might be playing a sport, taking photographs, or baking. In a paragraph, explain how you developed this skill. When you are finished, underline the adverbs you used.

**GO BEYOND** Work with three other students. Use the adverbs you underlined in your paragraph. Write each adverb on a separate slip of paper. Add any other adverbs you and your classmates can think of. Shuffle the slips, and place them face-down. Take turns drawing a slip and making up a sentence using the adverb on the slip.

# Comparing With Adverbs

Like adjectives, most adverbs have positive, comparative, and superlative forms. The **positive form** is the adverb itself (*soon*). The **comparative form** compares two things and usually ends in *-er* (*sooner*). The **superlative form** compares more than two things and usually ends in *-est* (*soonest*).

Some longer adverbs, such as *suddenly,* would sound strange with *-er* or *-est* added. The words *more* or *most* are used instead (*more suddenly* and *most suddenly*). The words *less* and *least* are also used for comparative and superlative forms (*less calmly, least calmly*). A few adverbs, such as *now,* cannot be compared.

## Example

The underlined words in these sentences are adverbs that are being used to compare.

Tim ran <u>faster</u> than John.
Is the turtle the <u>slowest</u> of animals?
The train will arrive <u>sooner</u> than the bus.
Penny organized her report <u>more clearly</u> than anyone else.
Of all the members on the team, Juan hits <u>most frequently</u>.

---

**PRACTICE 1** Write each sentence. Underline the adverbs that compare.

1. It rains most often in April.
2. That bell rings louder than this one.
3. Which engine runs more smoothly?
4. Detroit is farther than Columbus.
5. Val tries harder when the score is close.

**PRACTICE 2** Write each sentence. Use the correct form of the adverb in parentheses.

1. Lily jumped out of bed (eagerly) than she had the day before.
2. She could dress the (fast) of all the people in her family.
3. Because it had started to rain, her father had to drive (slowly) than he usually did.
4. However, they reached her grandmother's house (soon) than they had expected.
5. Lily had arrived the (early) of all the grandchildren.

**WRITE** What do you want to change about yourself? Is there something you would like to do better than you do it now? Write a paragraph describing what you would like to change. Use adverbs that tell how, when, and where, and adverbs that compare.

**GO BEYOND** Share with a partner the paragraph you wrote for the Write exercise. Ask your partner to examine your adverbs. Do they make your ideas clear and specific? Do you use a variety of different adverbs? Your partner should state which choices were good and why, and which ones could be improved. Discuss your partner's suggestions with him or her. Decide which suggestions you will use. Make your changes and rewrite your paragraph.

## A Narrow Fellow in the Grass

A narrow fellow in the grass
Occasionally rides;
You may have met him—did you not?
His notice sudden is.

The grass divides as with a comb,
A spotted shaft is seen,
And then it closes at your feet
And opens further on.

He likes a boggy acre,
A floor too cool for corn.
Yet when a boy, and barefoot,
I more than once at noon

Have passed, I thought, a whip-lash
Unbraiding in the sun—
When, stooping to secure it,
It wrinkled, and was gone.

Several of nature's people
I know, and they know me;
I feel for them a transport
of cordiality;

But never met this fellow,
Attended or alone,
Without a tighter breathing
And zero at the bone.

*Emily Dickinson*

What is described in the poem?
Which words help you see the "narrow fellow"?

**107**

# More About Adverbs

Adjectives tell about nouns, and adverbs tell about verbs. While a few adjectives and adverbs have the same form (*fast, much, early*), the most common adverb form ends in *-ly*. *Speedy* is an adjective: We had to wait at the crossing for a *speedy* train to pass. *Speedily* is an adverb: We waited at the crossing while the train passed *speedily*.

## Example

In the first sentence in each of the following pairs, the adjective form is incorrectly used. In the second sentence, the correct adverb form is used.

Ted's brother drives *careful*. (Incorrect)
Ted's brother drives *carefully*. (Correct)

Gretchen spoke *soft*. (Incorrect)
Gretchen spoke *softly*. (Correct)

When we called, the police came *quick*. (Incorrect)
When we called, the police came *quickly*. (Correct)

**PRACTICE 1**   Write each of the following sentences. Use the correct adverb form in place of the adjective form in parentheses.
1. Tim's uncle always works (careful).
2. The explosion sounded (loud) throughout the city.
3. Tell the children to play (quiet).
4. I am (near) finished with this job.
5. The pitcher turned (quick) and threw the runner out.
6. The witness was tired and could not think (logical).
7. I walked along the path as (careful) as a deer.
8. The rain clouds appeared (sudden).
9. The man reacted (irritable) to our question.
10. John acts (hasty) all the time.

**PRACTICE 2**   Add the adverb form of the word in parentheses to complete each sentence. Write each sentence.
1. Janice ran _____ and set a new school record. (powerful)
2. The men worked _____ for many hours. (steady)
3. If you want to learn how to do this, watch _____ . (close)
4. I put the glasses in the closet _____ . (careful)
5. Try not to act _____ . (foolish)

**WRITE**   Use each of the words below in a pair of sentences. In the first sentence, use the word as an adjective. In the second sentence, use it as an adverb. Add -ly if necessary.

terrible     rapid     late     awful     final

EXAMPLE     I had a very <u>easy</u> day. (adjective)
Joan caught the ball <u>easily</u>. (adverb)

**GO BEYOND**   Write a list of ten adjectives. Exchange your list with a partner. Write two sentences for each word. In the first sentence, use the word as an adjective. In the second, use it as an adverb. Check your work together.

## Practice

**A.** Write the adverb from each sentence. Does it tell how, when, or where?

1. Rick ran outside to play.
2. Seth left the room angrily.
3. Tina, the sweaters are on sale now.
4. Nick answered each question immediately.
5. Marge and Sally happily arranged some flowers.

**B.** Write an adverb that would complete each sentence. Then write whether the adverb tells how, when, or where.

1. Bring the book to me _____ .
2. Barbara walked _____ into the room.
3. Larry's lip swelled after he _____ fell off the swing.
4. Franny was not _____ hurt when she tripped.
5. Steve cooked some noodles _____ and put them in a bowl.

**C.** Use the correct form of each numbered adverb to complete each sentence. Write the sentence.

1. hungrily
   a. The sharks swam _____ around the tank.
   b. The boy grabbed at the sandwiches _____ than his sister did.
2. high
   a. Terry jumped _____ than Tess.
   b. Millie got the _____ mark in the class.
3. slowly
   a. The boys walked _____ .
   b. The dogs followed even _____ .
4. carefully
   a. You must handle a kitten _____ than you handle a cat.
   b. These instruments are tuned the _____ of all the instruments.
5. soon
   a. Mark must come home _____ than tomorrow afternoon.
   b. Please come at the _____ moment possible.

**D.** In each of the following sentences, an adjective form is placed in parentheses. Rewrite each sentence, using the adverb form.

1. The rain fell (steady) for hours.
2. Look (careful) before crossing.
3. If I run (quick), I can win this race.
4. We won the game (easy).
5. The fire broke out very (sudden).

## Composition

As people grow older, their views of many things change. One important change takes place in the way they view friends. What kind of friend did you look for when you were in first grade? What do you look for in a friend right now?

Think back to the time when you were in first grade. Identify qualities in a friend that were most important to you. Explain those qualities in a single paragraph. Then identify qualities that you now look for in a friend. Explain those qualities in a second paragraph. Use adverbs in your sentences.

## Advanced Challenge

Adverbs tell how, when, and where. Adverbs describe verbs.

Think of as many adverbs as you can that describe each of these verbs.

eat     walk     sleep     laugh

Make a list of the adverbs. Give yourself ten minutes. While you are thinking of adverbs, other students working on this activity will be making their lists.

At the end of ten minutes, count the number of adverbs on your list. Compare the lists with your classmates' lists. Were there any adverbs that were on everybody's lists? Which ones?

Look at all the adverbs on your own list. Decide which question each adverb answers—How? When? or Where? Make a chart to show which question each adverb answers. Which kind did you list most?

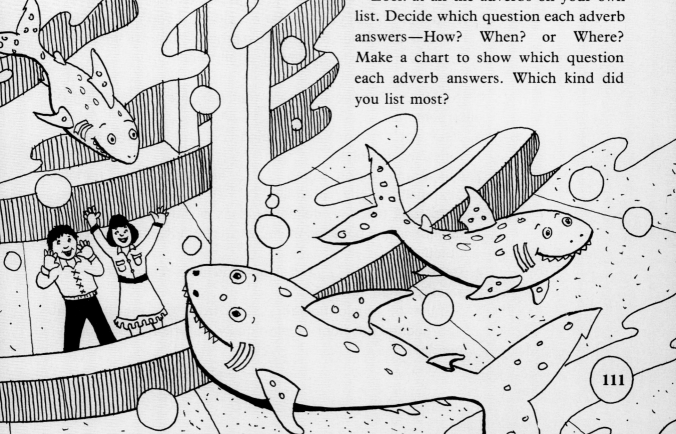

111

## MORE WORDS THAT DESCRIBE

It is often helpful to make a word list before you begin to write. Your list should include words that will fit into the kind of writing you plan to do. For a Halloween story, for example, you might list nouns like *ghosts* and *witches.* You might also list adjectives to describe them—*spooky, scary.* Adverbs that tell how ghosts and witches act might also be helpful. If you have a word list, you can check it whenever you need a particular word. Remember to think about the feeling each word suggests as well as its meaning.

EXAMPLE

Suppose you want to describe in a Halloween story how you crept to the door dressed in a ghost costume. You need a word that will tell your reader exactly how you moved. From the list in parentheses, you would probably choose the under-lined word (quickly, noisily, <u>stealthily</u>, cheerfully).

PRACTICE   Choose the word that best fits the meaning of each sentence.

1. "Get out of here!" he shouted _____ . (quietly, hastily, furiously, warmly)
2. The gentle moon sailed _____ across the sky. (jerkily, anxiously, quietly, carefully)
3. Beth took the tiny, delicate pieces of furniture out of the dollhouse and polished them _____ . (rapidly, briskly, gently, quietly)
4. Rain drummed _____ and steadily on the metal roof. (damply, weakly, often, noisily)
5. Strains of music flowed _____ from the elevator that approached our floor. (melodiously, surprisingly, suddenly, nearly)

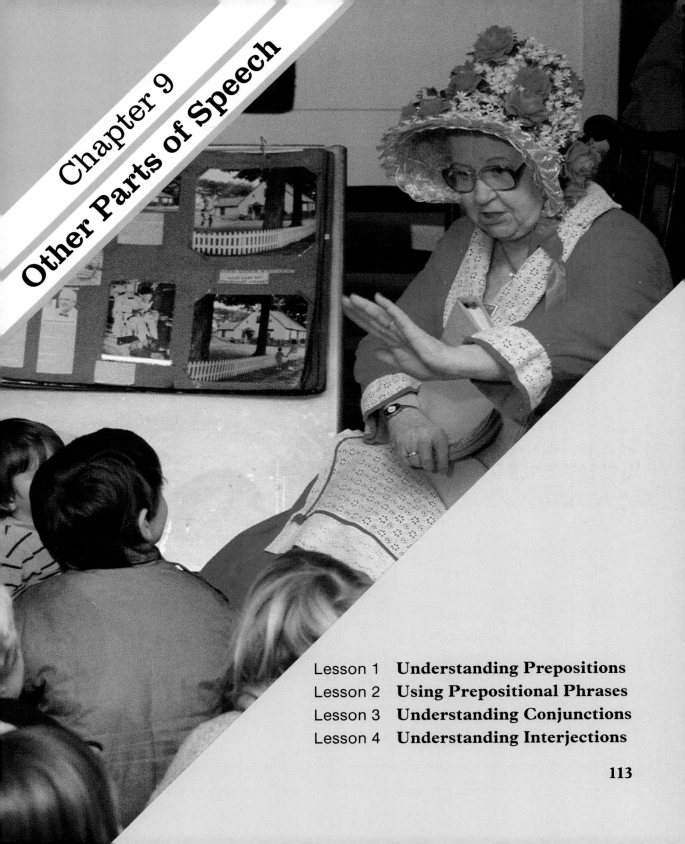

# Chapter 9
# Other Parts of Speech

Lesson 1  **Understanding Prepositions**
Lesson 2  **Using Prepositional Phrases**
Lesson 3  **Understanding Conjunctions**
Lesson 4  **Understanding Interjections**

# Understanding Prepositions

A **preposition** is a word that connects a noun or a pronoun to another word in a sentence. In the sentence *Ken did his homework at the table,* the preposition *at* connects the noun *table* to the verb *did*. The words *at the table* in the sentence form a prepositional phrase. A **prepositional phrase** is a group of words that begins with a preposition and ends with a noun or a pronoun.

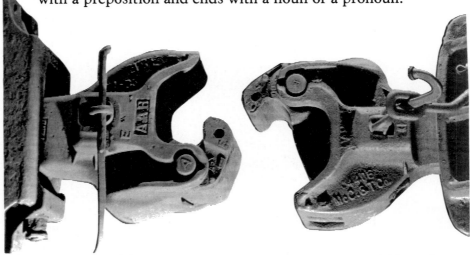

**Example**

Here are some of the more frequently used prepositions.

| | | |
|---|---|---|
| above | below | of |
| across | beside | on |
| after | between | over |
| against | by | through |
| along | down | throughout |
| among | during | to |
| around | for | under |
| at | from | until |
| before | in | up |
| behind | into | with |

**PRACTICE 1**  Write each sentence. Underline the prepositional phrase or phrases in each.

1. Nora carried the vase to the table.
2. The visitor from Japan enjoyed the baseball game.
3. A thunderstorm hit our area during the night.
4. The boy behind the tree is my brother.
5. We walked down the narrow road.
6. Flowers were planted along the path.
7. Jan swam toward the middle of the lake.
8. Chester threw a coin into the well, and it sank to the bottom.
9. The ball sailed over his head and bounced against the wall.
10. I read about her in the newspaper.

**PRACTICE 2**  Decide which of the two choices in parentheses is a prepositional phrase. Write the sentence, using the prepositional phrase.

1. The Fall Fair is held (every year, during September).
2. This year Joe went (alone, with me).
3. The displays are all (under a tent, outside).
4. Joe took pictures (all day, of the animals).
5. We met other students (from school, we know).

**WRITE**  Choose five prepositions from the list on page 114. Use each one to form a prepositional phrase. Then use each prepositional phrase to write a sentence.

**GO BEYOND**  Look around your classroom. Choose five things in the room to write about. They can be people or objects that you find especially interesting. Write a sentence about each that includes at least one prepositional phrase. Make your sentences as descriptive as possible. Exchange papers with a classmate. Underline the prepositional phrases on the paper you receive.

# Using Prepositional Phrases

You have learned that a prepositional phrase is a group of words that begins with a preposition and ends with a noun or pronoun (*up the hill, with them*). Prepositional phrases add information to sentences by telling *why, when, where, how,* or *which.* Prepositional phrases improve sentences by adding these kinds of details.

## Example

Read this selection from *Henry Huggins* by Beverly Cleary. Prepositional phrases are underlined.

His worse part had been in a Parent-Teacher program for National Brush Your Teeth Week. Henry had been really disgusted that day. He had to wear his best trousers and a white shirt to school, and he had to stay clean all day. Then he missed practicing with his football because the meeting was after school. Worst of all, he had to stand in front of all the mothers and teachers, bow, and recite:

I am Sir Cuspid,
My job is to bite.
Brush me twice daily
To keep me so white.

The kids called him Sir Cuspidor for a long time after that.

What kind of information does each prepositional phrase add to the sentence?

**PRACTICE 1**   Write each sentence. Underline each prepositional phrase in the sentence. Circle the preposition.
1. The dance recital was held at the school on Friday.
2. Ellie's mother and father went to the school with the Lang
   family.
3. Mrs. Lang searched for Ellie's name on the program.
4. "She's in the Dance of the Vegetables," Mrs. Lang told them.
5. "Yes, in a red costume," Mrs. Wayland beamed. "She's one of
   the radishes."

**PRACTICE 2**   Add a preposition to each group of words to
form prepositional phrases that will complete the sentences.
Write each sentence.

the entire auditorium        their son
his loudest voice            3:00 P.M.
tooth care

1. The Higginses were very proud _____ .
2. He recited a poem _____ .
3. He performed _____ .
4. He spoke _____ .
5. You could hear him _____ .

**WRITE**   Plan and write a story about a time when you took
part in a program. You can make up the story, if you wish. Tell
what the program was. What did you do? What happened? How
did you feel? Use prepositional phrases to add details to your
writing. Underline the prepositional phrases.

**GO BEYOND**   Make a classroom display called "Onstage."
Draw a picture to illustrate the story you wrote for the Write
exercise. Include both the story and the picture in the display.

# Understanding Conjunctions

A **conjunction** is a word that connects similar words or word groups in a sentence. A conjunction can also join two sentences. The word *conjunction* means "to join with." Common conjunctions are *and, but,* and *or.*

## Example

The underlined words in this paragraph are conjunctions.

> You <u>and</u> I can play this game. It's called Fat Cat. I've played it before, <u>but</u> I've forgotten what to do. We should read the rules on the box <u>or</u> on the special card. They are the same. You're supposed to draw cards from a pile. A purple card is worth one point, <u>but</u> a blue one is worth two points. Will you read the rules <u>or</u> should I read them?

What words or word groups are joined by each conjunction? What can players do when they are unsure of the rules of a game?

## Exercises

**PRACTICE 1** Write each sentence. Underline all the conjunctions.

1. Tony and Lynn played Fat Cat.
2. That game is easy to play, but there are rules to follow.
3. They could find the rules on the box or on a special card.
4. They read the rules and played the game.
5. Tony started out with more points, but Lynn won the game.

**PRACTICE 2** Rewrite each pair of sentences to make one new sentence. Join the sentences with *and, but,* or *or.* Use a comma before the conjunction.

EXAMPLE: Let's get together. Let's plan what we will do.

Let's get together, *and* let's plan what we will do.

1. Should we just talk? Should we plan a play?
2. One group could write a play. One group could produce it.
3. We could perform the play outdoors. The weather might not be good.
4. Cindy does not like Bob's ideas for a script. Bob does not like hers.

**WRITE** Write a paragraph describing a person, place, or thing. Tell at least three things about what you are describing, and make at least two comparisons. Use at least three sentences with conjunctions. Remember to use a comma before each conjunction that joins two shorter sentences to make a longer sentence.

**GO BEYOND** Work with a partner. Write a sentence at the top of a sheet of paper. It should not be a question. Then give the paper to your partner and name a conjunction. Your partner will write another sentence and connect it to the one you wrote, using the conjunction you named.

Then, on a new line, have your partner write a sentence and name a conjunction for you to use. Now it's your turn to add a sentence. Continue until you have several sentences, and then share the results with the rest of the class.

Each time you connect a sentence, remember to do these things:

1. Change the first sentence period to a comma before adding the conjunction.
2. Change the capital letter to a small letter on the first word of the sentence you are adding.
3. Be sure there is a period at the end of the new sentence.

---

*Other Parts of Speech*

# Understanding Interjections

A word or phrase used by itself to show sudden and strong feeling is called an **interjection**. Words that are normally used as other parts of speech can be used as interjections.

How do you feel when you say one of these words: *Wait! Ouch! Yippee!* In writing, a sentence that explains how the speaker feels usually follows an interjection. (*Wait!* I think the winner is coming into view. *Ouch!* You stepped on my toe. *Yippee!* I have a chance to go on a boat ride!) An interjection is usually followed by an exclamation mark.

## Example

**The Fourth**

Oh
CRASH!
my
BASH!
it's
BANG!
the
ZANG!
Fourth
WHOOSH!
of
BAROOOM!
July
WHEW!

*Shel Silverstein* (from *Where the Sidewalk Ends*)

Which interjections are used to suggest sounds?
Say the sentence that appears between the interjections.

**PRACTICE 1**  Number a paper from 1 to 5. Beside each number, write an interjection that fits each of the numbered situations below. You may choose from these interjections or make up your own.

1. You see a mysterious shadow.
2. A bucket of bolts falls off a truck.
3. The bus starts to leave without you.
4. You receive a ten-speed bike as a gift.
5. Your shoe gets stuck in a sidewalk grate.

**PRACTICE 2**  For each of these situations, write an interjection. Then write a sentence that explains its use. Use the three sample sentences on page 120 as an example.

1. Someone drops a heavy book on your foot.
2. A neighbor gives you $5.00 for cleaning up her yard.
3. Players from a team you beat tell you that you played well.
4. Someone has gotten you really angry.
5. Your dog is starting to chew on your new sneakers.

**WRITE**  Compose an original poem using interjections. Express strong feelings about a day or a place. Trade poems with a classmate. Do you feel the same way about the subject he or she wrote about?

**GO BEYOND**  Choose three interjections from the Practice or Write exercise, or make up three others. For each interjection draw a cartoon in which one person does something and another person responds with the interjection.

## Practice

**A.** Write each sentence and underline each prepositional phrase. Draw a circle around each preposition.

1. Nathan drove us around the city in his antique car.
2. We saw an unusual fountain in the park and flower beds beside the lake.
3. We stopped at a monument, and Arnie took pictures of us.
4. Nathan lives in a brick building with brown trim.
5. We walked through the garage and into the elevator.

**B.** Complete each sentence by adding a prepositional phrase.

1. The waves crashed _____ .
2. The sand blew _____ .
3. The sun shone brightly _____ .
4. Children were running _____ .
5. We went swimming _____ .

**C.** Combine each pair of sentences to make a new sentence. Use a comma and a conjunction (*and, but,* or *or*).

1. Chuck grows vegetables. Anne grows flowers.
2. The older students sang. The younger students couldn't hear them.
3. Annelise has a cat. Tim has a pet iguana.
4. Today we can go to the lake. We can stay at home to rest.
5. The dishes are very old. The silverware is new.
6. Mitch played the drums. Margot played the piano.
7. We will go to the zoo tomorrow. We might also go to the museum.
8. Luana bought a new dress. Her brother didn't buy anything.
9. The party was on Sunday. Leona went away on Saturday.
10. Dorothy drove to the airport. Susan met her there.

**D.** Write an interjection to go with each sentence.

1. _____ My grocery bag broke!
2. _____ I'm stuck!
3. _____ You can't go and that's final!
4. _____ There's a car coming.
5. _____ What a hit!

## Composition

A motto is a brief expression that tells about a belief. A motto expresses a guiding rule that one or more people live by. A well-known motto of the United States is *E pluribus unum,* which means "Out of many, one." It refers to the union of all the separate states.

Think about a motto that summarizes something you believe in or think of as important. State your motto and then explain in a paragraph why it is important to you.

## Advanced Challenge

As a group, the words that make up prepositional phrases tell about nouns or verbs. In other words, the phrases act as single-word adjectives and adverbs.

Write each of the following sentences. Draw one line under the prepositional phrases that tell about nouns and two lines under the phrases that tell about verbs.

1. The ship sailed under the bridge.
2. The door at the side of the building is the main entrance.
3. An accident at the intersection stopped traffic.
4. Marilyn hid behind a thick hedge.
5. The house around the corner belongs to the major.
6. An arrow flew through the air.
7. The section above the door needs paint.
8. He put the car in the garage.
9. The man in this picture is a friend of the family.
10. The trophies on this side of the room belong to Henry.

123

## DICTIONARY

A dictionary can show you what part of speech a word is. When you read the entry for *abide* in the Word Study for Chapter 5, you saw the abbreviations *v.* and *n.* used for *verb* and *noun*. A dictionary can also show you how to form and spell plurals, adjectives, adverbs, and irregular verbs.

EXAMPLE

**a tro cious** (ə trō′shəs). **1** very wicked or cruel; very savage or brutal: *Kidnaping is an atrocious crime.* **2** INFORMAL. very bad or unpleasant: *atrocious weather. adj.*—**a-tro′-cious-ly,** *adv.*—**a-tro′-cious-ness.** *n.*

This dictionary entry tells you that *atrocious* is an adjective (*adj.*). It also tells you how to form the adverb (*adv.*) *atrociously* and the noun (*n.*) atrociousness.

**loud** (loud). **1** making a great sound; not quiet or soft: *a loud voice, a loud noise.* **2** resounding; noisy: *loud music, a loud place to study.* **3** in a loud manner: *The hunter called long and loud.* **4** clamorous; insistent: *be loud in demands.* **5** INFORMAL. showy in dress or manner: *loud clothes.* 1, 2, 4, 5 *adj.* 3 *adv.*—**loud′ly,** *adv.*—**loud′ness.** *n.*

This definition tells you that *loud* can be used as either an adjective (definitions 1, 2, 4, and 5) or an adverb (definition 3).

PRACTICE   Use a dictionary to answer the following questions.
1. What part of speech is *deductive*?
2. What is one meaning for *on* used as an adjective?
3. How should you spell the adverb formed from *political*?
4. What is the plural of the noun *boss*?

**A.** Each underlined word is an example of a part of speech you studied in this unit. Beside the number of each underlined word, write the correct term from the list on the right.

1. Mom left a note <u>for</u> me.
2. I returned home <u>late</u> today.
3. "Meet David <u>and</u> me at Grandma's," it said.
4. She <u>invited</u> us to dinner.
5. I knew I would enjoy a <u>fabulous</u> dinner.

adverb
conjunction
preposition
adjective
verb

**B.** Write each sentence using the correct word form in parentheses.

1. The (Jacksons, Jacksons', Jackson's) are moving to Florida.
2. Dick has already called (he, him, his) parents.
3. Do you want (this, that, these, those) jacket I'm holding or (this, that, these, those) pants over there?
4. The (hospital, Hospital) is on (elm, Elm) (street, Street).
5. How many (dress, dresses, dresses') need repairs?

**C.** Write each sentence. Underline the main verb once. Underline any helping verbs twice.

1. Uncle Darrell usually visited us on Sundays.
2. Flight 342 from Toledo had arrived at Gate 3.
3. Tom is winning the game.
4. Frances chose these drapes.
5. The horses have eaten all of the hay.

# The Scholar

Fall Issue — Burke Elementary School

## Computers Hit School!

## Proofing Becomes Ea...

## Reading List
### for book reports....

*Where the Red Fern Grows*
— Rawls

*The Cat Ate my Gymsuit*
— Danzinger

*A Wrinkle in Time*
— L'Engle

*Tuck Everlasting*
— Babbitt

*Freaky Friday*
— Rodgers

## ?Question of the Day?

Who should decide the school lunch menu?

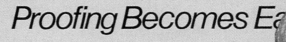

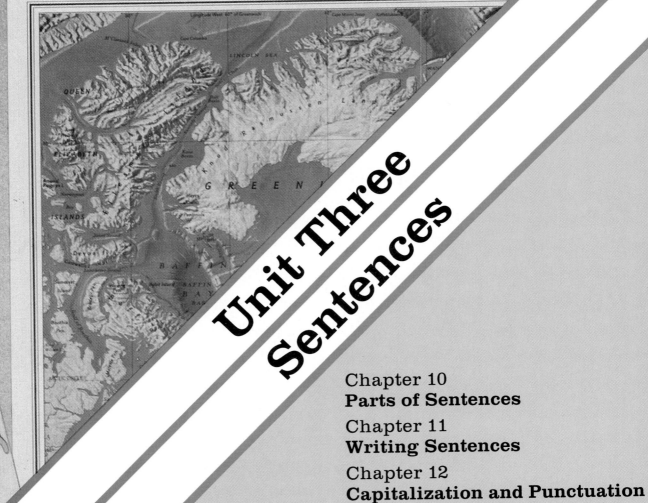

'Quote of the Week:'

"True ease in writing comes from art, not chance."
— Alexander Pope

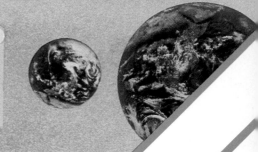

# Unit Three
# Sentences

Chapter 10
**Parts of Sentences**

Chapter 11
**Writing Sentences**

Chapter 12
**Capitalization and Punctuation**

# Sharing a Poem

**Calendar**

January shivers,
February shines,
March blows off the winter ice,
April makes the mornings nice,
May is hopscotch lines.

June is deep blue swimming,
Picnics are July,
August is my birthday,
September whistles by.

October is for roller skates,
November is the fireplace,
December is the best because
of sleds
and snow
and Santa Claus.

*Myra Cohn Livingston*

What is your favorite month of the year?
Why?

# Chapter 10
# Parts of Sentences

Lesson 1  **Four Kinds of Sentences**
Lesson 2  **Subjects and Predicates**
Lesson 3  **Objects in Sentences**
Lesson 4  **Subject-Verb Agreement**
Lesson 5  **Compound Sentence Parts**
Lesson 6  **Statements and Questions**

129

## LESSON 1  Four Kinds of Sentences

A sentence is a group of words that expresses a complete thought. There are four kinds of sentences. A **declarative sentence** makes a statement about something. It ends with a period. An **interrogative sentence** asks a question. It ends with a question mark. An **imperative sentence** tells or asks someone to do something. It usually ends with a period. The subject of an imperative sentence is usually not written. It is understood to be *you*. An **exclamatory sentence** shows strong feeling. It ends with an exclamation mark.

### Example

Read these examples of declarative, interrogative, imperative, and exclamatory sentences.

| | |
|---|---|
| DECLARATIVE | Joleen is the next batter. |
| INTERROGATIVE | Will she get a hit? |
| IMPERATIVE | Step up to the plate, Joleen. |
| EXCLAMATORY | We want a hit! |

*Sentences*

**PRACTICE 1** After the number of each sentence, write which kind of sentence it is: declarative, interrogative, imperative, or exclamatory.

1. Does your school have a gym team?
2. Mrs. Miller coaches the school team on Monday.
3. Be at the gym, dressed in a gym suit and ready to begin, at three o'clock.
4. My gym suit won't be here for another three weeks!
5. Wear a T-shirt and shorts instead.

**PRACTICE 2** Change each of the following sentences into the kind of sentence identified in parentheses. Write each sentence.

1. You should return the key tomorrow. (imperative)
2. The train will be late today. (interrogative)
3. Will the showers reach this area before morning? (declarative)
4. You should watch out for the holes in the road. (exclamatory)
5. You can keep this important date in mind. (interrogative)

**WRITE** The photographs on this page show people at work. Imagine that you are one of them. Write five sentences that tell about your work.

**GO BEYOND** Make up four sentences to illustrate the four kinds of sentences: declarative, interrogative, imperative, and exclamatory. Each sentence should tell about a responsibility you know you can handle or question a rule or practice that you believe ought to be changed. Share your sentences with your classmates.

*Parts of Sentences*

**Subjects and Predicates**

Every sentence has two parts—a **subject** and a **predicate**. The **complete subject** is made up of all the words that tell who or what the sentence is about. The **complete predicate** is made up of all the words that tell what the subject does or is.

The **simple subject** is the most important word in the complete subject. It is either a noun or pronoun. It answers the question *who* or *what* about the main verb in the sentence. The **simple predicate** is the verb in the complete predicate. The verb may be one word, or it may consist of a main verb and a helping verb.

**Example**

In these sentences, the complete subject is everything to the left of the line, and the complete predicate is everything to the right of the line. The simple subject and the simple predicate are underlined in each sentence.

The <u>man</u> in the brown hat/slowly <u>crossed</u> the street.
<u>Apples</u>/<u>grow</u> best in cold climates.
The <u>coach</u> of our football team/<u>has won</u> many league championships.
A large white <u>swan</u>/<u>was crossing</u> the road.

*Sentences*

**PRACTICE 1** Write each sentence. Draw a line between the complete subject and the complete predicate.

1. Scamp is a pet hamster.
2. The hamster escaped from his cage.
3. Scamp's owner searched the apartment for him.
4. The roaming pet was hiding.
5. A parent's bed is no place for a hamster.

**PRACTICE 2** Write each sentence. Draw a line between the complete subject and the complete predicate. Then underline each simple subject once and each simple predicate twice.

1. The Sanchez brothers get a weekly allowance.
2. They handle several different chores in return.
3. Paulo washes all the breakfast dishes.
4. Manuel washes the dinner dishes.
5. Both boys feed the family's pets daily.

**WRITE** Imagine that you are in a helicopter above the city or town in which you live. What do you see first? What do you observe as you look more closely? Describe the area as a whole. Then describe what your neighborhood looks like. Write at least five sentences. Be sure each sentence has a subject and a predicate.

**GO BEYOND** Work with five or six classmates to make up a group story. Set a time limit of five minutes. Have one person begin the story by saying the complete subject of the opening sentence. Have the next person add a complete predicate to that sentence. The third person will give the complete subject of the next sentence, and the fourth person will give the predicate. Continue in this way until the five minutes are up. You might want to create a serious story the first time and then make up a story that is funny or silly.

# Objects in Sentences

Some sentences are complete without any words after the verb: Father sang. Other sentences need words after the verb to complete their meaning: Father found a dollar. The word *dollar* is a **direct object**. A direct object is a noun or pronoun that follows an action verb and answers the question *what* or *whom*.

Sometimes a sentence contains an **indirect object** as well as a direct object. An indirect object is a noun or pronoun that answers the questions *to whom* or *for whom*. It appears before the direct object and after the verb. Look at this sentence: Father gave *me* a dollar. The pronoun *me* is an indirect object.

## Example

These sentences follow three patterns.

| SUBJECT | + | VERB |
|---------|---|------|
| Maya | | is drawing. |
| Your friends | | have left. |
| My dad | | teaches. |
| My sister | | paid. |

| SUBJECT | + | VERB | + | DIRECT OBJECT |
|---------|---|------|---|---------------|
| Maya | | is drawing | | a picture. |
| Your friends | | have left | | a message. |
| My dad | | teaches | | decimals. |
| My sister | | paid | | two dollars. |

| SUBJECT | + | VERB | + | INDIRECT OBJECT | + | DIRECT OBJECT |
|---------|---|------|---|-----------------|---|---------------|
| Maya | | is drawing | | me | | a picture. |
| Your friends | | have left | | you | | a message. |
| My dad | | teaches | | my sister | | decimals. |
| My sister | | paid | | the cashier | | two dollars. |

**PRACTICE 1** Write each sentence. Underline each direct object once and each indirect object twice.

1. The coach gave the racers a signal.
2. She blew a whistle.
3. The runners left the starting gate.
4. They crossed the finish line.
5. Mrs. McCarthy gave the winners a trophy.

**PRACTICE 2** Each numbered group of words in the list below follows the SUBJECT + VERB pattern. For each group write two sentences. Add a direct object to the first sentence. Add an indirect object and a direct object to the second sentence.

1. The young boy made
2. Sylvia wrote
3. Ben baked
4. My mom gives
5. She sent
6. Andrea taught
7. She will tell
8. Fred bought
9. They awarded
10. Bob has cooked

**WRITE** Write at least five sentences telling about things that have happened at school this week. Use a direct object in every sentence. Use an indirect object with the direct object in at least two sentences.

**GO BEYOND** Work with a partner. Exchange the sentences you wrote for the Write exercise. Have your partner underline the direct objects you wrote and circle the indirect objects.

# LESSON 4    Subject-Verb Agreement

The subject and verb in a sentence must be in **agreement**. That is, if the subject is singular, the verb must also be singular. If the subject is a singular noun and the verb is in the present tense, the verb will always end in -s: The bird *eats* at our feeder. The verb does not end in -s if the singular pronoun *I* or *you* is the subject: I *watch* the birds at the feeder. But the singular pronouns *he, she,* or *it* are always followed by a verb that ends in -s: She *watches* the birds at the feeder. Plural verbs do not have the -s ending: The birds *eat* at our feeder.

## Example

Notice the following sentences. Singular subjects and verbs are underlined once. Plural subjects and verbs are italicized.

Bob reads a book a week.
The cabin needs some work.
I believe his story.
The *wolves are* in this cage.
Most *citizens agree* with the mayor.
*They do* everything well.

**PRACTICE 1**  Write each sentence, using the correct word in parentheses.

1. The rain (falls, fall) quietly on the roof.
2. The boys (listens, listen) for the sound of thunder.
3. They (watches, watch) the rain hitting the street.
4. Larry (decides, decide) to play a record.
5. Hal (turns, turn) on the music.

**PRACTICE 2**  Number your paper from 1 to 10. Write *correct* after the number of each correct sentence. Rewrite each incorrect sentence to make the subject and verb agree.

1. The girls live in a big apartment building.
2. Rita love the elevator.
3. She like the city.
4. Carla complains about the crowds.
5. She miss the country.
6. The noise from the traffic bother her.
7. They talk about life in a small town.
8. Carla remember the quiet in a small town.
9. She enjoys so many different people, however.
10. The girls prefers the city but for different reasons.

**WRITE**  Imagine that a good friend is moving away. Write five sentences telling what you would miss about your friend. Use verbs in the present tense.

**GO BEYOND**  Work in groups of six. Take turns giving your opinions about a subject such as taking tests, year-round school, or air pollution. Then write a paragraph in which you state the opinions of the group members. Check your work to be sure that each verb agrees with its subject. When all members of the group have finished, take turns reading the paragraphs aloud. Has everyone reported the information accurately?

**Compound Sentence Parts**

The conjunctions *and* and *or* are often used to combine or compound basic sentence parts. A **compound subject** is made up of two or more nouns or pronouns joined by a conjunction: *Phil and Luis* rode the sled. A **compound predicate** is made up of two or more verbs joined by a conjunction: The farmers *plant, raise, and harvest* the grain. A **compound object** is made up of two or more nouns or pronouns joined by a conjunction. Both direct and indirect objects may be compounded: Phyllis loves *apples and pears.* Uncle Max sent *Ben and me* a letter.

When the subject of a sentence is a compound subject made up of two singular nouns joined by *and,* the verb is always plural: The *skirt and blouse* are new. When the conjunction *or* is used to form a compound subject made up of two singular nouns, however, the verb is always singular. The word *or* means "one or the other but not both": *Eleanor or Claire* has the book.

## Example

The compound sentence parts are underlined in these sentences.

COMPOUND SUBJECTS
Cans and paper littered the ground.
Carla and I are going.
Fred or Frank knows the score.

COMPOUND PREDICATES
The wind whistled and howled.
A large hole in the ground developed and grew.

COMPOUND OBJECTS
The store sold fabric and yarn. (direct)
She gave Rico and Anthony tickets to the game. (indirect)

**PRACTICE 1**  Underline the compound part in each sentence. Identify it as subject, predicate, or object.

1. Fish and whole grains have become popular foods.
2. This company makes and distributes sporting goods.
3. Brad or Will has a watch.
4. My father collects coins and stamps.
5. Plums, peaches, bananas, and cherries are in all the stores now.
6. I made Uncle Harry and Aunt Alice a tablecloth for their anniversary.
7. Men must wear jackets and ties in this restaurant.
8. Tim always orders chicken or turkey.
9. The men cut and raked the lawn.
10. This machine fills and seals the cans.

**PRACTICE 2**  Add a compound sentence part to each blank in the sentences. Write each sentence.

1. _____ and _____ are interesting animals.
2. Tim _____ and _____ the car.
3. We will buy some _____ and _____ .
4. Give _____ and _____ this report.
5. _____ or _____ can do this job.

**WRITE**  Write six original sentences. Write two sentences that contain a compound subject, two that contain a compound predicate, and two that contain a compound object.

**GO BEYOND**  Write one sentence that contains all of the compound sentence parts. In other words, your sentence should have a compound subject, a compound predicate, and a compound object. Exchange your paper with a classmate. Identify the compound sentence parts in each other's sentence.

# Statements and Questions

In declarative sentences, the subject usually comes first. The subject identifies the person, place, or thing that the sentence is about. It is followed by the predicate that tells what the subject is doing: The dog/has finished its dinner.

If a declarative sentence contains a helping verb or a form of *be,* it may be formed into a question by shifting the helping verb or the form of *be* to the beginning: *Has* the dog finished its dinner? *Is* the dog eating? If the declarative sentence has a one word verb other than *be,* the word *do* (*does* or *did*) is placed first: The teams play well. *Do* the teams play well? Doug runs fast. *Does* Doug run fast? The snow fell steadily. *Did* the snow fall steadily?

## Example

Notice how a question is formed from the declarative sentence in each pair.

The mechanics were fixing the car.
Were the mechanics fixing the car?

This is a new chair.
Is this a new chair?

The game ended.
Did the game end?

**PRACTICE 1** Change each statement to a question. Write the question.

1. A goose was standing in the shallow water.
2. The building was completed on time.
3. The rain stopped.
4. Diamonds are valuable and expensive.
5. The committee has completed its study.

**PRACTICE 2** Change each question to a statement. Write the statement.

1. Was the picnic enjoyable?
2. Does Jim know the rules?
3. Has the mail arrived?
4. Is Joan running around the track?
5. Will Tess buy some groceries for us?

**WRITE** Imagine that you are interviewing someone who has just returned from a visit to a place that has always interested you. Write five questions that you would ask that person about the visit. Begin all of your questions with a helping verb, a form of *be*, or a form of *do*.

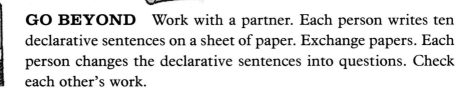

**GO BEYOND** Work with a partner. Each person writes ten declarative sentences on a sheet of paper. Exchange papers. Each person changes the declarative sentences into questions. Check each other's work.

## Practice

**A.** Write what kind of sentence each is—*declarative, interrogative, imperative,* or *exclamatory.*

1. Amanda wants to take dancing lessons again.
2. Did she enjoy her dancing lessons last year?
3. Please tell the teacher Amanda will be there.
4. I absolutely love that dancing class!
5. Can you study ballet at that school?

**B.** Write each sentence. Draw a line between the complete subject and the complete predicate. Then draw one line under the simple subject and two lines under the simple predicate.

1. My dad drives to work in a car pool with three other people.
2. The usual driver is Mrs. Sanchez.
3. Mr. Schwartz drives on Thursdays.
4. The blue and white car belongs to him.
5. A big traffic jam delayed drivers for two hours on Friday.

**C.** Write the sentence pattern that each numbered sentence follows—SUBJECT + VERB, SUBJECT + VERB + DIRECT OBJECT, or SUBJECT + VERB + INDIRECT OBJECT + DIRECT OBJECT.

1. Mom bought us clothes for school.
2. The happy dogs barked.
3. They bought a red jacket.
4. My little brother got a plaid shirt.
5. Our Aunt Amelia sent us clothes.

**D.** Write each sentence, using the correct word in parentheses.

1. Three mice (live, lives) under the subway tracks.
2. One always (keep, keeps) watch for trains.
3. A train (arrive, arrives) every few minutes.
4. Then the mice (run, runs) for their lives!
5. Passengers never (see, sees) the mice.

**E.** Rewrite each declarative sentence as an interrogative sentence.

1. Gerdy found a job through friends.
2. Our dog has gotten its shots.
3. Every telephone is working.
4. Costume jewelry is also called fashion jewelry.
5. My hair looks curly.

## Composition

Recall the time when a famous person visited the the area where you live. What activities were held to honor that person? How was he or she made to feel welcome? Who made all the arrangements for the famous person's visit?

Imagine that another famous person is about to visit. As junior mayor, you have been asked to plan the person's two-day stay. Where will the person eat and sleep? Who should he or she meet? What entertainment and activities can be scheduled? How can you make the person feel comfortable? Write a list of the arrangements you would make. State each arrangement in a single sentence.

## Advanced Challenge

When words are arranged in sentences, they appear in many different patterns. Three of the most common word patterns are subject + verb, subject + verb + direct object, and subject + verb + indirect object + direct object. Examples of each kind of word order are the following: Sam baked. Sam baked some bread. Sam baked me some bread.

Look through several different kinds of reading matter, such as magazines, books, or newspaper advertisements. Find five examples of each kind of sentence pattern.

Remember, as you look for your sentences, that not all sentences fit one of these three patterns. You will have to hunt carefully to find those that do.

Which of the three sentence patterns was hardest to locate? Which was easiest?

143

## DICTIONARY

What is the fastest way to look up a word in a dictionary? Certainly it is not by turning over page after page, looking for your word. Instead, use the **guide words** in heavy black type at the top of each dictionary page. The first guide word tells you the first entry word on that page, and the second guide word tells the last entry word. If your word is one that would come in alphabetical order between those guide words, it will be on that page.

EXAMPLE

Would *distract* be on a page with the guide words **distinction** and **dither**? Does *distract* come alphabetically between those two words? Yes, *distr-* comes after *disti-* and before *dit-,* so *distract* would be on that page.

PRACTICE   Tell where each word would appear—on the page with the guide words given, on an earlier page, or on a later page.

1. frown (**frolic/fruit**)
2. oldie (**Ohio/olden**)
3. exile (**exclude/exhaust**)
4. bait (**bag/balance**)
5. realist (**read/ream**)
6. expect (**expense/exponent**)
7. dingo (**dimple/dip**)
8. swab (**surliness/survive**)
9. irritate (**islet/issue**)
10. voyage (**vortex/vying**)

# Chapter 11
# Writing Sentences

Lesson 1   **Adding Words to Sentences**
Lesson 2   **Combining Sentences**
Lesson 3   **Avoiding Sentence Fragments**
Lesson 4   **Avoiding Run-On Sentences**
Lesson 5   **Avoiding Wordiness in Sentences**

# Adding Words to Sentences

Sometimes a sentence seems as plain as a bare wall: The sun slid behind the mountain. Just as you can decorate a wall with colorful pictures, you can bring a sentence to life by adding words that provide more information: The *fiery* sun slid *slowly* behind the mountain. When adjectives and adverbs are added to sentences, they add color and detail and catch the reader's attention.

## Example

In the following paragraph, a boy named Steve remembers a conversation he had with his grandfather. Notice how the underlined adjectives and adverbs are used to include important details in the paragraph.

Grandfather <u>slowly</u> shook his head. Billows of <u>snowy</u> <u>white</u> hair swept his forehead. "You seem to be a boy of <u>many</u> faces <u>lately</u>. I heard you and Hugh in a <u>loud</u> and <u>angry</u> argument over the <u>last</u> slice of pizza this noon. But then you <u>generously</u> lent him your <u>new</u> bike. Your <u>poor</u> mother must <u>constantly</u> remind you to do your <u>regular</u> chores. But your <u>new</u> teacher called to say he was <u>immensely</u> <u>happy</u> with how <u>carefully</u> you keep the <u>delicate</u> equipment in the laboratory. You have a <u>beautiful</u> voice and a <u>natural</u> talent for singing. But you listen only to the <u>noisiest</u> music."

Which of the underlined words are adjectives and which are adverbs?

Why is Steve "a boy of many faces"?

**PRACTICE 1** Complete each sentence by adding an adjective and an adverb. Write each sentence.

1. The _____ sailboat slipped _____ through the water.
2. Calvin had _____ forgotten the _____ letter.
3. _____ waves swept _____ over the pier.
4. On the horizon, _____ clouds _____ formed.
5. A _____ explosion _____ shook the valley.

**PRACTICE 2** Expand each sentence by adding an adjective and an adverb. Write each sentence.

1. The girl looked at the sign.
2. She read it and then stared at the roads.
3. At that point a boy stopped next to her.
4. He pulled a map from his pocket.
5. Just then the bus arrived, and people began getting off.

**WRITE** Make up five sentences about an older person that you admire. Give exact details about this person and why you might like to be like him or her. Underline the adjectives and adverbs that you use.

**GO BEYOND** Join a group of five or six classmates. Each of you should write the opening sentence for a story about an interesting person or an unusual animal. Pass the papers around the group, with each person adding a sentence to each paper to develop the story. Use exact details in each sentence you write. When your paper is returned to you, add a final sentence.

# Combining Sentences

No matter how long a sentence might be, it is a **simple sentence** if it has a single or compound subject and a single or compound predicate. In spite of its length, the following is a simple sentence because it has one subject and one predicate: In the early morning hours just before dawn, the *birds chirp* and *sing* in the bushes and trees around our house. The sentence is a simple sentence because there is only one subject (*birds*) and one predicate (*chirp* and *sing*).

A **compound sentence** is a sentence that is made up of two simple sentences joined together by the conjunctions *and, but,* or *or*. The single compound sentence that results has two separate subjects and predicates. A comma always comes before the conjunction in a compound sentence: The *men pushed* the boat away from the shore, and *they jumped* aboard.

Compound sentences offer you one way of avoiding short, choppy sentences. They allow you to put together in a single sentence two ideas that are closely related in some way.

## Example

Notice how the following pairs of simple sentences are joined together in a single compound sentence. The simple subjects and predicates are underlined.

The floodwaters rose. The dam finally collapsed.
The floodwaters rose, and the dam finally collapsed.

The letter was on the table. Mary forgot it.
The letter was on the table, but Mary forgot it.

We will rebuild the treehouse. We will take it apart.
We will rebuild the treehouse, or we will take it apart.

**PRACTICE 1** Write the following compound sentences. Underline each simple subject and simple predicate and circle each conjunction.

1. The weather was cold, but the air was clear.
2. The ice on the pond caught the sunlight, and it gleamed brightly.
3. I sat on a rock, and my sister laced my skates.
4. I will skate today, or I may never try again.
5. My friends helped me up, and I stepped carefully toward the ice.

**PRACTICE 2** Combine each pair of simple sentences into a compound sentence by using *and, but,* or *or.* Write each sentence, and remember to put a comma before the conjunction.

1. It was New Year's Eve. I decided upon some resolutions.
2. Brad enjoyed the piano. He hated the hours of practice.
3. The wind suddenly grew stronger. The lake became very rough.
4. I will leave on Saturday evening. I will wait until Sunday morning.

**WRITE** The sentences in Practice 1 begin a story. Finish the story. Use at least three compound sentences as you tell what happens.

**GO BEYOND** Work in groups of four. Read the story you wrote for the Write exercise. Have the members of the group find the compound sentences in your story.

### A-Ha!

Whatever is inside that sheet
Just gave a dreadful shout!

A-Ha, but what about those feet
That I see sticking out?

They help me guess who's hiding there,
Whose eyes are peeking through:

And how could anyone be scared of You!

*Dorothy Aldis*

Say the title of the poem.
Why is the exclamation mark in the title appropriate?

# Avoiding Sentence Fragments

A **sentence fragment** is a group of words that is punctuated as if it were a sentence. It is not a sentence, however, because it does not express a complete thought. Often the fragment is missing a subject or a predicate. Sometimes it is missing both. Sentence fragments should be avoided because they confuse the reader.

## Example

Notice the difference between the sentences and the sentence fragments below.

SENTENCES

They slowly climbed to the summit of the mountain.
The climbers could see a broad green valley below.
Sharp peaks of ice stood around them.

SENTENCE FRAGMENTS

Slowly climbed to the summit of the mountain. (no subject)
A broad green valley stretched below them. (no predicate)
On sharp peaks of ice around them. (no subject or predicate)

**PRACTICE 1**   After the number of each item, write whether the group of words is a sentence or a sentence fragment.

1. Amy walked slowly down the dirt road.
2. Kicking up little clouds of dust.
3. She had never given a speech.
4. Represent her class in the Veterans Day program.
5. Was already blushing.

**PRACTICE 2**   Three of the following groups of words are sentence fragments. Make each sentence fragment into a complete sentence. Write the new sentence.

1. Amy before the whole school.
2. She began speaking.
3. The silence around her.
4. Then she was finished.
5. Began to clap.

**WRITE**   What do you think was in the missing part of the torn newspaper picture on this page? Write a paragraph telling what would make the picture complete. Use your imagination. There is more than one correct answer for this exercise. Make sure you use complete sentences.

**GO BEYOND**   Work with six other students. Pretend to be a famous person the group knows about and let them guess who you are. First give them a category—for example, "I am a baseball star." Then offer a clue. If the others fail to guess correctly, give one or more easier clues. You must give each clue as a complete sentence.

# Avoiding Run-On Sentences

A **run-on sentence** is a group of words that is actually two or more sentences written as a single sentence. The individual sentences are not correctly separated from each other. In run-on sentences, two or more complete thoughts are written without a pause between them: Mom teaches at my school she is also the basketball coach.

Run-on sentences can be corrected by simply breaking the word groups into two separate sentences: Mom teaches at my school. She is also the basketball coach. It is sometimes possible to correct a run-on sentence by changing it into a compound sentence: Mom teaches at my school, and she is also the basketball coach.

## Example

Notice how the following run-on sentences have been corrected.

RUN-ON SENTENCES

Jason looked across the street he saw shadows on the lawn.
The junk tumbled from the closet it was too late to close the door.
I don't want to disappoint her I'm not a good player.

CORRECTED SENTENCES

Jason looked across the street. He saw shadows on the lawn.
The junk tumbled from the closet. It was too late to close the door.
I don't want to disappoint her, but I'm not a good player.

**PRACTICE 1**    After the number of each sentence, write either *correct* or *run-on.*

1. Jane has a picture of a former basketball star the player is Jane's mother.
2. Jane's mother won a trophy in high school Jane has a picture of her with it.
3. Her mother's parents were proud of their daughter and took pictures of her at some of the games.
4. Jane's mother is a basketball coach at Jane's school.
5. Jane's friends think she will be a good player because her mother was Jane is not so sure.

**PRACTICE 2**    Correct each run-on sentence. Write separate sentences or a compound sentence. Remember to place a comma before the conjunction in a compound sentence.

1. Mom expects me to try out she's already talking about how much fun the game is.
2. I never told her I don't like basketball I am an awkward player.
3. I get nervous when someone throws me the ball suppose I get hit in the face?
4. Still, I can practice before the tryouts possibly I may feel less clumsy.
5. I want to please my mother I don't want to let her down.

**WRITE**    Imagine that you are Jane in Practice 2. Write five sentences that tell what happens at the tryouts. Check your work for run-on sentences.

**GO BEYOND**    Find a paragraph of at least ten sentences in a book or magazine. Write the paragraph as a single sentence. Exchange the single-sentence paragraph with a partner. Correct and rewrite the paragraph you receive. Then check your work against the original version of the paragraph.

# LESSON 5  Avoiding Wordiness in Sentences

Sentences that are too wordy can confuse your readers and make their attention wander. Unnecessary words only get in the way, making your ideas hard to understand. Good sentences come directly to the point. They are clear and exact. They say exactly what you want to say.

*Which pack would you rather carry? Why?*

## Example

The first draft of a paragraph by a student named Marsha is wordy. Her second draft is more direct and exact.

FIRST DRAFT

Due to the fact that my parents' vacation is in the month of August, we will be taking a trip during that month. I wanted to go camping, but my parents seemed to be upset about this idea that I had. My mother and father said to me that they didn't want to have to do any cooking while they were on vacation. I guess we'll stay in motels to sleep, and then we can eat in restaurants. That way my parents can get a rest from what they do all the time.

SECOND DRAFT

Because my parents' vacation is in August, we will be taking a trip then. I like camping, but that idea upset my parents. They told me they didn't want to cook while they were on vacation. We now plan to sleep in motels and eat in restaurants. My parents do deserve a rest.

How did Marsha improve each sentence?
Why is Marsha satisfied with the vacation plans?

**PRACTICE 1**   Beside the number of each sentence, write *direct* or *wordy*.

1. Marsha's family has a real outdoor tent that is the color of blue.
2. Usually Marsha's family camps in May.
3. Everyone collects all the equipment that is needed for camping and then helps to pack it inside the old, green station wagon.
4. Marsha and her father begin the job of setting up the tent to sleep in as soon as they get there.
5. Marsha's mother gathers wood for their campfire.

**PRACTICE 2**   Rewrite each sentence. Omit any unnecessary words.

1. The baby of the whale is the biggest animal baby in the whole world.
2. A newborn baby blue whale may be as big as twenty feet long.
3. It may weigh more than a full-grown adult elephant weighs.
4. Not all of the animal mothers have babies that are big.
5. A 600-pound black bear may have a little cub that weighs as little as a pound on the scales.

**WRITE**   You are going on vacation. Where will you go? What will you do? What will you see? Write at least five sentences about your trip. Avoid wordiness.

**GO BEYOND**   Exchange with a partner the sentences you wrote for the Write exercise. What do you like about your partner's writing? Did your partner use any unnecessary words? Suggest what your partner can do to improve his or her writing. Listen to your partner's ideas about your writing. Use the best suggestions to help you rewrite your five sentences.

## Practice

**A.** Rewrite the paragraph below. Add an adjective, an adverb, or both an adjective and an adverb to each sentence.

The sun was shining. The beach was empty. A breeze blew from the ocean. The waves broke against the shore. We spread our towels on the sand. We would spend a day at the beach.

**B.** Combine each pair of sentences. Use *and, but,* or *or* to form a compound sentence.

1. Kenna is a fine gymnast. Sandy is an expert tennis player.
2. Mickey sang. Jill played the piano.
3. That would be a nice trip. The cost would be very high.
4. We may go to the beach. We may play softball at home.
5. Jim is taller and lighter. John can run much faster.

**C.** Rewrite each run-on sentence.

1. Nicky is my cat he is eleven years old.
2. The Susquehanna is an interesting river it flows through beautiful areas.
3. John agreed to the plan Betsy continued to object to it.
4. The television set is broken it has no sound.
5. Soccer is my favorite sport we play all the time.

**D.** Rewrite each sentence fragment as a complete sentence.

1. Pulled the covers over his head.
2. Paula and her young sister Eileen.
3. Heard the fire engine's siren.
4. In the early morning hours on my Uncle David's dairy farm.
5. Caught the ball and threw it perfectly to third base.

**E.** Beside the number of each sentence, write *direct* or *wordy*. Rewrite each wordy sentence.

1. My cousins and I went to the park where people play baseball that is on the other side of this town.
2. Peter forgot to give me my homework assignment.
3. Because I am sick, I will have to make up while I'm at home all the work I ordinarily do when I'm in school.
4. Myron and Libby helped Dad water the plants.
5. I borrowed a pencil from Jane.

## Composition

Write the rest of a story that begins with the paragraph below. Use adjectives and adverbs to make your sentences more lively and interesting. Use some sentences with compound subjects or compound predicates. Use at least one compound sentence.

Sunday morning began the way it always began. I woke up about eight o'clock. For a moment I thought I smelled breakfast. But it suddenly dawned on me that what I smelled was not breakfast at all. I jumped out of bed and ran to the door.

## Advanced Challenge

Find a book or a magazine and search for examples of simple sentences that are very long. Remember, no matter how long a sentence might be, it is a simple sentence if it only contains one subject and one predicate. Write down the longest simple sentence that you can find. Compare your sentence with the sentences that your classmates locate.

## DICTIONARY

You can't look up a word in a dictionary if you don't know how to spell it. True or false?

False. It is not always easy to look up a word whose spelling you don't know, but it certainly can be done. If you can spell the beginning of the word, you can find what page the word is on, especially if you use the guide words at the top of each page. Once you have found the correct page, you can quickly read down the page until you find the word itself. If you don't know how to spell the beginning of the word, think about the spelling of other words you do know that start with the same sounds. Then try each of the spellings until you find the right one.

EXAMPLE

Some sounds in English can be spelled in more than one way. If a word begins with a *k* sound, the word might start with either *k* or *c* (*kite, cat*). The sound *ow* can be spelled *ow, ou,* or *ough* (*owl, out, bough*). A *j* sound at the beginning of a word can be spelled with a *g* or a *j*. Check to see whether your dictionary has a guide to different ways of spelling sounds.

PRACTICE   Decide what you think is the right spelling for each word. Then check your work with a dictionary. Write the correctly spelled word.

1. jage, gaje, guage, gauge (type of measure)
2. cirus, sirrus, seerus, cirrus (type of cloud)
3. feable, feeble, feabel, feebel (weak)
4. ascend, assend, asend, ascind (go up)
5. tole, toal, toll, toel (fee for using a road or bridge)

# Chapter 12
# Capitalization and Punctuation

Lesson 1   **Capitalization**
Lesson 2   **Capitalization in Letter Writing**
Lesson 3   **Using Quotation Marks**
Lesson 4   **More About Writing Quotations**
Lesson 5   **Commas in Sentences**
Lesson 6   **Using Apostrophes**
Lesson 7   **Using Colons**
Lesson 8   **Proofreading Sentences**

# Capitalization

When a word begins with a capital letter, we say that it is **capitalized**. Capitalizing certain words sets them off from other words in a sentence or paragraph.

Here are rules for capitalization.

1. **Capitalize the first word in a sentence.**
2. **Capitalize the pronoun _I_.**
3. **Capitalize proper nouns and proper adjectives made from proper nouns (such as _Spanish_).**
4. **Capitalize a title before a person's name.**
5. **Capitalize the first word, the last word, and every other important word in the title of a book, play, story, song, or poem.**

## Example

These sentences illustrate capitalization rules.

FIRST WORD IN A SENTENCE
**Because** I want to write well, I work hard at my writing.

PRONOUN I
Last week **I** wrote and proofread a letter to my pen pal.

PROPER NOUNS
He is **James Chin,** and he lives in **Saginaw, Michigan**.

PROPER ADJECTIVES
The family is of **Chinese** origin.

TITLE BEFORE A PERSON'S NAME
His mother is **Dr.** Lucy Chin.

FIRST, LAST, AND ALL IMPORTANT WORDS IN TITLES
He told me about the book _**Fifth Chinese Daughter**_

**PRACTICE 1**   Rewrite this list. Capitalize where necessary.

1. english nobleman
2. *the house on the hill* (book)
3. eagle street
4. professor margaret ryan
5. is that you?

6. ms. maría garcía
7. mexican oil
8. president adams
9. *the sands of time* (book)
10. japanese car

**PRACTICE 2**   Rewrite each sentence. Capitalize correctly.

1. helen keller had a remarkable life.
2. she was born in tuscumbia, alabama, in 1880.
3. when she was less than two years old, an illness left her without sight or hearing.
4. with the help of anne sullivan, she learned to read and write.
5. helen wrote the book *out of the dark*, which told about part of her life.

**WRITE**   A local radio station is interviewing you. The producers want to know how young people use their free time. What are your hobbies? What games do you play? What do you do when you are not in school? Write a script of the interview. Include the questions and your answers.

**GO BEYOND**   Exchange papers from the Write exercise with a partner. Check each other's papers for correct capitalization. Return the papers and make needed corrections.

■   **Be sure that you capitalize all the words that require capital letters.**

# Capitalization in Letter Writing

Capitalization rules for the parts of a friendly letter are easy to remember: Capitalize the first word of the greeting and the closing. Capitalize all proper nouns and titles in the letter and on the envelope.

## Example

Kevin wrote this friendly letter to his pen pal.

> 18 Oak Street
> Tarrytown, NY 10591
> August 22, 19——
>
> Dear Peter,
>     How are you? I am restless. It's been so rainy lately that I don't get to play baseball much. Remember the fun we had playing at camp?
>     You must be enjoying your vacation with your aunt and uncle. Write and tell me about it.
>
>                         Your friend,
>                         Kevin

This is how Kevin addressed the envelope.

What rules did Kevin follow? To whom do *you* usually write friendly letters?

> Kevin McCarthy
> 18 Oak Street
> Tarrytown, NY 10591
>
>             Peter Henderson
>             % Mr. and Mrs. Alec Wayne
>             2041 Division St.
>             Burlington VT 05401

**PRACTICE 1**   Here are some of the words Peter capitalized when he answered Kevin's letter. Write the list. Beside each group, tell why he capitalized the word or words.

1. 2041 Division Street
2. September 1, 19—
3. Dear Kevin,
4. Your friend,
5. Burlington, VT 05401

**PRACTICE 2**   Rewrite the following letter. Correct the capitalization errors.

> 2020 River Street
> Fort Madison, ia 52627
> April 14, 19—

dear aunt susan,

   Thanks for talking with me last weekend. I needed someone to listen to me. Ever since my friend Meg moved away, I've been feeling sad. I feel better now.

   I hope to see you again very soon!

> love,
>
> Janice

**WRITE**   Mr. Wesley Nathan writes the advice column for your local paper. Your problem is that you have too many chores. Write a letter asking Mr. Nathan what to say to your parents. You want to be helpful because your parents work hard. You know you could probably do more during vacations, but now, between afternoon activities and homework, you don't have time.

**GO BEYOND**   Exchange with a partner the letter you wrote for the Write exercise. Check the letter your partner wrote and mark any words that are not correctly capitalized. Then pretend you are Mr. Nathan and answer your partner's letter.

# Using Quotation Marks

**Quotation marks** set off a speaker's exact words. When a quotation is part of another sentence, commas and end marks must be placed correctly before or after the speaker's words.

■ **Put quotation marks before and after a speaker's exact words. Use a comma to separate a quotation from words that come before or after it in a sentence.**
**Put a period or comma inside the closing quotation mark.**
**Put a question mark or exclamation mark inside the closing quotation mark if it is part of the quotation. Otherwise put the mark outside the closing quotation mark.**

## Example

Notice how quotation marks are used in the following sentences.

"Sal, please stop by my office."
Mother said, "Please keep your room clean."
"Watch for falling rocks!" shouted my father.
The man asked, "Can the town afford this?"
Did Patrick Henry say, "Give me liberty or give me death"?

**PRACTICE 1**  Write each sentence. Add quotation marks where they are needed.

1. We have decided to spend the day at the beach, Marion said.
2. Be careful shouted the police officer.
3. James asked, Do we meet at five o'clock?
4. Was it Ms. Ames who said This is the best class ever?
5. Our leader said Be sure to keep to the center of the path.

**PRACTICE 2**  Write each sentence correctly. Add whatever punctuation marks are necessary.

1. Who do you think won first prize Mia asked her father
2. Which one of you said I never make a mistake
3. Keep back from the edge, shouted Max
4. Fernando asked How far is it to Greenfield
5. Mr. Renfrew announced The final test will be given next Wednesday.

**WRITE**  What might be happening between the two people in the picture? What might each person be saying? Write their conversation. Every time the speaker changes, indent the sentence.

■ **Be sure that you used quotation marks before and after each speaker's words.**

**GO BEYOND**  Give the conversation you wrote to a partner to read. Proofread your partner's conversation for correct use of quotation marks and other punctuation. Then discuss how each other's ideas about what is happening in the picture were alike and different.

# More About Writing Quotations

A **divided quotation** is broken into two parts. A comma follows the last word in the first part and quotation marks go before and after each portion of what the speaker says: "I sing," she said, "but very softly." The second part of a divided quotation begins with a capital letter only if it begins a new sentence: "Bill enjoys singing," she said. "He always has."

No matter how short a direct quotation may be, the words of each new speaker should begin a new paragraph.

■ **Begin the second part of a divided quotation with a capital letter only if it begins a new sentence.**
**Begin a new paragraph each time the speaker changes.**

## Example

Lady Margaret Dinsmore starts the following conversation with Robin and Sir Peter, her husband. The selection is from *The Door in the Wall* by Marguerite DeAngeli.

"We have long awaited your coming, dear child, and now we are most happy that you have safely arrived."

"I shall make a sorry page, my lady," said Robin ruefully. "But I can sing, and I can read a little to while away the time for your lordship," he offered, "and I can pen letters for you."

Sir Peter kept Robin's hand in his and spoke directly to him. "Each of us has his place in the world," he said. "If we cannot serve in one way, there is always another. If we do what we are able, a door always opens to something else."

What shows that different people are speaking?
How does Sir Peter encourage Robin?

**PRACTICE 1**   Write the three sentences that are incorrectly capitalized. Correct the capitalization.

1. "Have you heard?" asked Bernie. "We won the game."
2. "Did you know," asked Ellen, "That our class won first place in the poster contest?"
3. "Let's try to arrive early," suggested Maria, "So that we get good seats."
4. "I'd like to go with you," said Antonio, "but I promised my dad that I'd wash the car."
5. "On Saturday afternoon," said Tom, "We play our first baseball game of the new season."

**PRACTICE 2**   Rewrite the following conversation. Add quotation marks, commas, and capital letters where necessary.

1. Oh dear complained the ant I'm so tired of working.
2. Why not sit in the sun with me asked the grasshopper and play awhile?
3. I will replied the ant but first I must gather food for winter.
4. You don't have to work so hard said the smiling grasshopper. winter is a long time coming.
5. Winter may be here sooner than you think warned the ant. I'll play when my work is done.

**WRITE**   Imagine that you have brought a famous person to speak to the class. You introduce that person to your teacher, and the three of you talk before class begins. Write the conversation.

■ **Be sure that you began a new paragraph each time the speaker changed.**

**GO BEYOND**   Divide into five groups. Have one person from each group write a quotation on the board. The quotation should illustrate a rule from this lesson. A correct sentence earns one point. See which group can score five points first.

# Commas in Sentences

**Commas** are used in writing to set off or to separate words, groups of words, and numbers from each other or from other words in a sentence. Learn and use the rules for commas.

■ 1. **Use commas to set off items in dates and addresses.**
2. **Use commas to separate items in a series.**
3. **Use commas to set off the names of people spoken to.**
4. **Use commas to set off introductory words.**
5. **Use a comma before the conjunction that combines the parts of a compound sentence.**

## Example

These sentences can serve as models for using commas.

DATES AND ADDRESSES
Ty was born on Wednesday, April 7, 1982, in Austin Texas.
He now lives at 2 Plum Road, Phoenix, Arizona.

ITEMS IN A SERIES
This morning we picked beans, cucumbers, and corn.
I have to go to school, to drum practice, and to a scout meeting.

NAMES OF PEOPLE BEING SPOKEN TO
Mario, will you do me a favor?
Let's play Cosmic Search after dinner, Angela.

INTRODUCTORY WORDS
Yes, you will receive an invitation.
Well, I am very pleased.

COMPOUND SENTENCES
Frances selected the seeds, and I planted them.
It will not rain today, but it will be cloudy.

**PRACTICE 1** Write each sentence. Add commas where they are needed.

1. Jerry sometimes I just don't understand you.
2. On April 20 1983 we stayed overnight in Chicago.
3. Jo vacuumed the floors the drapes and the furniture and I washed all the windows.
4. No you may not borrow my books.
5. The house in Kansas City Missouri had a den a library and a family room.

**PRACTICE 2** Write each of the sentences below, adding commas correctly.

1. Well it's not really what I expected.
2. I was born in Abilene Kansas on June 21 1979.
3. My sister aunt and uncle went to the game with me.
4. Jim Tom will turn out the lights and I will lock the door.
5. Mother packed a lunch of sandwiches fruit and cheese for us to share.

**WRITE** Plan and write a story about a trip on a space shuttle. Put yourself in the story, if you like. Include in your story a date, an address, and at least one series of items.

■ **Check your story to be sure you used commas correctly.**

**GO BEYOND** Divide into five groups. Each person should read aloud the story he or she wrote for the last exercise. The others in the group can tell what they like about each story. Discuss ways in which each story can be improved.

**Using Apostrophes**

As you already know, the apostrophe is used with nouns to show possession: Arthur's pen, the students' classes, the women's decision. Apostrophes are also used in forming **contractions**. A contraction is a single word formed from two words. The apostrophe shows that letters have been omitted. Some contractions are formed from a verb and the word *not* (*can not* = *can't*). Others are formed from a pronoun and a verb (*they are* = *they're*).

## Example

Study the following list of contractions.

| | | | | |
|---|---|---|---|---|
| I am | = I'm | | can not | = can't |
| you are | = you're | | he had | = he'd |
| he is | = he's | | she had | = she'd |
| she is | = she's | | have not | = haven't |
| it is | = it's | | is not | = isn't |
| we are | = we're | | are not | = aren't |
| you will | = you'll | | will not | = won't |
| they are | = they're | | does not | = doesn't |
| I will | = I'll | | do not | = don't |
| who is | = who's | | has not | = hasn't |

**PRACTICE 1** Rewrite each sentence, changing the underlined words to contractions.
1. I am not sure I understand you.
2. They will repair the bridge by morning because they are worried about the rush hour traffic.
3. What do you think you are doing?
4. This is not a good idea.
5. I think we are finished here.

**PRACTICE 2** Complete each of the following sentences by forming a contraction that uses the word in parentheses. Write each sentence.
1. We _____ cross this property. (will)
2. I _____ the slightest idea what he means. (have)
3. _____ my best friend. (she)
4. _____ those girls tall? (are)
5. We tried hard, but we _____ budge the rock. (can)

**WRITE** Write ten sentences of your own using the contractions listed in the Example. If you know some contractions not listed, use those. Be sure to use apostrophes correctly.

**GO BEYOND** Form into groups of five. Write each of the words in the first column of each list in the Example on a slip of paper. List a word only once. (*Does* will be on one slip, and *not* will be on one slip.) Each member of the group picks two slips of paper and forms as many contractions as possible from the words picked. For example, if you pick the word *I,* you might list *I'm, I'd, I'll,* and *I've.* Share your list of contractions with the other members of the group. See if they can think of any contractions that you missed.

# Using Colons

A **colon** is a stronger and more formal punctuation mark than a comma. A colon can be used to introduce a series or a list of items. A colon separates the numbers for hours and minutes when someone writes the time of day. A colon follows the greeting in a business letter.

## Example

The following examples show the uses of the colon.

INTRODUCING A LIST OR SERIES
At camp I signed up for these sports: swimming, archery, and riding.
The governor of our state works hard to do the following things: plan the budget, appoint officials, and approve bills.

WRITING THE TIME OF DAY
2:15 P.M.     6:30 P.M.

AFTER THE GREETING IN A BUSINESS LETTER
Dear Sir or Madam:     Dear Ms. True:
Dear Mr. Bower:

## Exercises

**PRACTICE 1** Beside the number of each item, write why a colon was used. Use the reasons listed in the Example.
1. We need the following tools: a screwdriver, pliers, and a hammer.
2. Will the following people please stand: Andrea, Terry, Rachel, and Felipe.
3. Dear Senator Ludlum:
4. Joseph can cook these foods: soup, omelets, and popovers.
5. Mr. Ozwald is catching a 6:00 P.M. plane for Chicago.

**PRACTICE 2** Rewrite each of the following items, adding colons where they are needed.

1. Post this announcement in these places the main office, the cafeteria, and the gym.
2. Dear Professor Nidetch
3. Baker School begins classes promptly at 830 A.M.
4. When you go to the laundromat, take the following items quarters, detergent, fabric softener, bleach, and a laundry basket.
5. I get up every morning at 730 A.M.

**WRITE** Imagine that you have been selected to serve as principal of your school. Write a notice to the students in the form of a letter. Tell some of the things that you expect to do. Include at least one list following a colon and one time of day.

**GO BEYOND** Work with a partner. Read your notices from the Write exercise to each other. Tell where you used colons and the reason for each use. Discuss each other's ideas about what you would do as principal of your school.

# Proofreading Sentences

Good writers edit their work. That is, they correct and improve it. **Proofreading marks** show the changes they wish to make.

You can use the following proofreading marks when you correct your own writing.

- Take out a letter.
— Take out a word.
∧ Put in a word or letter.
⊙ Use a period.
⋏ Use a comma, as in this line.
≡ Use a capital letter.
¶ Begin a new paragraph.

## Example

This is how a student corrected a written conversation.

"hank are you sure you know how to repair a watch?"

"Sure. It's easy. you jut take this thingamajig offf the back."

"Somehow I'm not sure you know what you're doing."

"At least I didn't drop my my watch in the fish tank!"

Explain each editing mark.
Would you let Hank repair your watch?
Why or why not?

**PRACTICE 1** Copy the sentences listed below. In each sentence find the error that can be corrected by using the instruction in parentheses. Then use a proofreading mark to make the corrections.

1. "Hank I wish you'd have more respect for your elders." (Use a comma.)
2. "Just because you're two days older than I am, you're hardly an adult," hank told me. (Use a capital letter.)
3. I took one last look at at my watch. (Take out a word.)
4. "Be kind to it It's the only one I own." (Use a period.)
5. "It'll be better than knew in five minutes," Hank assured me. (Take out a letter.)

**PRACTICE 2** Copy each sentence without correcting it. Then use proofreading marks to show any corrections.

1. Hank pried the back off the case
2. "so much for the thingamajig" he said
3. True to his word, he had the the watch fixed in less than five minutes.
4. "I don't believe it" I told him. "It's working!"
5. "Take a lesson from a child," told me, getting even for my remark about being his elder.

**WRITE** Write about a time when you tried to fix something. Your story can be funny or serious, true or imagined. Use at least two characters in your story and have them talk to each other. When you edit your story, use proofreading marks to show the corrections you will make. Then recopy your story.

**GO BEYOND** Draw a picture to illustrate the story you wrote for the Write exercise. Share your story and drawing with the rest of the class.

---

## Practice

**A.** Rewrite each sentence or letter part, using correct capitalization.

1. dear aunt terry,
2. marty and tom said that i was in charge.
3. our trip to montreal, canada, in july of 1982 was exciting.
4. the canadian people are very friendly, and many speak french.
5. mr. huard was a french canadian who loaned us a guidebook about travel in canada.

**B.** Rewrite each sentence. Add quotation marks to set off the words for the speaker.

1. Kathy yelled, Give me the ball!
2. Look out! I yelled. Here it comes.
3. It will be good to have you on our team, Kathy said.
4. Oh, no! I said. I can't come to practice.
5. Practice, said Kathy, is every Wednesday.

**C.** Turn this play dialogue into a written conversation. Use quotation marks and add words like *said* and *asked*.

MARY:   What time is the train due in?
DICK:   It's due at noon.
MARY:   Are you meeting your mother?
DICK:   No, Aunt Harriet is coming.
MARY:   I hope she enjoys her visit.

**D.** Rewrite each sentence. Add a colon or comma wherever one is needed.

1. Millie I'd like these things paper towels paper napkins cups and forks.
2. No the performance took place at 2 00 P.M. on February 20 1982.
3. Yes Henry will collect tickets.
4. Dear Sir or Madam
5. Robert give me some lotion and ice.

**E.** Combine each of the following pairs of words into a contraction.

1. can not
2. did not
3. it is
4. I am
5. we are
6. he will
7. does not
8. who is
9. are not
10. has not

**F.** Copy this paragraph. Use proof-reading marks to show corrections.

marsha looked into her room, it was neat. "cleaned my room?" marsh said? "i did," said marshall from behind her! "it was my good deed for the month of october."

## Composition

Imagine that you write an advice column for a local newspaper. You have received a letter with the following request. Write a reply. Remember to treat the request for advice seriously.

Dear Adviser,

I really need help. I have two sisters and one brother. The problem is that the four of us fight constantly. For example, last evening I got home from school just before dinner. My sisters and brother were watching television. I told them that I had to watch the news to complete a current events assignment, and I switched the channel. A fight broke out, and my father had to stop it. This sort of thing happens all the time.

Please help me. I need peace and quiet.

Sincerely,

A Student

## Advanced Challenge

Look over the writing you have done in the past few weeks. Find a capitalization or punctuation rule that you have trouble remembering when you write. Study and learn that rule.

Now write ten exercise items that let you practice the rule. Look at the Practices in the lessons of this chapter to see the kinds of items you should write.

Make up an answer sheet on a separate piece of paper to accompany the items in your exercise. Trade exercises with a partner. You should both agree on the correct answer for each of the exercises.

Keep your exercise and answer sheet for review and practice.

## DICTIONARY

What happens when you start writing a word at the end of a line on your paper and don't have enough room to finish it? As you probably know, you can divide many words. You put a hyphen (-) at the end of a syllable and write the rest of the word on the line below. Remember these rules about dividing words.

1. Never divide a one-syllable word.
2. If a word is one that always has a hyphen, *only* divide that word at the hyphen, no matter how many syllables the word has.
3. Do not divide a word in a way that separates just one letter from the rest of the word.

How can you tell what letters in a word form syllables? If you look up the word in your dictionary, you will see that the word has extra space, a little line, or a dot, between each syllable.

EXAMPLE

Where can you divide the word *dictionary*? If you look up the word, you may find that your dictionary divides it this way: **dic-tion-ar-y**. Therefore, you can divide the word after *dic* or after *tion* and put the rest of the word on the line below. But you should not divide **dictionary** after *ar* and leave *y* by itself on the next line.

PRACTICE   Use your dictionary to learn how to divide these words. Write the words with dots or spaces to show the divisions.

1. remember
2. gymnastics
3. dungeon
4. isthmus
5. grouchily
6. banana

**A.** Write the following sentences. Draw a line between the complete subject and the complete predicate.

1. My Grandmother Nagy was born in Hungary.
2. We piled the sleeping bags and camping gear in the truck.
3. The huge, noisy crowd moved slowly down the street.
4. A blue-and-white striped blimp floated in the sky.
5. The ocean liner sailed slowly into the harbor.

**B.** Read the word groups below. Write whether each is a *sentence, sentence fragment,* or a *run-on sentence.*

1. The silver plane on the runway.
2. Three robins landed near the feeder.
3. Like Mary Ellen, so many times before.
4. Larry plays violin Jack is on flute.
5. They want to vacation in New Mexico it is so beautiful.

**C.** The following paragraph has many errors. Use proof-reading marks to show all the corrections that need to be made.

Dear sir or madam
In your adversising you say "we have the best service. smith's stamp service, howerver, does not gve good service. sox months ago i ordered stamps from iraq, india, and spain. Ive received five bills, but no stamp.

# Unit Four
# Paragraphs

Chapter 13
**Elements of Paragraphs**

Chapter 14
**Descriptive Paragraphs**

Chapter 15
**Factual Paragraphs**

Chapter 16
**Building Paragraphs**

183

## Brontosaurus

The giant brontosaurus
Was a prehistoric chap
With four fat feet to stand on
And a very skimpy lap.
The scientists assure us
Of a most amazing thing—
A brontosaurus blossomed
When he had a chance to sing!

 The bigger brontosauruses,
Who liked to sing in choruses,
Would close their eyes
And harmonize
And sing most anything.)

They growled and they yowled,
They deedled and they dummed;
They warbled and they whistled,
They howled and they hummed.
They didn't eat, they didn't sleep;
They sang and sang all day.
Now all you'll find are footprints
Where they tapped the time away!

*Gail Kredenser*

What sounds did the Brontosaurus make when it sang?
Why did the Brontosaurus disappear?

# Chapter 13
# Elements of Paragraphs

Lesson 1 **The Paragraph**
Lesson 2 **Main Ideas in Paragraphs**
Lesson 3 **Adding Details to Paragraphs**

**The Paragraph**

A **paragraph** is a group of sentences about one main idea or topic. The first word in a paragraph is indented, or set in from the left margin. This shows the reader that the indented sentence and those which follow are related.

Because a paragraph talks about a single idea, all the sentences in a paragraph must explain or add to that idea. As a group, all the sentences in a paragraph help the reader to understand the main idea that the writer wants to make.

*Which picture does not belong with the others? Why?*

## Example

Here is a paragraph that presents information about a kind of fish.

Most salmon do not spend their entire lives in one body of water. Both Pacific and Atlantic salmon hatch from eggs in cold, clear rivers. After a while the young salmon travel downstream to the ocean, where they spend most of their lives. Years later they fight their way up river to the place of their birth. They are responding to the urge to spawn, to leave eggs of their own to hatch. They leave the fertilized eggs that produce the next generation of salmon.

What is the main idea that the paragraph talks about?
What do you think happens to the salmon after they spawn?

**PRACTICE 1** The paragraph in the Example tells how salmon live. Decide which three sentences below could be part of that paragraph. Write the three sentences.

1. Some baby salmon are only a few weeks old when they start downstream.
2. Salmon can be smoked or canned.
3. The adult salmon will swim against the river current to return home to spawn.
4. After spawning, the exhausted salmon die.
5. Some people use colorful bait to catch salmon.

**PRACTICE 2** Tell which sentences belong in a paragraph about the dangers in the life of salmon at sea.

1. At sea the salmon are often in danger.
2. Larger fish eat the young salmon.
3. Some salmon die in polluted waters.
4. Female salmon lay their eggs in nests which they dig in the bottom of a shallow stream.
5. People who fish for a living and those who do sportfishing catch many salmon.

**WRITE** In a paragraph, tell about the dangers that another living creature faces. You may choose a bird, a beast, or a human being. List at least three things that might harm that creature. These could be the dangers they face from their natural enemies, a shrinking food supply, or other changes in the environment. Be sure to indent the first word of your paragraph.

**GO BEYOND** Draw or find a picture to illustrate the paragraph you wrote. Then form a group and make a classroom display of all the paragraphs and pictures that were done.

# Main Ideas in Paragraphs

A **topic sentence** is a sentence that tells what the main idea in a paragraph is. The topic sentence tells the reader what the paragraph is about.

A topic sentence can actually appear anywhere in a paragraph. But because it helps the reader to know what the main point of a paragraph will be, the topic sentence often comes first. When you are learning to write paragraphs, it is a good idea to put the topic sentence at the beginning.

## Example

Read the following paragraph.

Many tame animals share the work of human beings. In some parts of the world, horses are used to plow the land and to get people from place to place. In some places oxen are also used for plowing and for pulling heavy loads as well. Wherever sheep are kept, trained dogs watch over them and herd them together at the shepherd's command. Reindeer are used in the world's Arctic regions to pull sleds over long distances. In the world's desert regions, camels carry all kinds of loads and people, and they are also used to plow the land.

What is the topic sentence of this paragraph?
What other things do tame animals do for people?

**PRACTICE 1**  Write these sentences in order. Start with the topic sentence.

1. She escaped from slavery in 1849.
2. During the Civil War, which began in 1861, she served as a nurse, a scout, and a spy for the Union Army.
3. If she had been caught, Tubman could have been jailed or killed for aiding the slaves.
4. Harriet Tubman was a brave woman.
5. During the 1850s she helped free about 300 slaves.

**PRACTICE 2**  Write each sentence that would belong in a paragraph with the following topic sentence.

TOPIC SENTENCE     It took courage for Ben to defend Neena.

1. He knew his friends didn't like her because she dressed differently and spoke with an accent.
2. They wouldn't like him if he helped her.
3. She was new to the school and to their ways, and she needed a friend.
4. Neena played the piano.
5. He decided to be her friend—no matter what happened.

**WRITE**  In a single paragraph, tell about something that used to frighten you but no longer does. Explain how you overcame your fear. Remember to state the main idea at the beginning of your paragraph.

**GO BEYOND**  Work with a partner. Read each other's paragraph from the Write exercise. Try to explain the main idea of your partner's paragraph. If the main idea is not clear, work with your partner on rewriting the paragraph. Make sure the topic sentence is a clear statement of what the paragraph is about.

**Adding Details to Paragraphs**

Each of the sentences that follows the topic sentence in a paragraph must support or add information about the topic sentence. These **supporting sentences** do their job by explaining, by offering details, or by giving examples.

The information that you offer in the supporting sentences should be definite and exact. Sentences that include definite and exact information allow your reader to get a clear picture of the point you want to make. They tell your reader why you came to the conclusion expressed in the topic sentence.

## Example

Here is a paragraph about life in the desert. The topic sentence is underlined.

All life must adapt to the dryness of the desert. Plants are widely scattered so that they will not use up what little water there is. Some plants, like the mesquite, get water from deep beneath the surface. Most desert animals cut their water intake by feeding at night when it is cooler. Camels live for months on water produced when the fat in their humps breaks down.

How does each sentence support or add information to the topic sentence?

In what ways do living things adapt to the conditions that surround them?

**PRACTICE 1** Three of the following sentences supply supporting information for the topic sentence. Write each of those sentences.

TOPIC SENTENCE    We had a wonderful time at the beach.

1. There were big waves, and my sister Rachel and I spent the afternoon jumping into them.
2. The sky was light blue with few clouds.
3. My little brother Leonard and my mom made a huge sand castle.
4. My big brother Joe collected all the different types of shells he could find.
5. He keeps them in a large glass jar on his desk.

**PRACTICE 2** Only four of the numbered sentences belong together in a paragraph. Write a statement telling why each sentence does or does not belong.

TOPIC SENTENCE    Mountains add much to our lives.

1. They offer beautiful scenery as we hike and camp.
2. The grass on their slopes feeds our animals.
3. Surveyors can measure their height.
4. Wood from mountain forests warms our homes.
5. Swift mountain streams generate the electricity that lights many of our homes.

**WRITE** Tell about a place you like to visit. Write a paragraph explaining where the place is and what it looks like. Make sure your supporting sentences develop the topic sentence.

**GO BEYOND** Draw or find pictures to illustrate the paragraph you wrote for the Write exercise. Use your writing and illustrations for a bulletin-board display.

## Practice

**A.** Rewrite the paragraph below, leaving out any sentence that does not support or add information about the main idea.

The squirrel made his way across the yard. He darted among the leaves. Oak trees are often the last to lose their leaves. His cheeks were full of nuts that he had collected across the street. With just a few more nuts the squirrel would be set for winter. Some winters are quite cold, while others are quite mild.

**B.** For each topic sentence below, write two sentences that add details.
1. Playing a musical instrument is more difficult than it looks.
2. I wish I could get through one winter without catching a cold.
3. Which kinds of animals come in a variety of colors or sizes?
4. I would rather own a pony than a dog.
5. Our class has found several ways to earn money.

**C.** Write the number of each sentence that belongs in a paragraph about sailing.
1. In some areas even frostbite sailing— sailing in cold weather—is popular.
2. Sailing is one of the most popular water sports.
3. Tennis is a more popular sport in my community.
4. Gliding along the water in any kind of sailboat, from the smallest to the most luxurious, is sheer pleasure.
5. White-water canoeing is another popular water sport.

**D.** Write the topic sentence from the paragraph that follows. Then write two sentences of your own that add details to the topic sentence.

Many people today are involved in exercise programs for fitness. Running and jogging are inexpensive sports, requiring only a good pair of running shoes. Dancing—from ballet to aerobics—is perhaps more popular than at any other time in history. Tennis and racquetball, which require stamina and coordination, provide a good workout. Being fit is not just a fad. It's a matter of good health.

## Composition

A paragraph may be written to present a personal opinion of the writer. Usually the opinion is stated in the topic sentence. The supporting sentences offer information that shows why the writer holds that opinion.

An example of an opinion expressed in a topic sentence is "Crown Point is the best place to spend a vacation day." Sentences supporting that topic sentence will tell about the beautiful beach, the picnic places, the nearby playing fields, and the local food specialties.

Think about an opinion you hold. Ask yourself why you hold it. Jot down your reasons. Then state the opinion in a topic sentence. Develop a complete paragraph, using the reasons in supporting sentences.

## Advanced Challenge

Search through some books, magazines, or newspapers to find a paragraph that has a clear topic sentence. The paragraph should be at least five sentences long. You might have to search a bit for a paragraph with a clearly stated topic sentence.

Write the topic sentence at the top of a sheet of paper. Then make a list of all the other sentences, but not in the order in which they appeared in the original paragraph.

Challenge a partner to write a paragraph, putting the supporting-detail sentences from the list in the correct order. Read your partner's paragraph. Does the paragraph your partner wrote make sense? Is it different from the original paragraph? Is is better than the original?

While your partner is working with your list of sentences, you should be doing the same with his or hers.

### DICTIONARY

A dictionary is set up in a way that makes it as easy as possible to locate the words you want. To begin with, all the words in a dictionary are arranged in alphabetical order. Also, as you have seen, there are guide words on each page to help you find the page you need as quickly as possible.

Once you have found the page that includes the word you want, the final step is to scan the page, checking on the alphabetical arrangement of the words. If you are trying to find the words *dentist, dental,* and *dentifrice,* look for words that begin with *dent–.* Then look at the fifth letter in each word. Since the fifth letter in *dental* is *a, dental* will be listed before *dentifrice* and *dentist.* And since the sixth letter in *dentifrice* is *f,* that word will come before *dentist.* Keep in mind two-word entries, such as *postage stamp,* are arranged in alphabetical order, letter by letter, just as if they were one word. The entry *postage stamp* will appear after *postage* and before *postal.*

PRACTICE  Put the words in each group in alphabetical order.
1. monetary, money, monumental, morose, moose
2. lawyer, lariat, lawlessness, lacerate, laugh
3. fog horn, fogginess, fog, fog bank, foggy
4. civilized, civilian, civility, civilize, civilization
5. indivisibility, indivisible, individual, individuality, individualism

# Chapter 14
# Descriptive Paragraphs

Lesson 1   **Writing Descriptive Paragraphs**
Lesson 2   **Describing Persons and Places**
Lesson 3   **Describing Events**
Lesson 4   **Revising Descriptive Paragraphs**

**195**

# Writing Descriptive Paragraphs

A paragraph that describes a person, a place, an object, or an event is called a **descriptive paragraph**. In a descriptive paragraph, the writer tries to help the reader picture what is being described. To do this, the writer tells how something looks, sounds, feels, tastes, or smells.

When you write a descriptive paragraph, use exact and colorful details. These will allow your reader to experience what you are describing.

## Example

Here is a descriptive paragraph that focuses on a scene.

> The lake changed all at once. Its smooth, glossy surface had been undisturbed by the gentle breeze blowing from the west. But the ink-dark clouds that suddenly appeared brought a powerful companion with them. As they hovered over the lake, a tree-bending gale was suddenly born. It vacuumed up sand and dust from the beaches and whipped it into the faces of the fleeing bathers. Waves three or four feet high sprang up and crashed against the rocky shores, exploding into fans of mist and spray. The wind screamed, thunder rumbled, and the lake's surface was spanked by the punishing rain.

What details help you to picture the scene?
What details help you to hear what is happening?

**PRACTICE 1**   Each of the following sentences contains a detail or details that appeal to the reader's senses. Write the detail and identify the sense that it appeals to.

1. The bridge groaned as the truck inched its way across.
2. The rubbery skin of the large fish brushed against me.
3. The golden skin of the freshly caught trout glistened in the pan.
4. The white flaky mounds of fresh fish melted in our mouths.
5. The wind-blown snow against our faces felt like tiny needles.

**PRACTICE 2**   Write the more descriptive sentence in each pair.

1. a. The slender runner crouched in readiness.
   b. The runner got ready to go.
2. a. The starting gun went off with a loud noise.
   b. The starting pistol cracked the stillness.
3. a. He took off when the pistol fired.
   b. He started to run.
4. a. Panting, he burst through the tape at the finish line.
   b. He crossed the finish line.
5. a. The crowd cheered as he accepted the gold medal.
   b. He walked forward and received his prize.

**WRITE**   In a paragraph describe a person in action—working, enjoying sports, or busy with some activity. The person may be real or imaginary. Use exact details in your paragraph.

**GO BEYOND**   Work in groups of three or four. Exchange the paragraphs that each person wrote for the Write exercise. Note the details in the paragraph you receive. Be prepared to explain to each member of the group how well the details allow you to picture the person being described.

*Descriptive Paragraphs*

**Describing Persons and Places**

When you write a descriptive paragraph, it is important to present the details in an order that helps the reader follow what is being described. If you are describing persons and places, you can arrange details in **space order**—from top to bottom, for example, or from left to right, or from near to far.

Decide in what order you want to describe a person or a place before you begin writing. That way you will find it easy to organize the details of your paragraph.

## Example

In this selection, the writer uses space order to describe a place.

Ursula tapped lightly on Jennifer Parker's door. "Yes, come in," a faint voice answered. Ursula opened the door and stepped in. What a cheerful room, she thought, glancing around. On her left was a large four-poster bed, framed between two floor-to-ceiling windows. A canopy of white ruffles arched above it. The ruffles matched those on the window curtains. Beside the bed, on the right, she saw a marble-topped table, just big enough to hold a book and a brass reading lamp. There, in the center of the room, she saw a fireplace with a softly glowing fire and a large yellow cat curled up on the hearth, plainly enjoying the warmth. To the right of the fireplace, Ursula saw a gray-haired woman, seated in a Boston rocker, with another, but smaller, yellow cat on her lap. Both the woman and the cat seemed to be smiling at her.

In what order does the writer present the details of this scene? Why do you think Ursula tapped lightly on Jennifer Parker's door?

**PRACTICE 1** Here is a list of things named in the paragraph in the Example. Write them in the order in which they were presented.

1. a fireplace
2. a table with a reading lamp on it
3. the smaller, yellow cat
4. a four-poster bed
5. a gray-haired woman

**PRACTICE 2** Read the scenes listed below. Imagine what each would look like. Decide what the best order for describing the details of each scene would be—top to bottom, left to right, or near to far. Write your answer next to the number of each scene.

1. a line of people waiting to buy tickets to a movie
2. a football player in uniform
3. an old guitar leaning against a wall
4. a lighthouse keeper looking out to sea
5. the dashboard of a car
6. children playing a game of tug-of-war
7. standing on a stage, looking out over an audience
8. a row of stores
9. a snow-capped mountain
10. a basketball court

**WRITE** Choose one of the scenes listed in Practice 2. Write a descriptive paragraph about it. Make sure you arrange your details in the order that you chose as best for that scene. Remember, you want the reader to be able to picture clearly what you are describing.

**GO BEYOND** Write each sentence from the Write exercise on a separate strip of paper. Exchange sentences with a partner and see whether he or she can put them in the right order. Discuss any differences. Have you discovered better ways to arrange each other's sentences?

# Describing Events

Descriptive paragraphs often describe an event. When you describe an event, it is usually best to present the details in a **time order**—what happens first, what happens second, and so on. Time order makes it easier for your readers to follow what is happening.

## Example

Here is a paragraph that focuses on an event and allows the reader to share in it.

The ball players watched gloomily as the giant yellow machines rolled across the playing field. One machine extended a claw and scratched away the pitcher's mound. The players huddled together in silence, remembering their wins and losses. Then the machine grabbed several more shovelfuls of grass and dirt and home plate.

Which sentences tell what the ball players saw?
Which sentences tell what the players thought or felt?

**PRACTICE 1**   Write the sentences in time order. Start with the topic sentence below.

TOPIC SENTENCE    Once the alarm sounded, the firehouse came alive.

1. Before twenty seconds had passed, the trucks rumbled down the driveway, lights flashing and sirens wailing.
2. As the fire fighters reached the burning house, tongues of flame licked out from the upstairs windows.
3. The two electronically operated doors rolled upward.
4. The engines of the two trucks came to life seconds apart.
5. The six fire fighters ran as one to the place where their equipment was stored.

**PRACTICE 2**   Write the sentences below in time order. Then add two more events that could have happened after Tanya entered the classroom. Make sure the events you add are also in correct time order.

1. She was glad no one saw her on the way to school.
2. At home that morning Tanya had cut off her long braid of silky black hair.
3. At first none of her classmates noticed the change.
4. Tanya edged hesitantly into the classroom.

**WRITE**   Write a paragraph with the following topic sentence: I couldn't believe what happened. The event you describe can be real or one from your imagination. Be sure to present the details in time order.

**GO BEYOND**   Work in groups of three or four. Listen as the members of the group take turns reading their paragraphs from the Write exercise. Evaluate each other's paragraphs. Be prepared to suggest how each paragraph could be improved.

**Revising Descriptive Paragraphs**

A descriptive paragraph must have a wealth of details so that the reader can easily picture what is being described.

In the first draft of a descriptive paragraph, you might not include enough details or you might not present details in a logical order. That is why it is always necessary to revise what you have written. In your first draft, for example, you might present only a general or overall view of your topic. When you revise what you have written, you can pay closer attention to the details you present. You can then see to it that the details are as colorful and as accurate as you can make them.

Careful revision produces paragraphs that make your topic come alive for a reader.

## Example

Notice the differences between these two drafts.

FIRST DRAFT

The spider's web caught my attention. It looked as if it was made of thread. Dew was still on the web. The sun hit the dew. The web moved gently in the breeze. It hung between two tall blades of grass.

SECOND DRAFT

The spider's web caught my attention. Its delicate threads hung between the two tall blades of grass. It glistened in the sun as it moved gently in the soft breeze. The dewdrops that clung to it reflected the morning light.

What makes the revised paragraph different from the first draft? What other words or phrases can be used to describe a spider's web?

**PRACTICE 1**   Three of the following sentences are from the first draft of a descriptive paragraph and two are from a revised draft. Identify the two sentences that have already been revised. Then revise the remaining three first-draft sentences.

1. The large wave moved toward the shore.
2. In a blinding flash, lightning filled the sky and turned the night into day.
3. It was hard to drive in the fog.
4. Shadowy fingers stretched out across the yard as the sun dropped out of sight.
5. The wind caught the kite.

**PRACTICE 2**   Revise the numbered sentences that make up the following descriptive paragraph.

TOPIC SENTENCE      Sue Ann and I built a snow house.

1. We decided where the walls would go.
2. We built the walls of pieces of snow.
3. We made a roof of cardboard.
4. Then we made a doorway.
5. We put a rug on the floor and looked at our work.

**WRITE**   Carefully observe some object such as a plant, an animal, a picture, or a piece of furniture. You might find it helpful to write down a list of words that describe the object. Then write a descriptive paragraph about it. Be sure to revise your paragraph so that a reader will be able to picture the object clearly.

**GO BEYOND**   Share your description from the Write exercise with a classmate. Does he or she recognize the object? If not, think about how you can describe it more clearly. Think about other details you can add that tell how your object looks, sounds, tastes, or smells.

## Sleet Storm

TIC-TIC-TIC!
The sound of the sleet
Fell like the beat
of tiny feet,
Racing and chasing down the street:
The quick sharp beat
Of a million hoofs
Clicked and clattered
Across the roofs.
The sleet storm fell
Through a day and a night
With a tic-tic-tic
That was fast and light.

On the second morning
A cold sun shone
On a glittering, crystal,
Frigid zone.
Each bush and branch
Was icily hung
With the frozen song
The sleet had sung.
The branches swayed
With their icy load
Where millions of diamonds
Flashed and glowed.
Steep roofs shone
With a blinding glare.
Fringed with icicles
Everywhere.

But the tic-tic-tic
Of the sleet was still,
Caught on each glistening
Valley and hill.

*James S. Tippett*

Why is the poem divided into three stanzas?
What is the main idea in each stanza?

## Practice

**A.** Write the more descriptive sentence from each pair.

1. a. Marvin's snake crawled out of its cage and got lost.
   b. Slithering into the night, Marvin's snake disappeared, never to be found.
2. a. Chuck and Melissa are good cooks.
   b. Chuck and Melissa prepare some tasty meals.
3. a. The icy water trickling down her dry throat felt good.
   b. She was glad to cool her throat.
4. a. Terrified and beyond control, the monkey swung wildly from limb to limb.
   b. The monkey swung from limb to limb.
5. a. Clutching his throat and choking, the man collapsed.
   b. The man fell to the ground, holding his throat.

**B.** Rewrite the paragraph below. Add details to make it clearer and more specific. Arrange the sentences in an order that will give the reader a clear picture of what is being described. Write an opening sentence that will catch the reader's attention.

We went shopping to buy Dad a present. The stores were crowded. The snow was falling. Traffic was snarled. When we finally got home at 4:30 P.M., we were tired and freezing. The temperature was almost zero.

**C.** Rewrite the following paragraph. Put the sentences in correct time order.

Finally it landed. We stood at the window eagerly watching for the plane. My sister and I arrived at the airport ten minutes before our cousins' plane was supposed to arrive. Slowly it taxied toward the building. The door opened, and Sue and Ernie were the first ones out. The ground crew moved the boarding steps up to the plane. Delighted to see them, we ran to our cousins and hugged them.

## Composition

Think of a very striking or unusual person, place, or thing. Write a topic sentence stating what is striking or unusual about your subject. A topic sentence about a person might be "Harold's clown costume causes everyone to notice him." A topic sentence about a place might be "Craven Park is amazingly well kept." A topic sentence about an object or an animal might be "The aardvark is a strange-looking animal."

Develop a paragraph by describing your subject. Describe your subject in a way that uses space order. The details of your paragraph should be arranged from left to right, top to bottom, or from near to far.

## Advanced Challenge

In a novel or short story find a descriptive paragraph of a place. Create a diorama based on the description in the paragraph. A diorama is a small scene, or setting. You can create one in a shoe box or similar box. Paint or crayon the background or attach colored paper to the box. Use cardboard or heavy paper for any figures in your scene so that they will stand up.

List the details from the descriptive paragraph that you included in your diorama. Make a second list of any details that were not mentioned in the paragraph but that appear in your diorama. For example, a paragraph about a room may not mention the floor, but since every room has one, you would put one in your diorama.

Compare the two lists. What did the author assume you would know or guess about the place or thing described? Would the paragraph be better if the author had included these details? Why, or why not?

### DICTIONARY

What does *to see red* mean? It could mean to see the color red, but it is an **idiom,** or a group of words that has an un-expected meaning. As an idiom, *to see red* means "to be angry." The expression may have come from the belief that the color red makes bulls angry.

In some dictionaries idioms are shown in heavy black type. In others they are marked *idiom* or *id.* or *colloq.* To look up an idiom, decide what its most important word is. Read the diction-ary entry for that word. You may have to look up more than one word in an idiom before you find the phrase and its meaning.

Suppose you read *She really hit the nail on the head* in a story about a quiz show, not about building. The meaning you might expect the phrase to have does not make sense in regard to a quiz show. What is the most important word in the phrase? Try looking up *hit*. You will find something like this.

**hit, 1 a:** to reach with or as if with a blow **b:** to come in contact with <the ball ~ the window> **hit the nail on the head:** to be exactly right.

PRACTICE   Use a dictionary to find the meaning for each of the following idioms.

1. see eye to eye
2. play it by ear
3. find oneself
4. on the tip of one's tongue
5. put down roots

# Chapter 15
# Factual Paragraphs

Lesson 1 **Writing Factual Paragraphs**
Lesson 2 **Limiting a Topic**
Lesson 3 **Order in Factual Paragraphs**
Lesson 4 **Revising Factual Paragraphs**

**209**

# Writing Factual Paragraphs

A **factual paragraph** is one that informs or explains. To write a factual paragraph, you must first gather the information that you want to pass along to your reader.

You probably know enough about some topics to write factual paragraphs about them. For other topics you might be able to gather the information you need by observing with your own eyes. But for many topics you will have to collect the information you need from books and magazines.

The topic sentence in a factual paragraph usually appears near the beginning. It explains the purpose of the paragraph. The other sentences develop the topic sentence.

## Example

Read the factual paragraph below.

The shape of a wing makes it possible for a heavy airplane to fly. An airplane wing is curved on its top side and flat underneath. The air that flows over the top of the wing must therefore travel farther than the air that flows under the wing. The air that travels a greater distance reaches a higher speed. The slower moving air underneath the wing has greater pressure or push than the air above. This pressure under the wing lifts the plane into the sky and keeps it there.

What sentence explains the purpose of this paragraph?
Where could you get the information used in this paragraph?

**PRACTICE 1**   Choose the sentence in each pair that would be the better topic sentence.

1. a. Birds need feeding stations when food is scarce.
   b. Before setting up a station, find the best location.
2. a. For most people, that adds up to about 121 days a year.
   b. Most people spend a third of their lives sleeping.
3. a. A computer can store a family's monthly budget.
   b. The computer is a useful machine.
4. a. Mammals share a lot in common.
   b. All mammals have backbones and are warm-blooded.
5. a. The Sears Building is 1,454 feet high.
   b. The world's tallest building is the Sears Building.

**PRACTICE 2**   Read the following questions. Choose one question that you would like the answer to. Describe what you would have to do to get an answer to the question.

1. Why are the leaves on trees green?
2. What is a platypus?
3. How do oysters make pearls?
4. Who was Amelia Earhart, and what did she do?
5. What causes thunderstorms?

**WRITE**   Choose the question in Practice 2 that you are most interested in answering. Gather the information that you will need to answer it. Write your answer in the form of a paragraph. Begin with a topic sentence, and use the information that you have gathered to write supporting sentences.

**GO BEYOND**   Write three questions that you would like to have answered. Each question should ask for information about something that exists in the world. As a class, examine all the questions. Vote on the most interesting one. As a class project, gather as much information as possible to answer the question.

# Limiting a Topic

The purpose of a factual paragraph is to give information to a reader. Because people want and need to know about all kinds of things, there are countless topics that you could write a factual paragraph about.

There is one important thing to remember in choosing a topic for a factual paragraph. You must be sure to choose a topic that you can actually develop in a single paragraph. Many topics cover so much information that you could never write about them in a single paragraph. A topic like "Dogs as Pets" would be far too broad for a paragraph. A narrower topic, however, such as "The Beagle as a Pet" could be developed in one paragraph.

## Example

Study this list of topics. Those in Column 1 are far too broad for one paragraph. Those in Column 2 could be developed in a single paragraph.

| 1 | 2 |
|---|---|
| Collecting Stamps | Choosing a Stamp Album |
| Growing Flowers | Planting Marigolds |
| Eating and Health | A Balanced Breakfast |
| The History of American Coins | The Flying Eagle Penny |
| Flags of the States | The Maryland State Flag |
| Home Projects | Building a Birdhouse |

**PRACTICE 1** Each of the broad topics listed below is followed by two narrower topics. Write the narrower topic that could best be developed in a single paragraph.

1. The Cat Family
   a. Feeding a Kitten
   b. The Cats of Africa
2. Fishing for Fun
   a. Freshwater Fishing
   b. Finding a Trout Stream
3. Cooking
   a. Making Fresh Bread
   b. Baking

4. Safety
   a. Smoke Detectors
   b. Safety at Home
5. Hobbies
   a. Launching a Kite
   b. Flying Kites

**PRACTICE 2** Choose one of the narrower topics that you identified in Practice 1. Or choose a narrow topic of your own. Choose a topic that you have some interest in or some knowledge about. Then do the following.

1. Make a list of what you already know about the topic.
2. Identify other people who might have some knowledge about the topic that they might share with you.
3. Make a list of the kind of books that could supply you with more information about the topic.
4. Write a brief plan that you could follow to gather the information that you would need to write a factual paragraph about the topic.

**WRITE** Follow the plan that you wrote in Practice 2, and gather information for your factual paragraph. Use the information to write your paragraph.

**GO BEYOND** Use the paragraph you wrote for the Write exercise for a classroom display. Draw or find pictures to illustrate your paragraph.

# Order in Factual Paragraphs

In many factual paragraphs, the supporting sentences will be arranged in time order. Time order will allow a reader to easily follow a paragraph that tells how something works or that presents the important events in a person's life.

Not all factual paragraphs, however, can be arranged in time order. If, for example, you are writing a paragraph about the California redwood tree, you might tell your reader about their size, their age, and the various efforts to keep them safe. Which information you present first is up to you. You might decide to present what you think is the most interesting or important piece of information about the tree first *or* last. The important thing is to group your sentences in an order that makes your meaning clear.

## Example

Notice the order in which the supporting information is presented in the following paragraph.

The common housefly is among the fastest of all flying insects. The buzzing that a housefly makes is the sound of its wings beating in the air. These wings allow the housefly to move at a speed of about four and a half miles per hour. The insect can fly even faster than that for short distances to escape its enemies. These enemies include many kinds of birds and, of course, human beings.

Why does the order of the supporting sentences make the paragraph easy to follow?

What other order could the writer have used to present the information?

**PRACTICE 1**   Study the topic sentence below. Then arrange the supporting sentences in an order that is easy to follow.

TOPIC SENTENCE    A flying squirrel can glide through the air, but it cannot really fly.

1. It uses its broad flat tail to guide it from tree to tree.
2. On each side of its body, a fold of skin connects the front and back legs.
3. Flying squirrels cannot gain height by gliding.
4. They always finish lower than where they started.
5. When the squirrel stretches out its legs, the folds of skin form "wings."

**PRACTICE 2**   Only one kind of order is possible in this paragraph. Study the topic sentence and then arrange the supporting sentences.

TOPIC SENTENCE    Opening a savings account is easy.

1. After that, Ms. López deposited the money for me.
2. First, I filled out a form.
3. Finally, Ms. López gave me my new passbook.
4. I asked Ms. López at the bank how to open one.
5. Then I signed my name on the form.

**WRITE**   Imagine that you have a job. Write a paragraph that tells how you do the job. Be sure to write a topic sentence and to arrange the supporting sentences in a clear order.

**GO BEYOND**   Work with three classmates. Choose a topic you each know something about. One person in the group gives a topic sentence for a factual paragraph. Each of the others adds three supporting sentences. As a group, decide upon the order in which the supporting sentences should be presented.

**Revising Factual Paragraphs**

Like any other kind of writing, the first draft of a factual paragraph should always be **revised**. Revision gives the writer the opportunity to improve what has been written.

When revising a factual paragraph, it is especially important to be sure that all of the supporting sentences develop the topic sentence. The topic sentence in a factual paragraph tells the reader what information the paragraph will give. Sentences that do not supply this kind of information weaken the paragraph because they cause the reader's interest to wander.

## Example

Compare the following drafts.

FIRST DRAFT

One of the most dangerous enemies of the human race is the common housefly. Some other kinds of flys are also dangerous. This insect carries many germs within its body or on the hairs of its body. Not all the germs are harmful. When a fly touches any person or object, it leaves these germs behind. The germs that a fly carries can cause serious diseases such as sleeping sickness, malaria, and typhoid fever.

SECOND DRAFT

One of the most dangerous enemies of the human race is the common housefly. This insect carries many germs within its body or on the hairs of its body. When a fly touches any person or object, it leaves these germs behind. The germs that a fly carries can cause such serious diseases as sleeping sickness, malaria, and typhoid fever.

What sentences that were in the first draft have been removed? Why were the sentences removed?

**PRACTICE 1**   For each topic, write the letter of the item that does not develop the topic.

1. Precious Metals
   a. gold   b. lead   c. silver   d. platinum
2. Green Vegetables
   a. beans   b. peas   c. squash   d. spinach
3. Citrus Fruits
   a. limes   b. grapefruit   c. oranges   d. plums
4. Planets
   a. Mars   b. the moon   c. Saturn   d. Mercury
5. Shade Trees
   a. maples   b. oaks   c. pines   d. elms

**PRACTICE 2**   Use the following sentences to write a paragraph. Leave out the sentence that does not belong with the rest. Arrange the sentences in an order that a reader can easily follow.

1. This happens because braces are made from wires and rubber bands.
2. Pressure can slowly change the position of a tooth.
3. Braces put constant pressure on teeth.
4. Permanent teeth usually appear around age 6.
5. An orthodontist adjusts the pressure of the wires and rubber bands from time to time.

**WRITE**   Reread a factual paragraph that you have written. Be sure that each supporting sentence develops the topic sentence. Revise the paragraph, making whatever changes are necessary.

**GO BEYOND**   Work in a group of four or five. Exchange the paragraphs you revised in the Write exercise. Discuss the changes you would make in each other's paragraphs. Then use the group's best suggestions to make changes in your own paragraph.

## Practice

**A.** Write the five sentences in an order that makes sense for a paragraph. Put the topic sentence first. Indent the first word. Have the sentences with supporting details follow in logical order.

1. Diamonds, the best-known precious gems, are the hardest gems.
2. Most sapphires have a deep blue color.
3. Precious gems are a fascinating subject.
4. Rubies, the deep red stones, complete the quartet of precious gems.
5. Emeralds are rarer and more costly than diamonds.

**B.** Write the sentences in an order that makes sense for a paragraph. Put the topic sentence first. Indent the first word. Have the sentences with supporting details follow in logical order.

1. In 1878 Carruthers met and married Lucinda Indes.
2. Upon entering the United States, Carruthers signed on with a company exploring the western territories.
3. Twenty years later Bruce and Lucinda had founded a boarding school that still bears their name.
4. Bruce Carruthers came to the United States from Scotland in 1874.
5. He worked as a cowboy from 1874 to 1878.

**C.** Revise the factual paragraph that follows by removing any sentences that do not develop the topic sentence. Then write the revised paragraph.

The pumpkin is a very old and useful autumn crop. Native Americans taught the early settlers how to raise the pumpkin and how to use it for food. The pumpkin grows from vines that spread along the ground. The meat of the pumpkin is used in puddings and soups. It is also used in pies that have become a traditional part of the winter holiday season. Mince pie is also a traditional favorite. The seeds of the pumpkin are toasted and provide a very special fall treat. Popcorn is a popular fall treat, too. And then, of course, there are the jaunty jack-o'-lanterns that people carve out of pumpkins for Halloween.

## Composition

Write a factual paragraph that explains how to do something or how something works. You might, for example, explain how to build a birdhouse or how to keep a healthy aquarium. You might even want to explain how a thunderstorm forms or how a boomerang returns to the person who throws it.

Since a factual paragraph must be accurate, make sure you understand your topic completely. If you do not understand it fully, learn more about it from a reference book. Be sure to arrange the sentences in your explanation in a clear order. That lets a reader follow your meaning more easily.

## Advanced Challenge

Look for a factual article on a topic that would be interesting to younger children. Decide how old the children should be to enjoy the subject. Ask a librarian or another adult to help you find magazines with suitable articles.

Read the article carefully and decide what are its most important ideas and supporting details. Now, simplify the article. Rewrite it so that it can be understood by younger children. You will have to write shorter, easier sentences. A good way of doing this is by breaking a compound sentence into two short sentences. You may also have to use simpler words and add new sentences to explain any difficult terms. To make your article shorter, leave out the less important details.

Give your article to a younger child, to a school librarian, or to the teacher of a lower grade.

## DICTIONARY

Many words have more than one meaning. When you use a dictionary to look up the meaning of a word, you should read all the meanings listed in the entry. These meanings are numbered. Look to see if an example sentence is given for each meaning to show you how the word is used. Often the example sentence will be enclosed in brackets or printed in italic type.

EXAMPLE

**cul ti va tion** (kul′tə va′shən). **1** preparing land and growing crops by plowing, planting, and necessary care: *Better cultivation of soil will result in better crops.* **2** condition of being prepared by plowing, planting, etc: *Only half the farm was under cultivation.* **3** giving time and thought to improving and developing (the body, mind, or manners): *the cultivation of good study habits.* **4** result of improvement or growth through education and experience; culture. *n.*

How many meanings are listed here for the word *cultivation*? How many have something to do with the mind?

PRACTICE   Use a dictionary to answer the following questions.
1. What is poetic license?
2. What does orbit have to do with a person's eye?
3. How many meanings can you find for slough?
4. What kind of person might be scolded for acting like a slug? Why?
5. What does culture have to do with germs?

220

# Chapter 16
# Building Paragraphs

Lesson 1   **Choosing a Topic**

Lesson 2   **Developing a Topic**

Lesson 3   **Revising What You Write**

Lesson 4   **Proofreading What You Write**

221

# Choosing a Topic

Before you begin to write, you will need to choose a topic. One way to do this is to try **brainstorming** by yourself. That is, for ten or fifteen minutes try thinking of *everything* you could write about the topic. List on paper as quickly as possible the ideas that you come up with, without deciding whether these ideas are good or bad. Just write down everything that comes to mind that you know something about. When the time is up, read through all your ideas and then pick the subject that interests you most.

Next, choose a topic, a part of the subject, to write about. Your topic should be narrow enough to tell about in one or two paragraphs. Think about what you will write. Get a clear picture of your topic in your mind before you begin to write.

## Example

A student described this experience.

I watched a drop of water trickle down the vein of a leaf and splash onto the ground. Another formed. Fresh and clear, it ran to the tip of the leaf and hung there. I stuck out my hand. The coolness spread slowly over my hot, sweaty palm. Another drop formed. It trembled but did not fall.

Why is the student's topic suitable for writing about in one paragraph?
What makes this personal experience interesting to a reader?

**PRACTICE 1**  In each pair below, decide which topic is narrow enough to write about in one or two paragraphs. Write the topic.

1. A Scary Dream, Dreams I Had Last Week
2. Skateboarding, How to Ride a Skateboard
3. Our Secret Club, Our Club's Secret Language
4. Our Family Pets, My Pet Gerbil
5. My Favorite Cousin, My Favorite People

**PRACTICE 2**  Prepare to write about something you know from first-hand experience. Follow these directions.

1. Take fifteen minutes to brainstorm for ideas. Write every idea you think of.
2. From your list, choose the three subjects that interest you most.
3. For each subject, select a topic that is not too broad to tell about in one paragraph.
4. Think of titles for your three topics. Write the titles.
5. Save your list for the next exercise.

**WRITE**  Choose one of the three topics you selected in the last exercise and write a paragraph about it. Before you begin writing, take a few minutes to plan what you want to say about that topic.

**GO BEYOND**  Sit quietly for one minute, looking and listening carefully. Then write down as many words as you can that describe what you saw, heard, and felt. Get together with a classmate. Compare what each of you wrote. What sights, sounds, and feelings do your lists have in common? How do your lists differ? Would some of your observations be good topics for writing that is based upon personal experience? Why do you think this is true?

# Developing a Topic

In this lesson you will choose a topic and write a first draft that tells about a personal experience. When you write about a personal experience, you will tell your reader what happened to you or to someone you know. You will be telling a story. When you tell a story, no matter how brief, you must present the events in the order in which they took place.

When you plan a brief story, you will have to decide where it begins and where it ends. You will also have to begin your story with a sentence that catches the reader's attention. Use your senses to help you record exact and vivid details. Make sure that the details in the sentences support the opening sentence.

## Example

A student named Mark wrote this first draft, the beginning of a story about a personal experience.

We were at a school picnic. A group of us swam out to the float. It had a diving tower. Debbie dived from the tower. She asked me whether I was going to dive. I didn't want her to think I was a coward. I told her I would dive. I had never dived such a distance in my life, and I was scared.

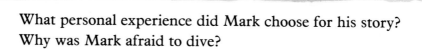

What personal experience did Mark choose for his story?
Why was Mark afraid to dive?

**PRACTICE 1**  Use the Example to answer the following questions. For each question, write *yes* or *no* and one sentence to explain your answer.

1. Is Mark's personal experience interesting?
2. Does Mark's first sentence catch the reader's attention?
3. Does Mark present the events in the order in which they took place?
4. Do the details in each sentence support the paragraph's opening sentence?
5. Do all the sentences relate to the paragraph's main idea?

**PRACTICE 2**  Build another paragraph for Mark's story by writing these sentences in order.

1. Finally, I closed my eyes, pushed with my toes, and sailed into space.
2. Then I walked out on the board and looked down.
3. For a few minutes I stood on the board, trying to decide if I wanted to make such a scary dive.
4. First, I climbed the six steps to the platform.
5. I seemed to be a mile above the water!

**WRITE**  Perhaps, like Mark, you would like to tell about trying something for the first time. Write a first draft about an experience that you had. Start with a sentence that catches the reader's attention. Use as many of your senses as you can to provide good details. Tell your story in two or three paragraphs. Save your paper for the next lesson.

**GO BEYOND**  Find or draw one or two pictures to illustrate your story. At the bottom of each picture, write a sentence that tells what part of the story the picture shows. (You may quote a sentence from the story, if you wish.) Save the pictures for Lesson 4.

**Revising What You Write**

The first draft of your writing gives you something to work with. It lets you decide what part of your story works well and what part might need improvement. It is sometimes helpful to ask others to suggest improvements. Others may see things that you overlooked.

Not all the suggestions that others make will be equally helpful. Choose the best ideas. Use those ideas as well as your own to revise your writing.

### Example

Here is the revised draft of Mark's personal experience.

I was in big trouble! We were at a school picnic at Iron Mountain Lake. After my classmate Debbie dived from the six-foot tower on the float, she looked at me and asked if I was going to dive.

I told her that I would because I didn't want her to think I was a coward. In fact, I told her that I loved to dive and was very anxious to do it. Actually, I had never dived from that height before, and I was scared silly.

What did Mark do to improve the second draft of his personal experience?
How does Mark feel about diving?

**PRACTICE 1** Compare Mark's first and revised drafts. Then write your answers to the following questions.
1. What is the topic of the first paragraph in the second draft?
2. What two new details appear in the first paragraph of the second draft?
3. Why did Mark start a second paragraph?
4. Why would the reader be interested in Mark's experience?
5. Why is the revised draft better than the first draft?

**PRACTICE 2** Write a paragraph describing Mark's dive. Use one of the two opening sentences below. Then write sentences that answer the questions asked in items 1-5.

OPENING SENTENCES      To my surprise, the dive was great!
What a terrible dive!

1. How did Mark feel while in the air?
2. What did he think while in the air?
3. How did he enter the water?
4. How did the water feel to him?
5. How did he feel when he came up for air?

**WRITE** Work with a partner. Exchange first drafts of the stories each of you wrote for the last lesson. Tell what you like about your partner's story. Then tell how you think it could be improved. Add the best of your partner's suggestions to your own ideas. Revise your story. Write a neat final copy of the story.

**GO BEYOND** Finish the story about Mark's dive. How did he feel? What was Debbie's reaction? How did the story end?

Give your paper to someone to read. Listen to their suggestions for improving what you wrote. Then revise your conclusion to the story about Mark's dive. Save your work.

# Proofreading What You Write

Before you share something you have written, you should revise it. Revising often means big changes, such as writing more about a limited topic, changing the order of sentences, and adding or removing sentences.

Before you share something that you have written, you should also **proofread** your work. When you proofread, you correct errors in spelling, capitalization, and punctuation. Proofreading must always come before a final draft. A proofread piece of writing is a sign that you care about your reader.

You can use proofreading marks to show corrections before you prepare a final draft of your writing. These symbols are helpful to you as you work.

| | | | |
|---|---|---|---|
| ≡ | make a capital letter | ∧ | insert word or letter |
| ¶ | begin a new paragraph | ⋏ | use a comma |
| ℯ | take out a letter | ⊙ | use a period |

## Example

An eleven-year old student named Julia wrote, edited, and proof-read this paragraph.

My best friend is very special. She is honest and I feel that I can always trust her. Ada understands me better then anyone else does, but we still argue sometimes. Even best friends can't agre all the time. When I get made she usually teases me by saying, "Hey, dragon, your ears are steaming." That's my friend ada.

What proofreading corrections did Julia make?
Why does Julia think Ada is a special kind of friend?

*Paragraphs*

**PRACTICE 1** There are one or more proofreading marks in each sentence. Rewrite each sentence correctly.

1. My best friend is very special.
2. She is honest and I feel I can allways trust her.
3. Ada understands me better than anyone else but we still argue sometimes Even best friends can't agree all the time.
4. When I get mad, she usually teases me by saying "Hey, dragon, your ears are steaming
5. That's my frend ada.

**PRACTICE 2** There is an error in each of the following sentences. Write each sentence and add the proofreading mark that shows the mistake.

1. Ada and i met in kindergarten.
2. Together, we have gone to visit her grandparents played racquetball and helped her dad plant a garden.
3. This sumer we are hoping to go to camp
4. I know we woould have a good time.
5. Ada and I both expect that our parents will let us go?

**WRITE** Go back and find what you wrote for the Go Beyond exercise in Lesson 3. Decide if you want to write another revision of the ending you wrote for the story about Mark's dive. Proofread your last revision, marking each mistake with the appropriate symbol. Make all the necessary corrections and write a final copy of your work.

**GO BEYOND** Use the story about Mark's dive to make a classroom display. The display should feature the story ending you proofread for the Write exercise and the pictures you collected for the Go Beyond in Lesson 2. Think of a title for the display such as "These Are Our Experiences."

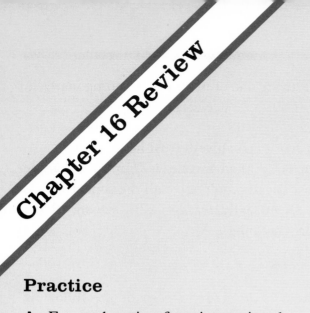

## Practice

**A.** For each pair of topics, write the letter of the one that is narrow enough to tell about in one or two paragraphs.

1. a. parks in our area
   b. our neighborhood park
2. a. musical instruments
   b. the clarinet
3. a. growing roses
   b. raising flowers
4. a. holiday fun
   b. a very special holiday
5. a. swimming
   b. how I learned to swim

**B.** Proofread the following paragraph. Use proofreading marks and make all necessary corrections.

Popcorn is a good snack, it is better than many others. Popcorn provides important fiber. It is low in calories too? A cup of poped popcorn has fewer than fifty calories is not fattening it tastes wonderful too.

**C.** Imagine that the following paragraph was written by a classmate. Tell the classmate, in writing, one thing you like about the paragraph. Tell, also, how you think the piece of writing could be improved.

Swoosh, and we were off! "Disneyland, here we come," said my sister Linda. Disneyland is in California, and we live in New Jersey, it would be a long flight. Mom had brought her knitting. She likes to knit. You should see the sweater she made me!

## Composition

You have probably read fables such as "The Tortoise and the Hare" and "The Fox and the Grapes." Fables are brief stories that teach a lesson. They end with a moral, a statement that tells what the lesson is.

Stories that are based on personal experience can also teach a lesson. A story from your own experience can end with a moral. Look at the morals listed below. Think about a personal experience that you have had that showed the truth of one of these morals, and then tell the story.

1. People can accomplish more together than they can alone.
2. Things are not always as they seem.
3. No act of kindness is ever wasted.
4. A person may talk a good game but not always play one.
5. There is no substitute for hard work.

## Advanced Challenge

When you write, it is important to get your reader's attention quickly. One way to do this is to have a strong opening sentence.

Select three magazine or newspaper articles. Look at the first paragraph of each and the opening sentence of that paragraph in particular. Then write two new opening sentences for each paragraph, followed by the sentences of the original writers. Then copy each paragraph with its original opening sentence.

Give all the paragraphs to a partner. See if your partner can tell which opening sentences were the author's and which were the ones you wrote.

Was your partner able to tell your writing from the author's? Why? Do you feel any of the sentences you wrote were better than the originals? Why or why not?

## COMPOUND WORDS

How many words can you think of that contain the word *space*? You can probably think of a good many, especially since you are living in the space age—the time in which people are exploring outer space. Compound words are words that are made up of two or more other words. They are often formed when new things are invented or when new places are discovered or explored.

EXAMPLE

*Spacecraft, spaceship,* and *airspace* are words in which the word *space* is combined with another word.

PRACTICE   Form as many compound words as you can by adding another word to each numbered word. Then use your dictionary to find even more compound words.

1. motor
2. man
3. car
4. boat
5. berry
6. sky
7. road
8. side
9. sun
10. light

**A.** Write the sentences that would belong in a paragraph with the following topic sentence.

Dolphins are astonishingly intelligent mammals.

1. Dolphins can live to the ripe old age of 35 years old.
2. Scientists have discovered that dolphins communicate by making underwater sounds.
3. Some dolphins have learned to imitate human speech.
4. Whales and dolphins are members of the same animal family.
5. Fishermen have seen dolphins leading schools of tunas away from their carefully placed traps.

**B.** Study the list of topics named below. Would you use space order or time order to arrange the details of a paragraph on each topic? Write your answer next to the number of the topic.
1. a class trip to a Wild West show
2. the front of a department store
3. a clown in full costume
4. a funny dream
5. the view down a dirt road

**C.** Each of the topics listed below is too broad to be covered in a single paragraph. Think of a narrower focus for each topic. Write your answer.
1. Winter Sports
2. Important Inventions
3. Snakes
4. Famous Explorers
5. Training a Pet

# Write A Mystery Story

## List of Characters

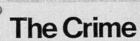

## The Crime

DUE DATES

Outline due Friday.

First Draft due two weeks later.

Final due one week thereafter.

**Clues**

**Where It Happened**

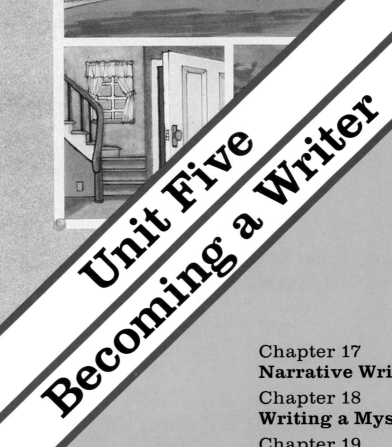

# Unit Five

# Becoming a Writer

Chapter 17
**Narrative Writing**

Chapter 18
**Writing a Mystery**

Chapter 19
**More About Mysteries**

# The Process of Writing

Learning to be a good writer is something like learning to ride a bicycle, fly on a trapeze, play a piano, or build a bookcase. To do any of these things well, you must first know what to do and then practice it.

Earlier this year, you learned that writing is a process. A process is a series of steps you have to take to reach a goal. Your goal may be writing a report, a story, or a poem. By following the steps in the writing process, you can write something that you and others will enjoy reading.

There are four major steps in the writing process. They are **prewriting, organizing, writing,** and **revising.** Each step prepares you for the next step, so they should be done in order. Don't rush. Good writing takes time.

**PREWRITING**  The first step in the writing process is prewriting. Prewriting includes choosing the topic you want to write about. You might want to start by brainstorming, or listing as many ideas as fast as you can think of them. If you already have a general topic, you might need to narrow the topic to something that is manageable.

Maybe you have to write a report on an invention. In prewriting, you would list all the inventions that interest you. Suppose you decide that you want to write about the telephone.

You realize that you don't have the space to write everything about the telephone. So you narrow your topic still further—to what the first home telephones were like. Now you are ready to list the questions that you want to answer in your report. These questions will guide your search for information.

Besides deciding what to write, you should also ask yourself these questions:

Who am I writing for? My teacher? My classmates? Somebody else?

Why am I writing this paper? To explain? To be funny? To tell an exciting story? To give my opinion?

**ORGANIZING**   The second step in the writing process is organizing. When you organize, you pull together all the things you thought about and discovered in prewriting. Check to see if you have collected enough information to answer the questions your report was supposed to answer. Arrange your information in the order in which you want to write about it. Throw away any material that does not relate to your topic.

If you are writing a story, put the events that will take place in order. Make sure your story has a beginning, a middle, and an end.

Before you finish organizing, you should have asked yourself these questions:

Which ideas and details help to develop my report or story? Which will not?

In what order do I want to present these details and ideas?

237

**WRITING**   The third step in the process is writing the first draft. At this point you will be able to see how the plan you developed for organizing your information is going to work. When you are writing your first draft, don't worry too much about spelling, grammar, and punctuation. That can all be fixed later. Just think about getting all your ideas and information down on paper.

When you have finished your first draft, read it over and ask yourself these questions:

Will my beginning interest readers?
Have I kept to my topic? Do I have enough details to make my points clear? Are they in the correct order?
Do I have a good ending?

**REVISING**   The last step in the writing process is revising. Read over what you have written. Pretend you are reading your report or story for the first time.

Ask yourself if any of your ideas or facts could have been written more clearly. Decide if any information needs to be moved to a different place in the paper. Mark any spelling, punctuation, or grammar errors that need to be corrected. Make the changes that would help your reader understand more clearly what you want to communicate. Now write your final draft for publishing.

Publishing doesn't always mean printing a book. It can mean simply sharing what you have written with others. For example, you can read your work to the class, display it on a bulletin board, or put it in a class writing folder for others to read.

# Chapter 17
# Narrative Writing

Lesson 1 **The Nature of Stories**
Lesson 2 **Prewriting a Story**
Lesson 3 **More About Prewriting**
Lesson 4 **Organizing a Story**
Lesson 5 **Writing the First Draft of a Story**
Lesson 6 **Revising a Story**

**239**

# The Nature of Stories

From almost the very beginning of time, people have been fascinated by stories. Stories allow people to enter an imaginary world that is more exciting than the ordinary world. You may never be a famous detective, solving difficult mysteries. You may never become involved in unexpected and exciting events in faraway places. But stories let you experience all these things and more.

Not all stories deal with adventure and excitement. Many tell how someone like yourself reacts to ordinary challenges and difficulties. You are interested in these kinds of stories, too, because nothing is as fascinating as people. And so you closely follow the story of a young person who learns the true meaning of friendship, or you closely follow the story of a young person with a handicap who learns to turn it into a strength.

In the next few lessons, you will write a story of your own. To do it, all you will need is a little bit of imagination.

## Example

Read the following summary of a story.

Tom is a young boy who has never been able to play any sport very well. He has tried many times but always failed. His failure makes him very unhappy. Whenever it comes time to choose sides for a game, no one wants him. One Saturday afternoon he is in a movie theater when a fire suddenly breaks out. He remains calm and leads several people to safety. He receives a lot of praise for what he did and learns that the ability to play a game is not the only ability that people admire.

Would this story be of interest to you? Why or why not?
What other events would make the story more interesting?

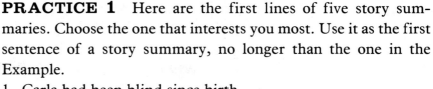

**PRACTICE 1**   Here are the first lines of five story summaries. Choose the one that interests you most. Use it as the first sentence of a story summary, no longer than the one in the Example.

1.  Carla had been blind since birth.
2.  The camping trip started out well, but it suddenly became full of danger.
3.  Professor Bach had worked on her invention for years.
4.  A message in a language no one understood crackled over the spaceship's radio.
5.  The theft had startled the city.

**PRACTICE 2**   What story that you read recently or saw on television have you liked a lot? Identify the story, and then briefly explain why you liked it.

**WRITE**   Find a story idea in Practice 1 or come up with one of your own. You might use a personal experience for a story idea or you might use an idea that comes from a story you are familiar with. Write a brief summary of the story you might write that uses your idea.

**GO BEYOND**   Work in groups of five. Each person presents the story summary prepared for the Write exercise. The other members of the group react to the summary and suggest changes and improvements. Using the group's best ideas, revise your story summary. Keep it for the next lesson.

**Prewriting a Story**

Every story has at least one character and a plot. The **characters** are the people in the story. The **plot** is the events that take place in the story. Every story also has a **setting**. The setting is where the action in the story takes place. A brief story will probably have a single setting. A longer story may have several settings because the action is likely to shift from place to place.

Once you have an idea for a story you would like to write, think about the setting. It can be either an ordinary place or an unusual one. It can be a place you know well or one that you invent. Using details that appeal to the senses will help bring your reader into the setting that you create.

## Example

This description of a setting comes at the beginning of a story.

It was late one winter afternoon, and the sun was slowly sinking below the horizon. Shadows from the trees, like black and gray pickup sticks, fell across the soft new snow. The wind was dying, and the temperature was dropping toward zero.

A twelve-year-old farm girl, Kim Sanders, was trudging home through the snow. Her family lived in an old frame farmhouse at the end of a narrow dirt road. Because the county snowplow had not yet reached the back roads, the school bus had dropped her off on the main road. She walked the mile to her house with only the brave, busy chickadees for company.

Where does the story take place?
What might Kim be thinking as she walks home?

*Becoming a Writer*

**PRACTICE 1**  Write a detail from the Example that tells about each of the following.

1. the time of day
4. the land
2. the seasons
5. the girl's house
3. the weather

**PRACTICE 2**  From each pair of sentences, choose the one with the better descriptive details, the one that gives the reader a clearer picture of the setting.

1. a. The flat land stretched out of sight under a hot sun.
   b. The land spread out for as far as Ken could see.
2. a. The land was empty except for four large green areas.
   b. The land was empty except for four green spots arranged like bases in a huge baseball diamond.
3. a. There were no clouds, just three things that looked like bicycle wheels.
   b. A gray circle, looking like an immense bicycle wheel, hung in the sky above each green base.
4. a. Every hour or so puffs of smoke rose from the green bases toward the gray wheels.
   b. Ken saw smoke go up into the sky.
5. a. As the smoke rose, there was a funny smell in the air.
   b. At the same time, a scent that seemed to be part fuel and part flowers filled the air.

**WRITE**  Look at the story summary that you prepared in the Write exercise in the last lesson. Write a full description of the story setting. Keep your description and summary for the next lesson.

**GO BEYOND**  Draw a picture of the setting of your story. If you think of more details than you thought of for the Write exercise, add them to your written description.

**More About Prewriting**

What happens in a story is really controlled by the characters in the story. What they think, what they say, and what they do determines the shape of the story. For this reason, the writer very carefully selects details to reveal to the reader the personality of each character.

## Example

Here is how a character in a story might be introduced.

Perhaps he should put his shoes on first when he got up, Dr. Bumble thought. That way he wouldn't be embarrassed by wearing one brown shoe and one black one, as he had yesterday. It was just that he always started by taking off his pajamas, and by the time he got to his shoes, his mind wandered and . . .

Bambi and Bruce, the good doctor thought, skipping to a more important topic. He just had to hire some adults. It could be downright dangerous letting twelve-year-olds take charge of a machine so powerful that . . .

But as for now . . . How could he possibly get his pants on over his shoes?

What have you learned about Dr. Bumble?
What does your knowledge of Dr. Bumble tell you about the kind of story this is likely to be?

*Becoming a Writer*

**PRACTICE 1** Write only the actions Dr. Bumble might take.

1. fumble absentmindedly for a pen or pencil
2. wear a tailored suit, crisp shirt, and matching tie
3. open a desk drawer containing last week's forgotten sandwich
4. quickly dictate from memory last week's many activities
5. wear a pair of ragged tennis shoes with his new suit

**PRACTICE 2** Ken is curious, stubborn, and very organized. Write the two sentences below that do not agree with that description.

1. Ken checked to make sure that he had enough water.
2. Then Ken said, "Let's get moving. I'm anxious to see what those puffs of smoke mean."
3. He wanted to go to first base, but Arthur easily convinced him to move toward third base instead.
4. As they jogged along on the path, Ken kept repeating, "At first base, we must look for other people."
5. Arthur tried to show him the bicycle wheels glowing in the dark, but Ken was not interested.

**WRITE** Think about two characters that you plan to include in your story. Tell what each character looks like. Then list five actions that tell the kind of person each is. Finally, write a conversation between the two characters. Let the reader know what each character thinks. Remember to use quotation marks and to begin a new paragraph whenever the speaker changes.

**GO BEYOND** Read to a partner your conversation from the Write exercise. Tell your partner what your characters are like. Then have your partner play the part of one of your characters, and you play the other part. Continue the conversation the characters are having, making up the dialogue as you go along.

# Organizing a Story

Now you are ready to plan the plot of your story. Remember, a story's plot is the series of events that take place as the story unfolds.

As you sketch out the events in your story, keep in mind that every story presents a problem that the characters must solve. The problem might be that a character has gotten into a dangerous situation and must get out of it. Or it might be that the character is misunderstood and must find a way to prove herself or himself to others.

Whatever problem the plot in a story might present, events happen before the problem is made clear to readers. And certain events must happen afterwards so that the problem can be solved. All the events make up the plot.

## Example

The following passage from Madeline L'Engle's *A Wrinkle in Time* presents the problem that the story deals with.

> School was all wrong. She'd been dropped down to the lowest section in her grade. That morning one of her teachers had said crossly, "Really, Meg, I don't understand how a child with parents as brilliant as yours are supposed to be can be such a poor student. If you don't manage to do a little better, you'll have to stay back next year."
>
> During lunch she'd roughhoused a little to try to make herself feel better, and one of the girls said scornfully, "After all, Meg, we aren't grammar-school kids anymore. Why do you always act like such a baby?"

What is the problem that this story's plot will have to solve? What two events tell you about the story's problem? How are they related?

**PRACTICE 1**   Read the following sentences. Three of them express problems that a story's plot could solve. Two do not. Write the three sentences that express problems.
1. Janet was walking quickly along the street.
2. Ben had only two minutes to try to stop the train.
3. Gail had finally understood that no one knew how she felt.
4. The guards watched closely as the big jet took on needed fuel.
5. It was time for Tony to stand up for his beliefs.

**PRACTICE 2**   In Practice 2 of Lessons 2 and 3, you met two boys who had set out to explore one of the green spots that they had seen in the distance. Here are sentences from the next part of that story. Write the sentences in an order that make sense.
1. What had looked like grass was actually a tall green fence.
2. The trip to first base took almost all night.
3. They decided to find a way inside the fence.
4. Hearing a grating noise, they turned just in time to see part of the fence disappear.
5. The fence looked cool, but it was too hot to touch.

**WRITE**   You have already written a story summary and a description of the setting and characters for your story. Now identify the problem that your story will solve. Then list the events that will take place before the problem is made clear to the reader. Next, list those events that will take place after the problem is made clear and that will take the reader to the end of the story. Make sure that all the events in your plot outline are smoothly related to each other.

**GO BEYOND**   Write each event from the list you developed in the Write exercise on a small slip of paper. See whether a classmate can arrange them in the order in which they will take place. Discuss whatever changes might be necessary.

# Writing the First Draft of a Story

You have already done a lot of work on your story. You know *where* your story will take place, *who* will be in it, and *what* will happen. Now you are ready to write the first draft.

As you write your first draft, be sure to include details that appeal to the senses of sight, sound, smell, taste, and touch. Those details will make your setting, characters, and action believable.

## Example

A fifth-grader named Stephanie wrote the following paragraphs as the first part of her story.

> ### Underground Turnaround
>
> Kim and her friend Ernestine were camping with Kim's family. The girls, who had planned to go on a cave tour, were disappointed when the park guide got sick and had to cancel the trip.
>
> "Let's explore the cave on our own," suggested Kim, the more daring of the two.
>
> Ernestine stopped writing in her notebook long enough to look at her friend. "I don't think that would be wise," she said.

How does the first paragraph get your attention?
How could the opening be improved?

*Becoming a Writer*

**PRACTICE 1**   Use the Example to answer these questions. For each question write *yes* or *no* and one sentence to explain your answer.

1. Is the topic of Stephanie's story interesting?
2. Did Stephanie start her story with an interesting sentence?
3. Did Stephanie show what her characters are like?
4. Did Stephanie use her senses well in telling details?
5. Can you guess what will happen next in the story?

**PRACTICE 2**   Here are some notes that Stephanie wrote for her story. Write *setting, characters,* or *plot* beside each number to tell what that note describes.

1. go into cave, using flashlights
2. black, cold, scary
3. Kim leads bravely; Ernestine follows, always writing in notebook
4. twist and turn down into cave
5. water dripping from roof
6. Ernestine wants to go back; Kim keeps on going
7. lose their way
8. Kim scared, doesn't know what to do
9. Ernestine calm; has drawn a map in her notebook
10. find way out again

**WRITE**   Beginning with an interesting sentence, write your story. Follow your plans for the setting, characters, and plot.

**GO BEYOND**   Work in groups of three or four. Read your story to the group. Ask the group members what they like about your story. Ask how they think you can improve it. Use notes to show the changes you plan to make. Keep your work for use in the next lesson.

**Revising a Story**

A first draft is only a beginning. Good writing usually demands a second or even a third draft. Each following draft should be better and more polished than the draft before it.

Family, friends, and classmates can suggest ways to improve your writing. You will have your own ideas, also. For best results, combine your ideas with those of others. Rewrite your story until you are satisfied with it.

## Example

Here is the second draft of Stephanie's story opening from page 248.

> "Let's explore the cave on our own," Kim said, her brown eyes snapping with excitement. "It's not our fault the dumb guide got sick and couldn't take us!"
>
> Ernestine stopped writing in her notebook long enough to stare at her friend. "I don't think that would be wise," she said uncertainly.
>
> "Well I'm going to. Are you coming or not?" Kim, the more daring of the two, stepped into the inky blackness of the cave.
>
> Ernestine closed her notebook with a shiver. This was a bad idea, something told her, but she shrugged and forced herself to follow Kim into the unknown.

How did Stephanie improve the opening of her story?
How does each character feel as she starts into the cave?

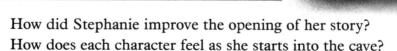

**PRACTICE 1**   Here are the next five sentences of Stephanie's story. Write them in order.

1. The two girls turned and twisted their way deep within the earth.
2. It's cold, Ernestine thought as she entered the cave, and she listened to a rustling sound overhead—like bats flapping about.
3. As Ernestine approached the cave she could see the beam of Kim's flashlight inside, bobbing along the dark tunnel.
4. "Put that notebook away and come on!" Kim called impatiently.
5. Ernestine stopped just inside the entrance, turned her light on the notebook, and wrote another scientific observation.

**PRACTICE 2**   Here are five notes that tell what happened at one point in Stephanie's story. Write them as sentences. Add details that show how the characters act and what they say.

1. Kim realizes she's lost
2. Kim admits she's scared
3. Ernestine tells her not to worry; she knows the way out
4. Ernestine tells Kim she drew map of route in notebook
5. Ernestine leads way out; Kim follows

**WRITE**   Use the notes you added to your story during the last lesson. Revise and rewrite the story. Proofread the story, correcting spelling and punctuation errors.

**GO BEYOND**   Share your stories with a younger class in one of the following ways.

1. Prepare a Story Hour for the class. Read your story to the students.
2. Tape your story. Give the tape to a teacher of a younger class.

### Abraham Lincoln
### 1809–1865

Lincoln was a long man.
He liked out of doors.
He liked the wind blowing
And the talk in country stores.

He liked telling stories,
He liked telling jokes.
"Abe's quite a character,"
Said quite a lot of folks.

Lots of folks in Springfield
Saw him every day,
Walking down the street
In his gaunt, long way.

Shawl around his shoulders,
Letters in his hat.
"That's Abe Lincoln."
They thought no more than that.

Knew that he was honest,
Guessed that he was odd,
Knew he had a cross wife
Though she was a Todd.

Knew he had three little boys
Who liked to shout and play,
Knew he had a lot of debts
It took him years to pay.

Knew his clothes and knew his house
"That's his office, here.
Blame good lawyer, on the whole,
Though he's sort of queer.

"Sure, he went to Congress, once.
But he didn't stay.
Can't expect us all to be
Smart as Henry Clay.

"Need a man for troubled times?
Well, I guess we do.
Wonder who we'll ever find?
Yes—I wonder who."

That is how they met and talked,
Knowing and unknowing.
Lincoln was the green pine.
Lincoln kept on growing.

*Stephen Vincent Benét*
*and Rosemary Benét*

252

What words are used here to describe Lincoln?
Would you use some of the same words in a class report about Abraham Lincoln?

## Practice

**A.** Choose the sentence from each pair that contains more interesting details.

1. a. The dog growled.
   b. The snarling dog bared his teeth.
2. a. Margaret's hair was the color of corn silk.
   b. Margaret had blond hair.
3. a. Out from under the bush crawled a black-clad figure.
   b. Someone came out from under the bush.
4. a. The sun was bright.
   b. The sun glared on the water like a million stage lights.
5. a. A crowd stood at the gate.
   b. The milling crowd waited restlessly at the locked gate.

**B.** Think of a well-known story. It can be an old story or a new one—perhaps from a popular movie. Then follow these directions.

1. Summarize one event in the plot of the story.
2. Describe the setting of the story.
3. Identify the main characters.
4. Tell whether the story is one of adventure, suspense, or everyday problems.
5. Explain how you identified the kind of story.

**C.** Imagine that the main character in your story is a teenage girl named Leslie. She is athletic, confident, and impatient. Write the three actions that agree with that description.

1. immediately decided to take the left fork in the road
2. jogged to the next camp site
3. lazily listened to the others as they tried to agree on where to pitch their tents
4. was the first to volunteer to take the survival course
5. kept wondering if her choice would turn out right

## Composition

Read the sentences below. Each one suggests a plot for a story.

a. The king died, and then the queen died suddenly, but no one knew why.

b. After a month of climbing, the two explorers reached the top of the mountain and found something completely unexpected.

c. We heard a radio broadcast in a language no one could identify.

d. Alana fell asleep—and woke in a sunless world.

e. At 20,000 feet the passengers heard a loud buzzer.

Now choose one of the sentences you read and do each of the following things.

1. Select a setting for the plot, and describe the setting in five or six sentences.

2. Invent at least two characters for the story, and describe each in three or four sentences.

3. Describe the story plot in five or six sentences.

4. Write an opening sentence for the story.

## Advanced Challenge

There are many different kinds of stories as you know from your own reading. Among the stories you have learned about, there are stories that tell about great adventures. There are also stories that are filled with mystery and suspense. And there are stories that deal with everyday problems and easily recognizable people. Think of a story that you would like to write that fits each of the three types.

For each of your three story ideas, plan a one- or two-sentence description of each of the following elements.

setting
main characters
plot

Write the setting, characters, and plot descriptions for each story on a separate piece of paper. Do not label the papers with the story types. Give the three papers to a partner. See if your partner can match the descriptions with the types of stories. Did any of them give your partner trouble? What caused the problem?

255

## WHERE DO WORDS COME FROM?

Do you know what a macadamized road is? It is a road made of small broken stones, pounded into a solid mass with a hard surface. The name comes from John L. McAdam, who disliked the dirt roads around his home so much that he invented a better kind of road. Many words for things we use, eat, enjoy, and wear come from people's names.

PRACTICE   Try to find out the origin of each of these words. Use your dictionary, the big dictionary in your school or public library, an encyclopedia, and books about words.

1. graham cracker
2. Morse Code
3. diesel engine
4. St. Bernard dog
5. macadamia nut
6. cardigan
7. gardenia
8. sandwich
9. Ferris wheel
10. Murphy bed

# Chapter 18
# Writing a Mystery

Lesson 1   **Prewriting a Mystery Story**
Lesson 2   **Organizing a Mystery Story**
Lesson 3   **Writing a Mystery Story**

# Prewriting a Mystery Story

Mystery stories ask questions. What really happened? Who did it? How will the bad guys be caught? Mystery stories are puzzles. One kind of mystery story is about a search. This kind of mystery asks, Where is it? The main character in this kind of story looks for something valuable, like a rare coin or an old diary or an important letter. *Nate the Great and the Missing Key* by Marjorie Weinman Sharmat is a mystery story about a search. In this story, Nate the Great uses the clues in a strange message to help him in his search.

## Example

Here is the message used by Nate the Great.

What is Nate the Great looking for?
Why is a strange message like this effective in a mystery story?

**PRACTICE 1** Which of these places would be good places to hide a key? Which of these places fit the clues given in the example?

1. in the false bottom of a wooden box
2. in a large jar filled with pins, needles, and shiny buttons
3. on a rubber band around a doorknob
4. in a jar of jelly in a refrigerator
5. on the collar of a large, fierce dog

**PRACTICE 2** Nate the Great's clues are a riddle in the form of a poem. There are other kinds of clues in mystery stories. Here is a list of items that might be searched for. Match each item in this list with a clue in the second list.

1. pirate treasure     a. muddy paw prints
2. lost gold mine     b. an old map with a ship on it
3. pet dog     c. the dying words of an art thief
4. oil painting     d. a message in secret code
5. top-secret plans     e. a picture carved in a rock

**WRITE** You can write your own mystery story. Your story, like *Nate the Great and the Missing Key,* will be a simple one, written for second or third graders. Start by making three columns on a piece of paper. In the first column, list things that might be searched for in a mystery story. In the second column, write a good place where each thing might be hidden or lost. In the third column, write why each thing might be hidden or lost. Choose the thing that would make the best search for your mystery story.

**GO BEYOND** Think about the kinds of clues you will have in your story. Like the ones in the Example, your clues should be tricky, but not too hard. Write your clues. If your clues are found on a map or in a picture, draw the map or picture.

# Organizing a Mystery Story

Your mystery story needs a main character. It also needs a plot. The main character will use the clues you wrote to solve the mystery. The actions of the main character are the plot. These actions should grow out of the clues. If the clues say to find a place that is safe, round, shiny, and big, then your story should tell how the main character finds such a place. Your main character should not be able to figure out the clues right away. He or she should have a little trouble. That will make your story more interesting.

## Example

These are the kinds of notes you might make about a main character and a plot for a mystery story.

MAIN CHARACTERS     Nate the Great, a boy who calls himself a detective, dresses like Sherlock Holmes, and is pretty clever

PLOT     Nate's friend Annie and her big dog Fang come to Nate for help. Annie is planning a party for Fang's birthday, but she can't get in her house. Annie has a note from her friend Rosomund that tells where Annie's house key is, but Annie cannot understand the note. Nate says he will find the key.

Nate looks around Annie's house. He cannot find anything safe, round, shiny, and big.

Nate goes to his friend Oliver's house. Oliver collects shiny things, but he does not have the key.

Nate goes to a bank because banks are safe and big, and they are filled with round, shiny coins. The key is not there.

Nate looks in Annie's garbage can, but the key is not there.

Nate thinks the key may be hidden with other things that are shiny like keys. He has Annie look at Fang's dog collar. She finds the key.

Why is the main character in a mystery story usually clever? Why does introducing Fang at the beginning of the story make the end of the story better?

## Exercises

**PRACTICE 1**   Suppose you are writing the story about the hidden key. Think of three places you could have Nate look for the key that are not mentioned in the Example. Make sure each place you list fits the clues.

**PRACTICE 2**   Suppose, again, you are writing the story about the key hidden on the dog collar, but you do not want to use Nate the Great as your main character. Which of these characters could you use instead of Nate the Great? Which would seem silly in this story?
1. a fashion model from Paris
2. an eleven-year-old girl who reads Nancy Drew mysteries
3. the President of the United States
4. a boy whose family just moved in next door to Annie's family
5. an Eskimo named Nanook

**WRITE**   Think about the kind of main character your mystery story needs. This person should be someone your second- or third-grade readers will like. Write a sentence or two describing this person. Then write your plot. Tell each step your main character will take in solving the mystery.

**GO BEYOND**   Thinking about your plot may have given you new ideas. Look at the clues you wrote for Lesson 1 and see if you could change any to make your story more mysterious.

# Writing a Mystery Story

You have an idea for a mystery story—characters, plot, and clues. Now you're going to turn that idea into a first draft. You can bring your idea to life by showing what your characters say and do, rather than merely telling. For instance, instead of just telling readers what a character is like, show them. Show readers what the character says and does. Use **dialogue** to make your first draft lively. Dialogue is conversation between characters.

## Example

Here is more from the story *Nate the Great and the Missing Key*. You can see how the writer uses dialogue to show rather than tell her story.

> "That is a strange poem," I said.
> "Sometimes Rosomund is strange," Annie said.
> I, Nate the Great, already knew that.
> "You must go to Rosomund's house and ask her where she put your key," I said.
> "I went to her house," Annie said. "But it was locked, too. I rang the bell, but no one was home."
> "This is a big day for Rosomund and locked doors," I said. "Who else has a key to your house?"
> "My mother and father. But they went out for the day. They don't like dog parties," Annie said.
> I, Nate the Great, knew that dog parties are very easy not to like.
> But I said, "I will take your case."

What two things does Nate think that he doesn't say aloud?
What does the writer show about her character Nate the Great?

---

**PRACTICE 1** Rewrite these sentences as dialogue.

Julita said that it might be a good idea to call the police. Ernesto replied that the phone lines had been cut. Julita asked who could have cut them. Eric said he thought it might have been the men in the black van parked across the street. Ernesto said they should all leave the house by the back door.

**PRACTICE 2** Suppose you are writing about a character named Cecily. You want your readers to know that Cecily is a girl who likes sports and hates to sit still. Which of the following sentences would you use to show readers the kind of person Cecily is? Tell why you chose each sentence.

1. Inside Cecily's closet were a tennis racket, a bag of golf clubs, a deflated football, a pair of ice-hockey skates, and several baseball bats.
2. Inside Cecily's closet were a dozen party dresses, several volumes of her diary, three books of poems, a paint-by-number kit, and a large carton filled with jigsaw puzzles.
3. "Hurry up," said Cecily.
4. At her party, Cecily had us play Twenty Questions.
5. Cecily bounced from one foot to another as she waited in the outfield for the batter to hit or to strike out.

**WRITE** Use the notes on your characters, plot, and clues to write a first draft of your story.

**GO BEYOND** Review your first draft to see if you are telling rather than showing. If so, add more action and dialogue.

## Practice

**A.** Think of a mystery story you have read. What made the story a puzzle? What clues were there to help in solving the mystery?

**B.** Write the plot of a mystery story, movie, or television program. What unexpected twists are there in the plot? How do these twists make solving the mystery more difficult? Why does trouble in solving the mystery make the plot more interesting?

**C.** Describe the main character from a mystery story you have read. How does the author of the story show what the main character is like? Tell why you like or dislike the character.

**D.** Here are two versions of part of a story. Choose the version that shows rather than tells. Tell the reasons for your choice.

Kumi looked out the window for a moment. She noticed something odd and asked Roberto if he had noticed it.

Roberto stared out at the bright field of snow. He didn't notice anything unusual at all.

Kumi told him to look again at the tracks and to notice where they started.

Roberto was surprised. The tracks started in the middle of the field.

Kumi said that it looked as if two people had suddenly appeared from nowhere and walked up to the house.

Kumi looked out the window for a moment. Then her forehead wrinkled.

"Do you see anything strange about the tracks?" she asked.

Roberto stared out at the bright field of snow. After a minute, he shook his head.

"Where do the tracks start?" Kumi asked. Roberto's eyes suddenly opened wide. "In the middle of the field," he said.

Kumi nodded. "It looks like two people suddenly appeared from no-where and walked up to the house."

## Composition

Many mystery stories are based on a series of clues. Often the clues are like these.

The school janitor said he heard a noise "like a window breaking" at about four o'clock.

Mrs. Redbone, the sixth-grade teacher, saw Fred Derf running across the playground at about four-fifteen.

Butch McGillicuddy, the school bully, was mad because Fred Derf beat him in a race.

The principal, Ms. Washington, kept Butch McGillicuddy in her office until a quarter to four.

Add some clues of your own to this list. The finished list should tell a story. With your clues, a reader should be able to answer these questions:
What crime was committed? Who committed the crime? Why was the crime committed?

## Advanced Challenge

Using clues to solve a mystery occurs not only in stories but also in real life. Look up one of the following real-life events. (You can find information in an encyclopedia.) What mystery did the event involve? How was the mystery solved?

1. the discovery of the planet Pluto
2. the search for the ancient city of Troy
3. the discovery of America
4. the first classification of blood into groups
5. the discovery of how yellow fever is spread
6. the first translation of Egyptian hieroglyphics
7. the discovery that lightning is electricity

## CONTEXT CLUES TO MEANING

A good detective picks up clues from everything and anything. A good word detective does the same thing. Be a word sleuth. Use the context, the sentence or paragraph in which a word appears, to figure out the meaning of an unfamiliar word. (Do you know what the word *sleuth* means? Can you guess?)

PRACTICE   First, guess what each underlined word probably means. Then use a dictionary to check your work.

"What on earth is this odd-looking concoction?" asked Detective Jacobi. "It looks like something Alice might have drunk in Wonderland."

"Well," replied his devil-may-care assistant, who was always ready to take chances, "quaff it and see, why don't you?"

"You may be reckless, my friend, but I approach strange fluids with the utmost caution. Remember what befell our colleague Max when he imbibed the potion he thought was malted milk!"

The assistant, whose name was Jay Greatheart but who went by the alias of Supersnoop, shuddered. "You're right, Chief," he said, greatly subdued. "That was ghastly. To be transformed into a lizard—ugh!" Supersnoop turned away, recalling with sadness their friend's cruel fate.

"Well, then, what shall we do?" inquired Jacobi.

"Dispose of the noxious brew with the greatest dispatch."

"Done," said Jacobi, pouring it onto the floor, where it boiled into the wood and then vanished as if it had never been there.

# Chapter 19
# More About Mysteries

Lesson 1 **Revising the Beginning**
Lesson 2 **Revising for Clarity**
Lesson 3 **Revising for Errors**
Lesson 4 **Revising for Publication**

## LESSON 1    **Revising the Beginning**

Start revising the first draft of your mystery story by looking at the beginning. The beginning of a story should have two aims. It should get readers interested and give them information. A good way to accomplish these aims is with action or dialogue. That gets readers into the story right away. At the same time, the beginning should answer two questions: Who is the main character? What is the mystery?

## Example

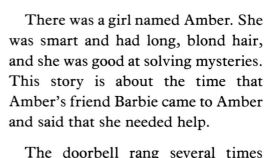

Here are the first draft and the revision of the beginning of a mystery story.

There was a girl named Amber. She was smart and had long, blond hair, and she was good at solving mysteries. This story is about the time that Amber's friend Barbie came to Amber and said that she needed help.

The doorbell rang several times before Amber put down the book she was reading and opened the door. Barbie was standing there. She looked lost.

"I need your help," Barbie said.

"What's wrong?" Amber asked.

"The necklace my mother gave me for my birthday is missing."

How do the two versions introduce the main character and the mystery?

Why is the revised version more interesting?

**PRACTICE 1**   Which of these sentences would be good ways to start a mystery story? Which would not? Why?

1. This story is about a treasure that was hidden.
2. The main character in this story is Willy the Whiz.
3. Roger looked at the empty drawer and rubbed his eyes in disbelief.
4. "Our five-hundred-pound gorilla has escaped," the zookeeper said.
5. The events I'm going to describe took place many years ago.

**PRACTICE 2**   Here are two versions of the beginning of a story. Which version is better? Tell why you chose that version.

Capt. Reynolds stared at the map spread out on the table.
"It's just an ordinary map," his assistant said.
"No," the captain said quickly. "If we know how to read it, this map will tell us where the stolen documents are hidden."

Capt. Reynolds stared at the map spread out on the table. The captain was a famous man who had been in the army and who now worked on top-secret cases for the government. He was tall and athletically built. He turned to his assistant and said, "This map will be a great help to us."

**WRITE**   Reread the beginning of your first draft. Does it identify the main character and make clear what the mystery is? If not, revise the beginning. Use action and dialogue to introduce the main character and the mystery.

**GO BEYOND**   Have a classmate read the beginning of your first draft. Can your classmate tell you who the main character is and what the mystery is? Does your classmate think the beginning is interesting? Use your classmate's suggestions to help make the beginning as good as you can make it.

# Revising for Clarity

The second step in revising your first draft is to look at it from the special point of view of your readers. You are writing your mystery story for second graders or third graders. For these readers, your story should be straightforward. You should stick to the basic plot and not wander. And you need to use words that your readers will know. You should not, however, be afraid to be **precise**. Call things exactly what they are. If a dog in your story is a cocker spaniel, write *cocker spaniel*, not just *dog*. Or better yet, give the dog a name, and use the name.

## Example

Here is part of the first draft of a mystery story and its revision.

"What's so valuable about the thing that's missing?" the officer inquired.

"Nothing really," said the coach. "It's just a four-leaf clover in a bit of glass. But Tim doesn't think he can pitch without it. People have had odd good-luck charms for thousands of years."

"What's so important about a lost good-luck charm?" Officer Peterson asked.

"Nothing really," said Coach Stephens. "It's just a four-leaf clover in a bit of glass. But Tim doesn't think he can pitch without it."

Why were words changed in the first paragraph?
Why were words removed from the second paragraph?

**PRACTICE 1**   For each number, choose the word or phrase you would more likely use in a story for second graders or third graders.

1. calculate, figure out
2. announced, said
3. talked about, discussed
4. squirrel, furry animal
5. dictionary, book

**PRACTICE 2**   Which sentences in this first draft wander from the basic plot and should be taken out? Write the selection, leaving out the sentences that wander.

"Tell me about the missing necklace," Amber said.

"It's a jade necklace," Barbie said.

Amber nodded. "I saw you wearing it at your birthday party. That cake your mother made was good. She gave me the recipe."

"I set the necklace on my dresser last night, and this morning it was gone."

**WRITE**   Reread your first draft. Look for words that would be too hard for your readers, for words that are not precise, and for places where you didn't stick to the basic plot. Make a note of anything that needs to be revised. Then make a list of words that could take the place of the words you thought were too hard or not precise enough in your first draft. Save your list.

**GO BEYOND**   Have a classmate read your first draft and lightly mark any words that would be too hard for a third grader, any words that are not precise, and any places where you didn't stick to the basic plot. Use your classmate's suggestions and your own ideas as a guide in revising your first draft.

**Revising for Errors**

Your mystery story is ready for editing. The spelling, the punctuation, the capitalization, and the word use all must be checked. You should pay special attention to the dialogue in your story. Everything a character says should be enclosed in quotation marks. Each change of speaker should be a new paragraph.

## Example

Here is part of a draft that needs to be edited. Checks show where corrections need to be made.

> Wendy point to the three fish tank on the table.
> "The note we found told us to look for glass walls, she said. They're they are."
> "Do you mean that the jewels are in the fish tank," Brad asked.
> Wendy nodded and said, we've been looking at them all along.

What are the mistakes that need to be corrected?
Why don't the words after "she said" start a new paragraph?

## Exercises

**PRACTICE 1**  Rewrite this paragraph as dialogue. Be sure to use quotation marks, commas, and question marks where they are needed. Begin a new paragraph each time the speaker changes.

Brad said that the jewels just looked like colored stones in the fish tank. Wendy agreed, adding that a good place to hide something is where people can see it. Brad asked if anyone had ever written a mystery story with that idea.

**PRACTICE 2** Rewrite the following part of a revised draft. Correct the mistakes. (Two mistakes are in spelling, two in punctuation, one in capitalization, and two in word use.)

"How did you now to look outside in the bushes for the wallet Randy asked.

Virginia point to their poodle Muggsy. "Muggsy brought a ball outside to play. If he took a ball outside, why not a wallet to?"

Randy smile and said, "good thinking."

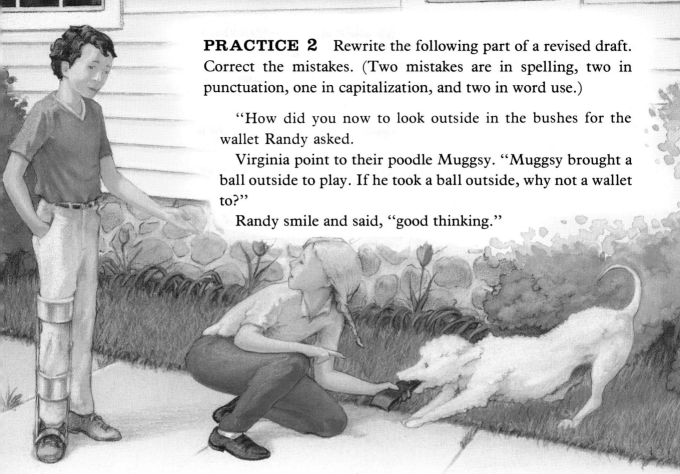

**WRITE** Carefully look over your revised draft. Check spelling, punctuation, capitalization, and word use. Look at each place where you used the word *said* or another word that means "said." Make sure you've used quotation marks where they are needed. See if you've begun a new paragraph each time the speaker changes. Mark each place where you need to make a correction.

**GO BEYOND** Have a classmate check your revised draft. Think about the kinds of mistakes you usually make. Tell your classmate to be on the lookout for those kinds of mistakes. Your classmate should mark any places where corrections are needed. Use your classmate's notes and your own to make a final copy of your story. Give your story a title.

## Raccoon

Crash goes the trashcan! Clatter and clacket!
What in the world can be making that racket?
I hurry to look by the light of the moon,
And what do I find? Why, a fine fat raccoon!
All through the garden the garbage he's strewn,
And he's eating his supper, that robber raccoon,
Eating so nicely without fork or spoon,
Why, his manners are perfect, that thieving raccoon!
And wasn't he smart to discover that pail?
And wasn't he smart to uncover that pail?
And isn't he lucky he won't go to jail
For stealing his dinner and making a mess
For me to clean up in the morning, I guess,
While he, the old pirate, abundantly fed,
Curls up in a ball fast asleep in his bed.

*Mary Ann Hoberman*

Why might a raccoon make a good mystery story character?

# Revising for Publication

You are ready to share your mystery story with your readers. But first, think about what you can do to help readers enjoy your story. For instance, telling readers a little about a story can make them want to read it. Drawing pictures for a story also can interest readers.

## Example

Here is how one fifth-grade writer told readers about her story.

This story is about the search for a valuable stamp collection. The stamps were hidden by the collector somewhere in his house, just before he died. The collector's granddaughter looks for them. Her only clue is some words her grandfather's parrot says over and over.

CRACKERS

Would you want to read this story?
Why or why not?

**PRACTICE 1**  Most of the following are good ways to help readers enjoy a mystery story. But some of them may not be right for your story. Choose the suggestions that would help your readers enjoy your story. Tell why you chose each one.

1. Draw pictures to go with the story.
2. Tell readers a little about the main character or the puzzle that will be solved.
3. Read the story aloud with a different reader for each character's dialogue.
4. Tell readers how the story ends.
5. Have readers stop reading just before the puzzle is explained. Ask them to guess how the story ends.

**PRACTICE 2**  Each of the following might make a good picture for a mystery story. But some of these picture ideas would not be right for your story. Choose the picture ideas that would help your readers enjoy your story. Tell why you chose each one.

1. a picture of the main character
2. a picture of the clue
3. a mysterious or scary picture
4. a funny picture
5. a picture that shows where the story takes place

**WRITE**  List things you could do to help readers enjoy your story. If your list includes telling readers about the story, write what you would say to them.

**GO BEYOND**  Have a classmate who has read your story look over the list you just wrote. Ask your classmate for any other suggestions that would help readers enjoy your story. Use your classmate's suggestions and your ideas to share your mystery story with readers.

6. small animal, gerbil
7. lunch, meal
8. shack, building
9. relative, Uncle Toby
10. vehicle, truck

**C.** Each sentence contains one error in spelling, punctuation, capitalization, or word use. Write each sentence correctly.

1. Emily whispered, "there's someone creeping around downstairs."
2. I throwed her a dirty look.
3. Where is my flashlight.
4. This is wear she was standing just before she disappeared.
5. She and Nancy has solved dozens of mysteries.
6. "What makes you think someone has found the treasure map" asked Della
7. "Someone," said Harry, "Left in a big hurry."
8. Its the only clue we've got.

## Practice

**A.** Which of these would be a good opening sentence for a mystery story?

1. "Look out!" Maria yelled, as the car swerved toward them.
2. Rick slowly pushed open the front door of the old mansion.
3. This story takes place in a small town in the Old West.
4. This mystery story tells how Alice figured out a very tricky clue.
5. "That's a lie," Detective Spinoza yelled.

**B.** For each number, choose the word or phrase that is more precise.

1. a zoo, the San Diego Zoo
2. ink spot, dark mark
3. popular sport, football
4. sandwich, food
5. sandwich, ham-and-cheese

278

## Composition

If you like to read mystery stories, you probably have a favorite detective. It might be Sherlock Holmes, Hercule Poirot, Encyclopedia Brown, Nancy Drew, or any of the dozens of fictional detectives. Once mystery readers find a character they like, they want to see their favorite in more adventures. What about the main character in your mystery? What further adventures could *your* detective have? Make a list of story ideas. If you think of one that sounds good, try writing a second mystery story.

## Advanced Challenge

Together with two or three classmates choose a fictional detective that you all like. Each of you should read a story or novel involving this detective. Then make a list of new story ideas for the detective. Either individually or as a group, choose one idea you like. Briefly write the plot of your story idea. If the plot sounds good, you could try writing the whole story.

## DICTIONARY

You know enough about dictionaries to write one yourself. In fact, that is what you will do when you get to the last Word Study. Here are some questions to help you review what you have learned.

PRACTICE   Use a dictionary to answer each question.
1. How do you spell the plural of *periphery*?
2. How many syllables are in the word *dinosaur*?
3. What adverb is made from the adjective *seasonal*?
4. What is a replica?
5. Which is the more common spelling, *code name* or *codename*?
6. What is the present participle of the verb *putty*?
7. Where is the Old World?
8. What did the word *husband* originally mean?
9. What is a synonym for the word *masticate*?
10. Can a horn be used as a container to hold something?

**A.** One sentence in each of the following pairs tells and the other shows. Write the sentence that shows.

1. a. Samantha asked if any of them had seen the accident.
   b. "Did any of you see the accident?" Samantha asked.
2. a. Samantha was careful about the way she handled the clues.
   b. Samantha wrapped the drinking glass in a handkerchief.
3. a. Tracy's jaw dropped open.
   b. Tracy expressed surprise.
4. a. The officer made an announcement about the investigation.
   b. "We've solved the case," the officer said.
5. a. Steven kept glancing at his watch.
   b. Steven was worried that we would be too late.

**B.** One sentence in each of the following pairs is from a first draft and one is from a final draft. Write the sentence that is from the final draft.

1. a. Philip said firmly, "Stay where you are."
   b. Philip said firmly, "stay where you are."
2. a. Look out, Ann yelled.
   b. "Look out!" Ann yelled.
3. a. The dog caught the knife in its mouth.
   b. The dog catched the knife in its mouth.
4. a. "There it is," Cathy said.
   b. "Their it is," Cathy said.
5. a. "You're the only one who can help us," Sheila pleaded.
   b. "Your the only one who can help us," Sheila pleaded.

281

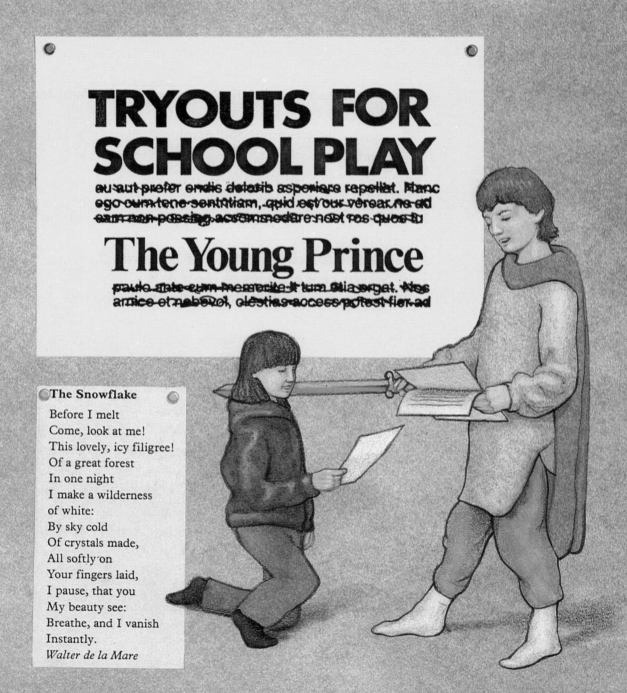

**Homework: Finish this sentence—**
**All of a sudden the lights went out....**

# TRYOUTS FOR SCHOOL PLAY

## The Young Prince

**The Snowflake**

Before I melt
Come, look at me!
This lovely, icy filigree!
Of a great forest
In one night
I make a wilderness
of white:
By sky cold
Of crystals made,
All softly on
Your fingers laid,
I pause, that you
My beauty see:
Breathe, and I vanish
Instantly.
*Walter de la Mare*

Best Story

A+ Fine Job!

A+ Excellent!

B Good Job

Chapter 20
**Descriptive Writing**

Chapter 21
**Writing for Special Purposes**

### The Snowflake

Before I melt
Come, look at me!
This lovely, icy filigree!
Of a great forest
In one night
I make a wilderness
of white:
By sky cold
Of crystals made,
All softly on
Your fingers laid,
I pause, that you
My beauty see:
Breathe, and I vanish
Instantly.

*Walter de la Mare*

Would you find a snowflake hard or easy to write about?
Why?

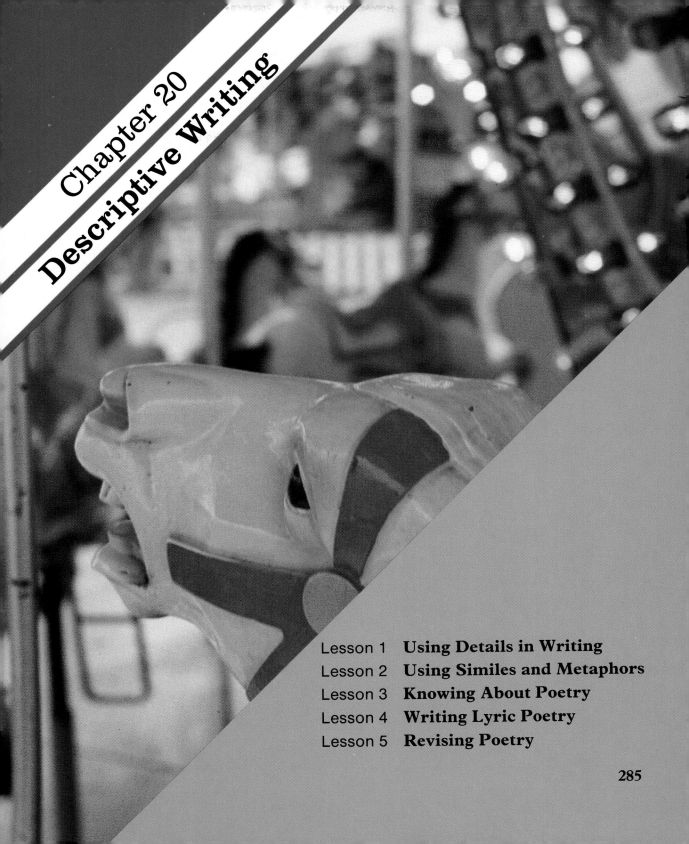

# Chapter 20
# Descriptive Writing

Lesson 1  **Using Details in Writing**
Lesson 2  **Using Similes and Metaphors**
Lesson 3  **Knowing About Poetry**
Lesson 4  **Writing Lyric Poetry**
Lesson 5  **Revising Poetry**

## LESSON 1  Using Details in Writing

There are five senses: sight, hearing, smell, taste, and touch. Each sense helps you experience your world and then show it to others. Why describe a store as "interesting" when you can write that it "has heaps of stuffed toys and gaudy games."

Let readers see, hear, smell, taste, and touch the world you describe.

**Example**

This paragraph is from Mildred Taylor's *Roll of Thunder, Hear My Cry*.

By the dawn, the house smelled of Sunday. By evening, it reeked of Christmas; a gigantic coon which Mr. Morrison, Uncle Hammer, and Stacey had secured in a night's hunt, baked in a sea of onion, garlic, and fat orange-yellow yams; and a choice sugar-cured ham brought from the smokehouse awaited its turn in the oven. In the heart of the house, where we had gathered after supper, freshly cut branches of long-needled pines lay over the fireplace mantle adorned by winding vines of winter holly and bright red Christmas berries. And in the fireplace itself, in a black pan set on a high wire rack, peanuts roasted over the hickory fire as the waning light of day swiftly deepened into a fine velvet night...and the warm sound of husky voices and rising laughter mingled in tales of sorrow and happiness of days past but not forgotten.

What kinds of details does the writer present?
What special memory do you have of a holiday?

**PRACTICE 1**   Tell which of the five senses the writer used in each detail. You may find that more than one sense is used to describe a detail.

1. fat orange-yellow yams
2. freshly cut branches of long-needled pines
3. peanuts roasted over the hickory fire
4. velvet night
5. warm sounds of husky voices and rising laughter

**PRACTICE 2**   Choose an object in your classroom to describe. Answer as many of the following questions about it as you can.

1. What color or colors is it?
2. What shape is it?
3. How big is it? What else is about the same size?
4. How heavy is it? What else weighs about the same?
5. What does it smell like?
6. What does it feel like?
7. Can it be tasted? If so, what does it taste like?
8. Does the object make a sound? What kind of sound?
9. Is there one particular thing you notice when you look at this object? What is it and why does it stand out?
10. Does the object remind you of an event or an experience? If so, what is it?

**WRITE**   Write a paragraph describing as fully as you can the object you observed in Practice 2.

**GO BEYOND**   Work in a group of five or six students. One at a time, read the descriptions each of you wrote. Do not tell what the objects are. Substitute *it* for the name of the object. See whether the group can identify each object.

# Using Similes and Metaphors

You can often create powerful descriptions by comparing or identifying one thing with something else.

A **simile** is a comparison that you can make by using the words *like* or *as*. For example, *the car was like a sleek black cat* is a simile. A **metaphor** goes one step further. It describes one thing by actually calling it something else. *The car was a sleek black cat* is a metaphor.

Remember, the two items being compared or identified must be different. If you write "Michael dresses like a cowboy," you are only making a comparison, not using a simile.

## Example

In this paragraph from Natalie Babbitt's *The Eyes of the Amaryllis,* the author uses simile and metaphor to create a colorful description.

The sky was a blaze of red and pink and orange, and its double trembled on the surface of the pond like color spilled from a paint box. The sun was dropping fast now, a soft red sliding egg yolk, and already to the east there was a darkening to purple.

Where in the paragraph did the author use simile and metaphor? What other simile and metaphor can you think of to describe the scene?

---

*Types of Writing*

**PRACTICE 1**  Choose the correct word or words in parentheses for each sentence. Use the paragraph in the Example for help. Write your choices.

1. Natalie Babbitt is describing a (pond, sunset).
2. The reflection of the sky in the pond is (like color spilled from a paint box, a ragged blaze of red and pink and orange).
3. The reflection is described in a (metaphor, simile).
4. The setting sun is a (dark purple, soft red sliding egg yolk).
5. The sun is described in a (metaphor, simile).

**PRACTICE 2**  Tell whether a simile or a metaphor is used in each sentence. Then explain what two things are being compared or identified with each other.

1. We played basketball in a building as hot as a sunlamp.
2. The crowd was roaring like wild animals.
3. Eli threw the ball like a speeding comet to Sammy.
4. Our coach's face became a storm cloud.
5. A fan's warning, "Watch that guy," was like the crack of a rifle.

**WRITE**  Use both a simile and a metaphor to describe each of these things.

1. the appearance of a tree
2. the sound of wind in the leaves or needles of a tree
3. the feel of a tree trunk

**GO BEYOND**  In a group of four or five students, play Challenge. The first player uses a simile or a metaphor to describe an object. Then she or he challenges another player to do the same for the same object. Each player challenged thinks of another simile or metaphor for the object. The challenging continues until a player cannot think of a simile or a metaphor. Then the last player chooses a new object to describe.

## LESSON 3  Knowing About Poetry

Poetry is a very special use of language that almost always appeals to the reader's senses. If you understand what poetry does and if you gain some experience in writing it, you will sharpen your ability to appeal to a reader in all kinds of writing.

There are many kinds and forms of poems. **Lyric** poems reveal feelings and describe objects and events. **Narrative** poems tell a story. Some poems contain words that **rhyme**: *sea, me*. Some have regular **rhythm**. Some are written in groups of lines called **stanzas**. Poems please with both sounds and ideas.

## Example

This poem, "City Rain," was written by Rachel Field.

Rain in the city!
  I love to see it fall
Slantwise where the buildings crowd
  Red brick and all.
Streets of shiny wetness
  Where the taxis go,
With people and umbrellas all
  Bobbing to and fro.

Rain in the city!
  I love to hear it drip
When I am cozy in my room
  Snug as any ship,
With toys spread on the table,
  With a picture book or two,
And the rain like a rumbling tune that sings
  Through everything I do.

What do you find pleasing about "City Rain"?

**PRACTICE 1**  These questions refer to the poem in the Example. Write your answers in sentences.
1. Is "City Rain" a lyric or a narrative poem?
2. How many stanzas does the poem have?
3. What rhyming words does it contain?
4. To what does the poet compare rain?
5. How does the poem make you feel?

**PRACTICE 2**  Write *thunder* and *lightning* as column headings. Under each heading write the following words that you are reminded of. Some words do not belong in either column.
1. drumming
2. neon sign
3. flashing strobe light
4. fire river
5. white lacy flakes
6. roar of a train
7. sunburst
8. moist green leaf
9. rumble of a truck
10. sky writing

**WRITE**  Choose an element of weather, such as rain, snow, hail, sunshine, or clouds, and a place, such as farm, fields, woods, beach, or pond. Write a poem about the effect one has on the other. Your poem may or may not rhyme. It may or may not be divided into stanzas. Use your senses to choose good details. Try to capture a feeling you have experienced in that situation. Save your poem for use in Lesson 5.

**GO BEYOND**  Since a poem creates a picture in the reader's mind, people often like to illustrate poems. Look through magazines. Cut out pictures that relate to the meaning and feeling of the poem you wrote in the Write exercise. If you cannot find the kind of pictures you are looking for in a magazine, you may want to draw your own pictures to illustrate your poem.

# Writing Lyric Poetry

One way to share your thoughts, feelings, and reactions to things is through poetry. A **lyric** poem is a short poem that expresses the writer's feelings. Lyric poems often use similes and metaphors to create sharp mental pictures.

## Example

Here is how one poet shares some thoughts and feelings about poetry.

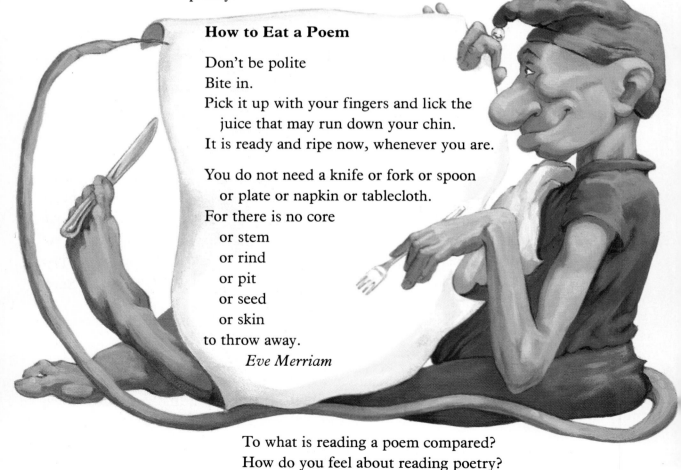

**How to Eat a Poem**

Don't be polite
Bite in.
Pick it up with your fingers and lick the
    juice that may run down your chin.
It is ready and ripe now, whenever you are.

You do not need a knife or fork or spoon
    or plate or napkin or tablecloth.
For there is no core
    or stem
    or rind
    or pit
    or seed
    or skin
to throw away.
        *Eve Merriam*

To what is reading a poem compared?
How do you feel about reading poetry?

**PRACTICE 1**  Write words from the poem in the Example that have the same meaning as each statement below.
1. Feel a poem through your senses.
2. Start reading right away.
3. Don't worry about table manners.
4. There are no leftovers with poems.
5. A poem can be enjoyed anytime you want.

**PRACTICE 2**  Make five comparisons. Match each item in the left column with one in the right column. Write the correct letter beside each number.

1. train in a tunnel          a. corn popping
2. rain on a metal roof       b. liquid crystals
3. air on a hot day           c. sharp forest perfume
4. the scent of a pine tree   d. underground mole
5. tears                      e. oven-hot air

**WRITE**  Choose something or someone you know well as a topic for a lyric poem. Then list some details about your topic. Include at least two comparisons. For example, if your topic is Thanksgiving, you might include details such as crisply browned turkey and hungry people. You might compare large helpings of food to mountains, or the hungry people to an attacking army. Write the first draft of your poem. Save your poem to use in Lesson 5.

**GO BEYOND**  Similes and metaphors make comparisons between unlike things. When you write a simile or a metaphor for a poem, be sure the comparison fits. For example, "the sea is a desert of water" works better than "the sea is a glass of lemonade." Work with a partner to write three similes or metaphors. Share what you have written with the class. Decide which similes and metaphors work well and which don't.

**Revising Poetry**

Poetry, like any other kind of writing, should be revised. Since a poem is meant to be heard, begin the revision process by reading it aloud softly to yourself. How does it sound? Do the words that are supposed to rhyme really rhyme? Does the poem have a regular rhythm? Should some lines be made longer or shorter?

After you have listened to the poem, study it carefully and ask yourself these questions: Are the ideas clearly expressed? Are the word pictures, or images, clear and strong? Is the main idea of the poem easy to understand? Make changes to improve your poem, proofread it, and then make a final copy.

## Example

This poem describes one person's feelings by making statements that contain clear images.

**Loneliness**

i walk
through a garden
rainbowed
with flowers
but
i only see gray
i'm out
in the sunshine
but it feels like night
during the day
it's as though
i am a flower
who hasn't been fed
who
wants to blossom
but
is
wilting
instead.

*Harlane Radler*

What feeling does the poet create by using the small *i?*
When have you ever felt like the person in the poem?

**PRACTICE 1**   Choose from the list the word or word group that correctly completes each sentence. Write each choice beside the correct number. Use the poem in the Example for help.

wilting      feels like night      but      small i      gray

1. Ms. Radler uses the _____ to show how small and helpless the person in the poem feels.
2. The speaker wonders why it _____ when she is outside in the sunshine.
3. Although rainbows and flowers suggest happiness and warmth, the speaker's world is _____ .
4. The speaker feels like a flower that is _____ .
5. Ms. Radler describes how mixed-up the person feels by repeating the word _____ three times in the poem.

**PRACTICE 2**   In the poem in the Example, the poet talks about being unable to enjoy the beauty of a garden, seeing gray, and being a wilting flower. Substitute your own examples for the three the poet offers. Find your own word pictures to create the feeling of loneliness.

**WRITE**   Choose a poem that you wrote earlier either in Lesson 3 or in Lesson 4. Then have someone read it aloud. Have you expressed your ideas clearly? Are you satisfied with the word pictures you have created? Have you used any similes or metaphors? Have you used details that would appeal to the reader's senses? Can you hear words that you would want to change or repeat? Revise your poem, changing words and lines that need improvement. Then rewrite it.

**GO BEYOND**   Decide as a class how to share your poems. Some possible ways are by making a class book, reading the poems to another class, or recording them on tape.

## Practice

**A.** Write the name of the sense being appealed to in each sentence.

1. The water threw little sparkles on the sides of the boats.
2. "Click, click," went the clock as time passed all too quickly.
3. My feet felt like leather after I had walked barefoot on the sand and sidewalks all summer.
4. Tart, tangy, and sweet, the fresh apple slices thrilled my taste buds.
5. The air was heavy with the perfume of the last day of summer.

**B.** Write the two things that are being compared in each sentence. Then write whether the comparison is a simile or a metaphor.

1. Mr. Terranova's hair was a snowy field.
2. His eyes were question marks.
3. The humid air was a steambath on that August night.
4. Becky's pitch to the catcher was like a shot out of a cannon.
5. The dinner that Marcy cooked smelled like burned rubber.

**C.** Complete each simile or metaphor.

1. The small ball bounced wildly, like a _____ .
2. The cat rolled over and curled his body like a _____ .
3. Eloise's little sister is a _____ , always making noise.
4. "Broom, broom," went the cars, speeding by steadily like _____ .
5. The children jumped around the gym, chattering like _____ .

**D.** Use the words below to complete each sentence. Write each sentence.

descriptive     narrative     rhyme
rhythm     stanza

1. Words that _____ end with the same sound.
2. A lyric poem is a _____ poem.
3. A _____ is a group of lines that belong together in a poem.
4. Poems have _____ , sometimes regular and sometimes not.
5. A _____ poem tells a story.

## Composition

When you describe a place, you explain how the things there look. You can also describe the smells that you find there and the sounds you hear. It might be possible, depending upon the place, to describe how things feel that you find there—the breeze against your face, for example, or sand curling between your toes.

Think of a place that you find interesting. List words and phrases that could be used to describe the place. Concentrate upon things that could appeal to a reader's senses. Use details that would make a reader see, hear, smell, taste, and feel. After you have as complete a list as you can make, write a lyric poem about the place. The poem should be no longer than ten lines. In your poem appeal to the reader's senses by using similes and metaphors.

## Advanced Challenge

A single word can often act as the starting point for an idea that can be developed into a poem. A single word can suggest others that will help the poem to take shape. The word snake, for example, might suggest the related words coil, slither, fangs, and crawl. Those five words could be used in a brief poem about snakes or about your personal reaction to snakes.

Prepare a list of five related words that could be used in a brief poem. Start with a noun and then write four other words that the noun suggests. The four other words can be nouns, verbs, adjectives, or adverbs. Exchange your list with another student. Use the five words you receive to write a brief lyric poem of no more than ten lines. Be prepared to share your poem with the class.

## WORD PARTS

Would you be angry if someone called you a *polyglot,* said you were too *ultra-ultra,* or called you *superhuman*? If you are a polyglot, you speak many languages. *Poly-* means "many," and *glot* is from a Greek word for tongue. If someone says you're ultra-ultra, though, the person is using a slang expression that means "stuck-up." *Ultra* means "extreme," "more than," or "beyond what is usual." It is a word in itself and is also used as a prefix, a group of letters added at the beginning of a word. As for being superhuman—well, *super* means "more than." Knowing the meaning of the prefixes *poly-, ultra-,* and *super-* can help you figure out the meanings of words that may at first look difficult.

EXAMPLE

Her clothes are *ultrafashionable*. She buys all the newest styles.

Spot must be a *superdog*! She climbed the mountain with us and then went for a long run with Mom.

Ms. Rodríguez drew a *polygon,* a figure with many sides, on the board.

PRACTICE   Guess what each underlined word means. Check your answer in your dictionary. Then write a sentence, like those in the examples above, that will clearly show the meaning of that word.

1. He went to a polytechnic school.
2. A new superhighway is being built through our town.
3. Their home was ultramodern.
4. The movie was about creatures with supernatural powers.
5. There are too many polysyllabic words on that page.

# Chapter 21
# Writing
# for Special Purposes

Lesson 1   **Writing a Book Report**
Lesson 2   **Writing a Friendly Letter**
Lesson 3   **Writing a Business Letter**
Lesson 4   **Writing Telephone Messages**

# Writing a Book Report

Writing a report is a way of sharing your ideas and opinions about a book. A **book report** helps others decide whether they would like to read the book or not.

Begin a book report by giving the title of the book and the author. Then tell whether the book is fiction or nonfiction. Next, tell what the book is about and identify the main characters. If the book does not have main characters, tell about the subject.

In the rest of the report, describe your reactions to the book. Tell briefly about any favorite part. In the last paragraph, explain why you did or did not like the book. Also, identify the type of reader who will probably enjoy reading the book.

## Example

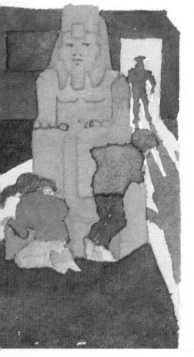

These paragraphs are from a book report.

E. L. Konigsburg's *From the Mixed-Up Files of Mrs. Basil E. Frankweiler* is a book of fiction. It is about a girl, Claudia, who runs away with her brother, Jamie, to the Metropolitan Museum of Art in New York City. Claudia plans the adventure because she feels that her family treats her unfairly. She is also bored. At the museum, the brother and sister meet Mrs. Frankweiler and help her solve a mystery.

My favorite part is when they are living in the museum. They take baths in a fountain and collect pennies from under the water to buy snacks. They sleep on a fancy canopy bed and hide their belongings under it. The children hide in the bathrooms when the guards lock up each night.

Anyone looking for an adventure story with a hard-to-solve mystery would like this book.

Would you like to read the book? Why or why not?

**PRACTICE 1** Choose the correct word or words in parentheses to complete each sentence. Write each sentence.

1. A well written book report includes (no opinion, your opinion) of a book.
2. A book report helps others learn whether they would like to (read, hear about) a book.
3. A statement about the title and the author belongs at the (beginning, end) of a book report.
4. A report about a nonfiction book should mention (the main characters, the subject covered) in the book.
5. The report should describe (briefly, completely) an interesting part of the book.

**PRACTICE 2** Answer the following questions about the book report in the Example.

1. What type of book is it, fiction or nonfiction.
2. What is the book about?
3. What is the setting of the book?
4. Who are the main characters?
5. Who would enjoy the book?

**WRITE** Choose one of the books you have read and liked. Write a book report about it. Follow the guidelines for writing a book report that are given in the introduction to this lesson. When you are finished, check to make sure you have included all the necessary information.

**GO BEYOND** Work in a group of four. Imagine that each person is a buyer for a different bookstore. Your job is to "sell" the book that you wrote about in the Write exercise, so that the "buyers" will want it for their stores. Read your report aloud. Answer any questions that the group members might ask.

# Writing a Friendly Letter

Friendly letters have five parts: **heading, greeting, body, closing,** and **signature.** The first word of the greeting and closing, state abbreviations, and all proper nouns and titles in the letter and on the envelope begin with capital letters.

In the middle of the envelope are the name and address of the person who will receive the letter. The name and address of the sender are in the upper left-hand corner of the envelope.

## Example

Notice how the parts of a friendly letter are placed on the page.

HEADING

GREETING

BODY

CLOSING

SIGNATURE

> 98 Vancouver Drive
> Saginaw, MI 48605
> May 13, 19--
>
> Dear Sue,
> We are definitely coming to visit you in the middle of July. Grandma Sanchez is coming to see our new baby. Grandma is then going to Mississippi to visit your family. Tom and I can come with her. I'm so excited. I have so much to tell you.
>
> Your cousin,
> Celia

ENVELOPE

> Celia Sanchez
> 98 Vancouver Drive
> Saginaw, MI 48605
>
> Susan Briggs
> 446 Western Avenue
> Vicksburg, MS 39180

**PRACTICE 1**   Write these headings, greetings, and closings. Use commas and capital letters where they are needed.

1. 27 beacon avenue
   crockett tx 75835
   april 3 19—
2. rural route 2
   plymouth mn 55401
   june 22, 19—

3. dear uncle dan
4. your nephew
   Chris
5. dear susan

**PRACTICE 2**   Rewrite the following letter and correct the six mistakes.

> 91 Cedar street
> Brigham City UT 84302
> June 15 1986

Dear Uncle Luke

    Here are the pictures of the family picnic we had last September. I think the picture of you and Chuck in the water fight is the best. I couldn't stop laughing when I saw the looks on your faces.

> your nephew
> Ted

**WRITE**   In a letter to a relative or a friend, tell what you have been doing at home and in school. Tell other news that could interest the person. Check and correct your work.

**GO BEYOND**   Bring an envelope and stamp to class. In the middle of the envelope, write the name and address of the person to whom your letter will go. Write your own name and address in the upper left-hand corner. Place your stamp in the upper right-hand corner. Mail your letter.

# Writing a Business Letter

The form of a business letter differs from the form of a friendly letter in three ways. Business letters have an **inside address** that tells to whom and where the letter is going. The greeting is followed by a colon (:). The closing is more formal than in a friendly letter. Some closings used in business letters are *Sincerely, Sincerely yours,* or *Yours truly.*

People often write business letters to ask for information or to express an opinion.

## Example

Notice how this letter is different from a friendly letter.

HEADING
> 31 Ocean Drive
> Myrtle Beach, SC 29577
> March 8, 19—

INSIDE ADDRESS
Delmont Record Company
5189 Derron Avenue
Memphis, TN 38118

GREETING
Dear Sir or Madam:

BODY
I have just heard your company's new record "Western Songs" by the Valley Singers. Will this group be doing more albums? I have never heard them before, but I think they are terrific.

CLOSING
SIGNATURE
> Sincerely,
> Kelly Stevens

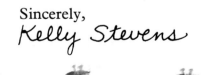

*Types of Writing*

**PRACTICE 1**   Correct the parts of a business letter below. Use capital letters and punctuation where they are needed.

1.  80 garden street
    lowell, ma 01852
2.  dear mr. bradley
3.  bradley bicycle company
    40 peachtree avenue
    atlanta, ga 30302
4.  yours truly

**PRACTICE 2**   Rewrite the following letter and correct the five mistakes. Add any missing parts.

> San Francisco, ca 94108
> May 4 19—

Central Computer company
20 Field Lane
Benavides, TX 78341

   I have seen a picture of your new computer, Model Y3. Please send me more information.
Yours Truly,

> Peggy Parker

**WRITE**   Make up the name and address of a company, and write a business letter. Express your opinion about one of their products, or ask for information. Check to make sure you have included all the parts of a business letter.

**GO BEYOND**   Work with a partner, and choose a famous person you both admire. Write a letter to the person and tell why you admire her or him.

# Writing Telephone Messages

Sometimes you answer the telephone and must take a message for someone else. When this happens, make sure you know the name of the person who is calling. Listen carefully to the message. Repeat it to the caller to make sure you have it right.

Write the message as soon as you complete the telephone conversation. Include whom the message is for, the name of the caller, the time, and all the information the caller gave. Remember to sign your own name to the message.

## Example

Read this telephone conversation.

JERRY:   Hello. This is the Adams' residence.

MR. SIMS:   Hello. Is your mother home?

JERRY:   I'm sorry, but she's at work. May I help you?

MR. SIMS:   This is Don Sims at the Auto Repair Shop. Could you give your mother a message? Tell her that her car is ready. She can pick it up anytime before 6:00 P.M.

JERRY:   Mom's car is ready, and she can pick it up anytime before 6:00 P.M. Is that right?

MR. SIMS:   That's it. Many thanks.

JERRY:   You're welcome. Good-bye.

This is the message
Jerry left for his
mother.

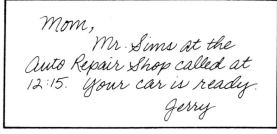

Mom,
Mr. Sims at the
Auto Repair Shop called at
12:15. Your car is ready.
Jerry

What information did Jerry leave out of the message?
What questions should you ask when you are taking a message?

**PRACTICE 1**   Four of the questions below would help you take a telephone message. Write the numbers of the questions.

1. Who is calling, please?
2. Would you call back when I'm not so busy?
3. Would you spell your name, please?
4. Is this the correct message?
5. Would you repeat that information?

**PRACTICE 2**   Find what is missing in the following message. Write the numbers of the missing information.

Peg, you got a call at ten o'clock about your lost puppy. He has been found. You can pick him up when you get home from school.

Peg, you got a call at ten o'clock about your lost puppy. He has been found. You can pick him up when you get home from school.

1. what the call was about
2. whom the call was from
3. who took the message
4. when the puppy can be picked up
5. where the puppy can be picked up

**WRITE**   Imagine that you are having a telephone conversation similar to the one in the Example. Write a conversation in which you are asked to take a message.

**GO BEYOND**   Work with a partner. Read aloud your conversations from the Write exercise. When you are the caller, your partner writes a message. When your partner is the caller, you write a message. Check each other's messages to make sure they are complete.

*Writing for Special Purposes*

## Practice

**A.** Read this part of a book report and answer the questions about it.

> *The Guilty Goose* by Myra S. Perkins is a fiction story about a girl named Gloria who raises geese as a hobby. There are many amusing events, especially when the creatures escape from their owner and cause a general uproar. My favorite part of the book is the part where Gloria is accused of stealing a gold watch. Naturally, it was one of her pets that did it.

1.  What is the name of the book?
2.  Who wrote the book?
3.  What is the book about?
4.  Who is the main character?
5.  What is the reviewer's favorite part of the book?

**B.** Write *C* beside the number of each correct part of a friendly letter. Rewrite each incorrect part.

1.  Dear Sherry:
2.  85 Hari Road
    Stark, NH 03582
    February 24, 19—
3.  62 marion road
    linden, NJ 07036
4.  sincerely
    Michael
5.  The Cortex Company
    21 Pimlico Way
    Colorado Springs CO 80909

**C.** Write *F* for each letter part that belongs in a friendly letter. Write *B* for each part that belongs in a business letter.

1.  The Wilmo Company
    30 Feather Drive
    Bolinas, CA 94924
2.  Dear Mr. Lucindas:
3.  Your friend,
4.  Yours truly,
5.  Dear Aunt Rebecca,

**D.** Write a business letter expressing an opinion about something you do not like or about a product that does not work well. Make sure you include all the parts of a business letter.

**E.** Find what is missing in the telephone message. Choose from the information below and rewrite the message.

> Maria, someone called about your class field trip.
>
> > Don

1. Please be at the school by 8:30.
2. Your teacher, Mrs. Ames, called at 10:30.
3. She lives on Speckle Street.
4. It will be next Friday.
5. The third grade took a trip yesterday.

## Composition

Think of something you would like to invent. Make up the name of a company that would manufacture your invention. Write the company a business letter describing your invention. Tell what it will do and why it is needed. Point out any special features. Ask the company to consider manufacturing or selling your invention. Make a drawing to go with your letter if you wish.

## Advanced Challenge

Think of a novel you enjoyed reading. Imagine yourself as one of the characters in it. Write a friendly letter to another character in that book. Tell about one event that takes place in the book. Use your imagination, and, if you like, go beyond the material in the book. For example, you, as that character, might give an opinion that is not given in the book. You could tell about something that is mentioned but not discussed in detail in the book.

Be sure to use the correct friendly letter form. Choose a closing that you think the character would be likely to use.

## WHERE DO WORDS COME FROM?

What state do you live in? Do you know how it got its name? Many of our states have names that come from Native American words. Others have names that come from other languages such as Spanish or Dutch.

EXAMPLE

Utah may have come from two Native American words. One, *eutah*, means "in the mountaintops." The other, Ute, means "hill people." Rhode Island comes from *roodt Eylandt*, Dutch words meaning "red island."

PRACTICE   Match the state names below with the names or other words they come from. If your state is not on the list, try to find out how it got its name.

1. Alaska            Queen Calafia in a Spanish legend
2. Arizona           Queen Elizabeth I of England, the "virgin queen"
3. Mississippi       *Vert Mont,* French, "green mountain"
4. Connecticut       King George II of England
5. Georgia           Alakshap, Eskimo word suggesting "mainland"
6. Virginia          arizonac, Native American, "small spring"
7. California        tanasi, Native American, "friends"
8. Vermont           michigamaw, Native American, "big water"
9. Tennessee         Quienticutt, Native American name of a river
10. Michigan         misisipi, Native American, "large river"

**A.** Each group of words explains a term you studied in this unit. Write the term that is explained.

1. a short poem with strong personal feeling
2. groups of lines in a poem
3. a poem that tells the events in a story
4. a comparison made by using the words *like* or *as*
5. a report explaining your ideas and opinions about a book

**B.** Tell whether a simile or a metaphor is used in each sentence.

1. He was as tall and proud as a giant redwood tree.
2. Lucy twirled around the dance floor like a spinning top.
3. The radiator was a snake hissing steam.
4. The clouds were giant puffs of cotton.
5. His heart pounded like a giant bass drum.

**C.** Rewrite these headings, greeting, and closings. Correct the mistakes.

1. your friend
2. 51 hovey street
   conyers ga 30207
   March 3 19—
3. dear melba
4. 16 pond avenue
   anderson in 46016
   may 5 19—
5. you son
   Danny

*Unit Seven*

*Study Skills*

Chapter 22
**More About Words**

Chapter 23
**Gathering Facts**

Chapter 24
**Writing a Report**

313

## Oh Yeah

I love to go to school
I love to get all A's
I never look forward
To any holidays.

I love to do my homework
It never makes me pout
Even when days are sunny
And all the kids are out.

I never say to my mother
I won't do this or that
I jump right up and obey
You can't call me a brat.

Oh Yeah!!!

*Richard Power*

Do you believe what the speaker in the poem is saying?
What tells you it is not true?

314

Lesson 1    **Using Words That
            Are Related**
Lesson 2    **Using Contractions**
Lesson 3    **Using Prefixes**
Lesson 4    **Using Suffixes**

**315**

# Using Words That Are Related

Knowing about synonyms, antonyms, and homophones will help you understand and use words more precisely. A **synonym** is one of two or more words that have similar meanings. The words *moist* and *damp* are synonyms. An **antonym** is one of two words with opposite meanings. The words *rude* and *polite* are antonyms. A **homophone** is a word that sounds the same as another word but has a different meaning and a different spelling. The words *flour* and *flower* are homophones.

A dictionary may list the synonyms for entry words. A thesaurus is a special kind of dictionary that lists only synonyms. As you learn more about words, you will notice how synonyms help you to express your meaning exactly.

## Example

In this passage from *The Phantom Tollbooth* by Norton Juster, people react to a suggestion. As you read the selection, look to see if the author uses synonyms, antonyms, or homophones.

> "Well, then," said Milo, not understanding why each one said the same thing in a slightly different way, "wouldn't it be simpler to use just one? It would certainly make more sense."
> "Nonsense."
> "Ridiculous."
> "Fantastic."
> "Absurd."
> "Bosh!" they chorused again and continued.

Are the responses to Milo's statement synonyms, antonyms, or homophones?

If you answered that the responses were synonyms or antonyms, explain how the words have similar or opposite meanings.

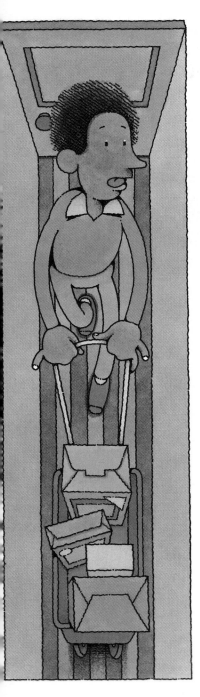

**PRACTICE 1** Write whether the words in each pair are synonyms, antonyms, or homophones.

1. excellent, terrible
2. brave, courageous
3. clean, dirty
4. road, rode
5. famous, well-known
6. due, dew
7. graceful, clumsy
8. find, discover
9. hair, hare
10. thankful, ungrateful

**PRACTICE 2** Write a synonym and an antonym for each of the following words. You may use a dictionary for help.

1. ancient
2. little
3. difficult
4. beautiful
5. amusing

**WRITE** Certain words are overused. Write the following paragraph, supplying synonyms for the words in parentheses. Use a dictionary or a thesaurus if you wish.

Lee felt (bad). She (liked) her new school, and she thought her classmates were (nice). She wanted to be friendly with several of them, but she didn't know how. She was quiet when she (really) wanted to talk. Her face (looked) serious, but she really (liked) to tell jokes and laugh. Some classmates decided that Lee wanted to be left alone. "Why do I act so shy?" Lee (said) to herself.

**GO BEYOND** Work in groups of four. Read the pairs of homophones below. Each person says a sentence that includes one of the words. The other group members in unison spell the word that was used. Continue taking turns until all the words have been used.

fare, fair        mail, male
hall, haul        right, write

# Using Contractions

A **contraction** is a word formed by joining two words and leaving out one or more letters. An **apostrophe** (') is used in place of the missing letters.

Some well-known contractions are forms of *be* or *have* that are joined with *not*—for example, is not = *isn't* and had not = *hadn't*. Others are formed by joining a pronoun and *will*—for example, I will = *I'll* and she will = *she'll*.

## Example

Here are some frequently used contractions.

| I am | I'm | is not | isn't |
|------|------|---------|--------|
| you are | you're | are not | aren't |
| she is | she's | has not | hasn't |
| we have | we've | had not | hadn't |
| they had | they'd | have not | haven't |
| he will | he'll | was not | wasn't |
| it will | it'll | were not | weren't |

What letter or letters were left out when each contraction was formed?

Which contractions that are not listed can you think of?

**PRACTICE 1**   Find and write the contraction from each sentence. Then write the two words from which the contraction is formed.

1. I didn't spoil your fun.
2. I can't read Roman numerals.
3. Larry wasn't fair.
4. I couldn't tell time when I was your age.
5. I didn't have anyone to play with.

**PRACTICE 2**   Rewrite the following sentences. Use apostrophes where they belong in the contractions.

1. Eli isnt the only boy in his family.
2. However, hes the oldest.
3. Its difficult to tell him apart from his younger brother.
4. Theyre both on the swimming team.
5. They both play the drums, and theyll soon join the school band.

**WRITE**   Think of a sentence that describes each of these situations. Include at least one contraction in each sentence you write.

1. a food that you do not like to eat
2. a place you will be visiting in the future
3. the prettiest thing you have ever seen
4. a person you would like to meet
5. something you do not think you will have to do when you are an adult

**GO BEYOND**   Join a group of four classmates. Share your sentences from the last exercise. See how many of your sentences are the same. The group should choose one sentence as best for each situation. Share your sentences with the class.

# Using Prefixes

A **prefix** is a group of letters added at the beginning of a word: *tri- + cycle = tricycle*. Adding a prefix changes the meaning of a word. Prefixes have their own meanings and are important building blocks of language. By learning the meanings of prefixes, you can add a great number of words to those you already know.

## Example

Here are some common prefixes.

| PREFIX | MEANING | EXAMPLE |
|--------|---------|---------|
| bi- | two, twice | bicycle |
| dis- | not, away | dishonest |
| in- | not | inexpensive |
| mis- | badly, wrongly | misspell |
| non- | not | nonsense |
| re- | back, again | reheat |
| semi- | half, partly | semicircle |
| sub- | under, below | subfreezing |
| trans- | across | transatlantic |
| tri- | three | tricolor |
| un- | not | unimportant |
| uni- | one, single | unicycle |

**PRACTICE 1** Match each numbered word with its meaning. Write the letter of the correct meaning.

1. dishonest
2. misspell
3. subfreezing
4. bicycle
5. tricolor
6. semicircle
7. transatlantic
8. nonsense
9. unicycle
10. inexpensive

a. across the Atlantic
b. half circle
c. one-wheeled vehicle
d. having three colors
e. not honest
f. not making sense
g. spell incorrectly
h. two-wheeled vehicle
i. not expensive
j. below freezing

**PRACTICE 2** Add one of the prefixes below to the word in parentheses to complete each sentence. Write the word with the prefix.

mis-　　in-　　non-　　un-　　re-

1. My brother feels very (comfortable) in a tie.
2. Taking a shower on a hot day always (freshes) me.
3. Dad has been working (stop) for five hours.
4. Johnny is an (experienced) skier.
5. My bread turned out badly because I (read) the directions.

**WRITE** Write four or five sentences about someone who misreads, misunderstands, or forgets to use a prefix and gets into trouble. Get help from a dictionary if necessary.

**GO BEYOND** Work in groups of four. Each group works with a different prefix introduced in the lesson. Together, the members write a word chain by listing as many words as possible that begin with the prefix. Compare word chains.

# LESSON 4  **Using Suffixes**

A **suffix** is a group of letters added at the end of a word. Like prefixes, suffixes have meanings of their own. Adding a suffix can even change a word to another part of speech. For example, adding the suffix *-ation* changes the verb *transport* to the noun *transportation*.

## Example

Here are some common suffixes. Notice how the spelling of a word may change when a suffix is added.

SUFFIXES USED TO FORM NOUNS

| WORD | SUFFIX | MEANING OF SUFFIX | NEW WORD |
|------|--------|-------------------|----------|
| occupy | -ation | action, condition | occup<u>ation</u> |
| science | -ist | doer, believer in | scient<u>ist</u> |
| instruct | -or | doer | instruct<u>or</u> |

SUFFIXES USED TO FORM ADJECTIVES

| WORD | SUFFIX | MEANING OF SUFFIX | NEW WORD |
|------|--------|-------------------|----------|
| poison | -ous | full of, marked by | poison<u>ous</u> |
| girl | -ish | like, suggesting | girl<u>ish</u> |

SUFFIXES USED TO FORM VERBS

| WORD | SUFFIX | MEANING OF SUFFIX | NEW WORD |
|------|--------|-------------------|----------|
| short | -en | make, become | short<u>en</u> |
| equal | -ize | make, cause to be | equal<u>ize</u> |

SUFFIXES USED TO FORM ADVERBS

| WORD | SUFFIX | MEANING OF SUFFIX | NEW WORD |
|------|--------|-------------------|----------|
| quick | -ly | in a certain way | quick<u>ly</u> |
| hour | -ly | every | hour<u>ly</u> |

*Study Skills*

**PRACTICE 1** Use the meaning of the suffix to help you write the meaning of each underlined word.

1. Mr. Lee's class was studying <u>multiplication</u>.
2. Len tried to <u>memorize</u> facts from the multiplication table.
3. Mr. Lee gave a test <u>weekly</u>.
4. In the beginning the tests were ten minutes long, but he decided to <u>lengthen</u> them to fifteen minutes.
5. Louis was a <u>perfectionist</u>, and he decided to get 100 percent on all the tests.

**PRACTICE 2** Add one of the suffixes below to the word in parentheses to complete each sentence. Write the sentence.

-ish    -ist    ize    -or    -ous

1. My birthday was a (joy) event.
2. Ask the (conduct) if this is our stop.
3. Jenny is an excellent (violin).
4. That was a (child) thing to do.
5. Andy, will you please (alphabet) these cards?

**WRITE** Using words that you formed in Practice 2, write new sentences. Make sure your sentences show that you understand the meanings of the words with suffixes.

**GO BEYOND** Work with a partner. You will need twelve index cards. On each of eight cards write a suffix used in this lesson. Number the other four cards 1 through 4. Put the cards in two stacks, facedown. One player starts by picking a card from the suffix stack and reading the suffix aloud. The player then picks a card from the number stack and says as many words with the suffix as the numeral on the card says. Shuffle the number card back into the stack after each turn. When the suffix cards have all been used, the activity is over.

## Practice

**A.** Write each sentence, using the correct homophone.

1. We walked up the (aisle, isle) toward the stage.
2. The prince is the (heir, air) to the throne.
3. I used two cups of (flour, flower) in the pineapple bread.
4. The party last night was (grate, great)!
5. I went outside to (shoo, shoe) the chickens back into the coop.

**B.** Write the contraction for each set of underlined words.

1. They are going to a museum.
2. It is on Huntington Avenue, or so I have been told.
3. They could not find the museum the first time they tried.
4. I will be glad when I have had a chance to see that art museum.

324

5. We have been looking forward to the exhibit of Irish art treasures.

**C.** Match each word in the first column with the correct meaning in the second column.

1. pianist          a. like a kitten
2. misspent         b. one-wheeled bike
3. submarine        c. spent wrongly
4. kittenish        d. write a drama
5. triangle         e. make longer
6. lengthen         f. underwater ship
7. happily          g. piano player
8. unicycle         h. figure with
9. inconsiderate       three angles
10. dramatize       i. in a happy way
                    j. not thoughtful

**D.** Write both a synonym and an antonym for each word.

1. orderly
2. plain
3. sad
4. quiet
5. heavy

**E.** Rewrite each sentence, using a synonym for each underlined word.

1. Marcia noticed the picture hanging on the wall.
2. Our club is planning an excellent show.
3. The costume is well made and very pretty.
4. The rainy skies made me feel gloomy.
5. Mr. Hagen has a merry personality.

## Composition

Each of the words listed below is overused. For each overused word write a synonym. Then use the synonym in a sentence. If the synonym that you use has a prefix, underline the prefix once. Underline a suffix twice if you choose a synonym that has one.

1. neat
2. throw
3. run
4. say
5. like
6. find
7. look
8. lose
9. little
10. tired

## Advanced Challenge

Word roots are words or word parts from which other words are formed. You use many in your spoken and written language every day. Many roots have meanings that come from other languages.

The Greek and Latin languages are the sources of many words in English. The word *telephone* is a good example. *Tele* comes from a Greek word meaning "at a distance." *Phone* comes from a Greek word meaning "sound" or "voice." Sometimes a root word can stand alone: *cent, script, verb.*

Think of as many words as you can that include *tele* or *phone*. Combine those parts with prefixes, suffixes, other word parts, or even other words. Then do the same for these roots.

| ROOT | MEANING |
| --- | --- |
| 1. graph | write |
| 2. port | door, carry |
| 3. dict | say, tell |
| 4. scope | see |
| 5. scrib | write |

Find three more word roots on your own. See how many words you can make from each.

**WORD PARTS**

*Mis-* as a prefix means "badly," "wrongly," or "unfavorably." *Dis-* means "apart from," "separated from," "not," or "the opposite of."

PRACTICE   Guess the meaning of each underlined word. Then check that meaning with the meaning given in a dictionary.

"The smile on your face does not <u>mislead</u> me, my friend," said the old man. "I sense some <u>discomfort</u> on your part—correct?"

"Yes, sir," said the youngster. "You have not <u>misread</u> my feelings. I have been <u>dishonorably</u> discharged.

"Oh, what a <u>miscarriage</u> of justice!" said the old man. "How did you fall into <u>disfavor</u>?"

"Alas," said his companion, "I <u>mishandled</u> so many tasks that my employer was <u>displeased</u>. She was probably right to <u>discontinue</u> me."

"And now?" said the old man.

"Now," said the youth sadly, "I will think about my <u>misconduct</u> and decide how to correct this <u>misimpression</u> of my behavior.

Lesson 1    **Finding Sources of Information**
Lesson 2    **Using a Dictionary**
Lesson 3    **Using an Encyclopedia**
Lesson 4    **Using Other Reference Books**
Lesson 5    **Using Library Card Catalogs**
Lesson 6    **Finding Facts in Books**

327

# Finding Sources of Information

Many sources of information can provide answers to your questions. One source is a newspaper. Newspaper articles cover many subjects and are often your best source for up-to-date information.

Another good source is people. Government officials, nurses, farmers, computer programmers—these people can supply information because of their jobs. Other people have seen or heard things, firsthand, that you would like to know about.

## Example

Willa's town is considering a law that would require all dogs to be on a leash. Willa and her classmates want to know whether the law is a good idea. Here are notes for their research.

QUESTIONS
How many dogs are in our town?
Have dogs caused much damage?
Who is for the leash law, and who is against it?

SOURCES
head of town animal shelter
citizens
editor of local paper
persons in town government

Why did the class select each source?
What other questions and sources might the students use?

*Study Skills*

**PRACTICE 1** Write the words *person* or *newspaper* to tell which would have information about each topic.
1. whether it was fun to be a child fifty years ago
2. what the high and low temperatures of one day are
3. what the cafeteria in a nearby factory is like
4. which films will be shown on public TV this week
5. which grocery store has the most items on sale

**PRACTICE 2** Match the groups. Beside the number of each group, write the kind of information it can give you.

GROUP
1. police department
2. fire department
3. emergency room at hospital
4. record department at town hall or county seat
5. water department or department of public works

KIND OF INFORMATION
a. the number of smoke detectors you need in your home
b. the system your town uses to supply water
c. how to protect your home from burglars
d. what to do if someone has a bad fall at home
e. the number of babies born in your town in the last year

**WRITE** Look through newspapers to see how these types of information are organized and written: weather forecasts, entertainment listings, advertisements about jobs. For each of these, write an example that follows the form used in the newspaper.

**GO BEYOND** Produce a newspaper for your class. Use your examples from the last exercise. Write other features found in a newspaper—local news, sports, comics, and so on.

# Using a Dictionary

A **dictionary** contains information about words. Each word listed in a dictionary is an **entry word**. Entry words appear in dark type and are always listed in alphabetical order.

Usually entry words are divided into **syllables,** or units of sound. In most dictionaries an extra space is placed between each syllable in a word. The entry word *passenger* would be written *pas sen ger* to show that it had three syllables. The syllable with the **accent** mark (✓) is stressed or said with more force.

Most dictionaries give the pronunciation, the part of speech, and the **definition,** or meaning, of an entry word. When a word has more than one spelling, dictionaries list these, too. Dictionaries may also list and explain synonyms and the origins, or history, of the entry words.

## Example

This dictionary entry for the word *figure* tells you many things.

**fig ure** (fig´yər), **1** symbol for a number. 1, 2, 3, 4, etc., are figures. **2** use numbers to find out the answer to some problem; calculate: *figure out one's taxes. Can you figure the cost of painting this room?* 3 **figures,** *pl.* calculations using figures; arithmetic: *She is very good at figures.* **4** amount or value given in figures; price: *The figure for that house is very high.* **5** form enclosing a surface or space: *Circles, triangles, squares, cubes, and spheres are geometric figures.* **6** form or shape: *In the darkness she saw dim figures moving.* **7** way in which a person looks or appears: *The survivor of the earthquake was a figure of distress.* **8** person; character: *Napoleon is a well-known figure in history.* **9** stand out; appear: *The names of great leaders figure in the story of human progress.* **10** picture; drawing; diagram; illustration: *This book has many figures to help explain words.* **11** a design or pattern: *the figures in the wallpaper.* **12** outline traced by movements: *figures made by an airplane.* **13** set of movements in dancing or skating. **14** figure of speech. **15** INFORMAL. think; consider: *I figured I should stop where I was.* **16** INFORMAL. to seem likely or to be expected: *They didn't come to our party; well, it figured.* 1,3–8,10–14 *n.,* 2,9,15,16 *v.,* **fig ured, fig ur ing.** [*Figure* came into English about 700 years ago from French *figure,* and can be traced back to Latin *fingere,* meaning "to form, shape."]

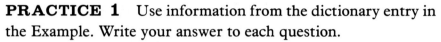

**PRACTICE 1** Use information from the dictionary entry in the Example. Write your answer to each question.

1. How many syllables are in the word *figure?*
2. Which syllable in the word *figure* has an accent mark?
3. How many meanings are given?
4. The word *figure* can be traced back to what two languages?
5. What is the meaning of *fingere?*

**PRACTICE 2** The word *figure* has a different meaning in each sentence. Write the number of each meaning as given in the Example.

1. Nellie can figure out how much each person must pay.
2. A skater must perform many special figures in the Olympics.
3. Is that figure a three or an eight?
4. Can you give me a figure on the cost of repairs?
5. Benjamin Franklin was a very important figure.

**WRITE** Find in a dictionary the meaning of *yeoman, equerry, crony, corporation,* and *attainment.* Write original sentences using at least three of those words. Give enough information to make the meaning of each word clear.

**GO BEYOND** Work in four groups. One member is the leader. Using a dictionary, take turns finding a word that no one knows. Each person then writes a made-up definition for the word, writing it as though it were from the dictionary. The leader writes the real definition, collects and shuffles all the definitions, and reads them aloud. Each person guesses which definition is correct. Each correct guess scores one point.

# Using an Encyclopedia

An **encyclopedia** contains articles about many topics. An encyclopedia may be contained in one book or in a set of books. Each book in the set is a **volume**. The index to an encyclopedia may be a separate volume.

All encyclopedia articles and volumes are arranged in alphabetical order. Letters or numbers on the spine, or edge, of each book guide readers to the correct volumes. **Guide words** at the top of each page show the topics covered on that page and help the reader locate articles quickly.

Since information about a topic may appear in more than one place, encyclopedia articles often contain cross-references. A **cross-reference** lists the other articles in the encyclopedia related to that topic.

## Example

Lynne, who is interested in swimming, read the following encyclopedia article.

**SKIN DIVING** Skin divers wear face masks and equipment that allows them to breathe while underwater. Some skin divers catch fish with spears. Others take pictures of fish and beautiful underwater scenery with special waterproof cameras. Other skin divers explore sea caves and shipwrecks.

Skin diving can be dangerous, and divers can drown. Take good instructions before skin diving on your own. Always have a partner with you when you dive. *See also* **DEEP-SEA EXPLORING; DIVING; SWIMMING.**

*Study Skills*

**PRACTICE 1**   Use these words to complete the sentences. Write the sentences.

letters          alphabetically          numbers          volume
articles         cross-reference         guide words

1. A _____ is one book in an encyclopedia set.
2. The spine of each book in an encyclopedia set has _____ or _____ on it.
3. A _____ lists the other articles in the encyclopedia related to a particular topic.
4. Encyclopedia articles are arranged _____ .
5. Readers use _____ on each encyclopedia page to find _____ quickly.

**PRACTICE 2**   Use the encyclopedia article in the Example to answer these questions.
1. What is the title of the article?
2. What letter will be included in the volume that contains that article?
3. What equipment do skin divers wear?
4. Why should a diver take a partner along?
5. In which other articles might you find facts about skin diving?

**WRITE**   Write an encyclopedia article of one or two paragraphs about your favorite sport, hobby, or activity. State your topic in the title. Use facts rather than opinions in your article. End with one or two cross-references.

**GO BEYOND**   Share the encyclopedia article you wrote in the Write exercise with three or four classmates. What did they like about your article? What could be improved? Revise your article and include it in a classroom encyclopedia. You may illustrate your article if you wish.

# Using Other Reference Books

You have learned how to use two reference books—a dictionary and an encyclopedia. There are other reference books. In a library the reference books are kept together in one area. Since they cannot be checked out, they must be used in the library.

An **almanac** is a one-volume reference book that contains brief facts on many subjects. For example, an almanac can answer questions about the tides, famous composers, world records, and state capitals. It is usually printed each year and tells much about the events of that year.

An **atlas** is a book of maps. It contains information on such topics as the crops, climate, and populations of various places.

A **biographical dictionary** contains information about well-known people. Many libraries have special biographical dictionaries that list well-known people in certain fields, such as sports or music.

A **thesaurus** is a dictionary of synonyms grouped according to ideas. It is especially helpful to writers and speakers looking for substitutes for overused words or phrases.

## Example

Joseph will be spending next summer on his grandmother's farm in Maine. He will plant and harvest vegetables and help with the haying. He went to the library for answers to these questions.

Which vegetables grow best in Maine?
How much rainfall is expected there each summer?

Which books would probably answer each question?
What else might these reference books tell Joseph about Maine?

**PRACTICE 1** Write the name of the reference book that correctly completes each sentence.

an atlas          a thesaurus          a biographical dictionary
an almanac        an encyclopedia

1. To find a map showing climate in Mexico, look in _____ .
2. Look for a synonym for the word *beautiful* in _____ .
3. Brief facts about the most important imports and exports of Mexico would be in _____ .
4. For detailed information about the geography, history, products, and people of Mexico, look in _____ .
5. _____ or _____ would contain information about Benito Juarez, one of the most famous Mexican presidents.

**PRACTICE 2** For each item listed, write two questions that you could answer by using that reference book.
1. an atlas
2. an almanac
3. a thesaurus
4. an encyclopedia
5. a biographical dictionary

**WRITE** Use the questions written in Practice 2 that you could answer by using an encyclopedia. Look up the information. You may have to look at more than one article to find an answer. In your own words, write a brief answer to each question.

**GO BEYOND** Make a class thesaurus. Each person should be responsible for one page. Choose an overused word. Write as many synonyms for that word as you can. Then show what each synonym means by using it in a sentence. Illustrate some of the words. Arrange and bind all completed pages in alphabetical order. Use the book as a class reference.

### The Horses

It has turned to snow in the night.
The horses have put on
their long fur stockings
and they are wearing
fur capes with high necks
out of which the device
of their ears makes four statues.

Their tails have caught flecks
of snow and hang down
loose as bedsheets.

They stand nose to nose
in the blue light that coats
the field before sunup
and rub dry their old kisses.

*Maxine Kumin*

Suppose you wanted to find out how horses survive in the winter. Where would you look for the information?

# Using Library Card Catalogs

A **card catalog** lists all the books in a library. Books are listed on three kinds of cards.

An **author card** has the author's name at the top, last name first. A **title card** has the title of the book at the top. A **subject card** has the subject of the book at the top. Each card may include a brief summary of the book.

All catalog cards are alphabetized by the first word on the top line. In the upper left corner of each card is a **call number,** usually one or more letters and numerals, showing where to locate the book.

## Example

Here are the three kinds of cards from a card catalog.

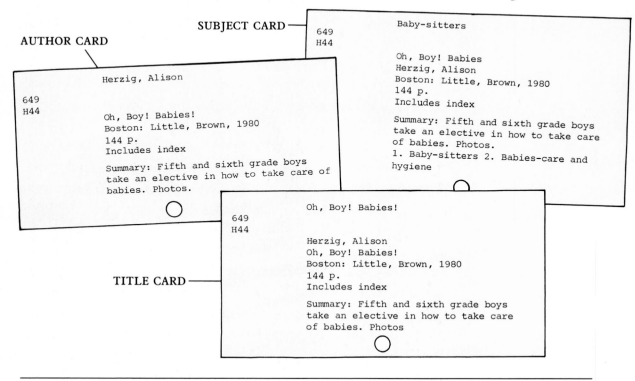

AUTHOR CARD

SUBJECT CARD

TITLE CARD

```
              Herzig, Alison
649
H44
        Oh, Boy! Babies!
        Boston: Little, Brown, 1980
        144 p.
        Includes index
        Summary: Fifth and sixth grade boys
        take an elective in how to take care of
        babies. Photos.
```

```
649          Baby-sitters
H44
        Oh, Boy! Babies
        Herzig, Alison
        Boston: Little, Brown, 1980
        144 p.
        Includes index
        Summary: Fifth and sixth grade boys
        take an elective in how to take care
        of babies. Photos.
        1. Baby-sitters 2. Babies-care and
        hygiene
```

```
            Oh, Boy! Babies!
649
H44
        Herzig, Alison
        Oh, Boy! Babies!
        Boston: Little, Brown, 1980
        144 p.
        Includes index
        Summary: Fifth and sixth grade boys
        take an elective in how to take care
        of babies. Photos
```

**PRACTICE 1**   Write the answer to each question about the catalog cards in the Example.

1. What is the title of the book?
2. Who is the author?
3. What is the subject of the book?
4. What call number does the book have?
5. What company published the book and when?

**PRACTICE 2**   What kind of catalog card would give you the best answer to each question: *author, title,* or *subject*?

1. Where could you find books about baseball?
2. Does your library have any books by Natalie Babbitt?
3. Where would you look for information about Canada?
4. Who wrote the book *Arilla Sun Down*?
5. Does the library have any mysteries that you have not read?
6. What is the call number for *All About Weather*?
7. Has John Fitzgerald written other books besides *The Great Brain*?
8. What is the name of Katherine Paterson's newest book?
9. Who wrote *Sing Down the Moon*?
10. What books does the library have on weaving?

**WRITE**   Choose two books that were mentioned in Practice 2. If possible, they should be books that you have not already read. Look up the books in the card catalog. From the information given on the cards, choose one of the books to read. Write a paragraph explaining your choice.

**GO BEYOND**   Choose a specific subject such as guitars or steamboats. Go to a library. See whether the subject is listed in the card catalog. If it is not, see if you can find it under a more general heading. List the titles, authors, and call numbers of at least four books about your subject.

**Finding Facts in Books**

Parts of a book guide you to the information within the book. Other parts give you important information about the publication of a book.

The **title page** is one of the first pages in a book. It gives the title, author, publisher, and the place of publication. The **copyright page** follows the title page and tells when the book was published. The **table of contents** lists the chapters or stories in the book in order.

At the back of the book you may find a glossary and a bibliography, as well as an index. The **glossary** is a small dictionary of special words found in the book. The **bibliography** is a list of other books on the same subject. The author may have used some or all of them as references. The **index** lists in alphabetical order all topics included in the book. The index also tells the pages on which the topics are found.

## ▬ Example ▬

Here are three pages from the front of a book. One page from the back of a book is shown on page 341.

TITLE PAGE

BILL STOTT

Write to the Point

AND FEEL BETTER
ABOUT YOUR WRITING

ANCHOR PRESS/DOUBLEDAY
GARDEN CITY, NEW YORK
1984

COPYRIGHT PAGE

ISBN: 0-385-19371-8
Copyright © 1984 by Bill Stott
All Rights Reserved
Printed in the United States of America
First Edition

Library of Congress Cataloging in Publication Data

Stott, Bill, 1940–
Write to the point.

Includes index.
1. English language—Rhetoric. 2. English language—Grammar—1950–
I. Title.
PE1408.S7665 1984   808'.042   83-24370

TABLE OF CONTENTS

1 WHAT COUNTS IN WRITING 1
  FIRST THINGS FIRST 2
  FAULTS 4
  A SECOND TRY 5
  CONFESSION TIME 6
  THE MESSAGE 7
  BAD WRITING 8
  GOOD BAD WRITING 9
  A PROTEST 11
  MY MISTAKE 14

2 HOW TO FIND SOMETHING TO SAY 20
  WHAT WE READ FOR 22
  CONTEXT 23
  CHANGING EXPECTATIONS 26
  SO WHAT? 30
  ORIGINALITY 35
  THE QUESTION AGAIN 38
  A B.A. FOR F.S. 41
  SEVEN SURVIVAL PLOYS 44

*Study Skills*

**PRACTICE 1**   Write which part of a book you would use to find each type of information.

1. the titles of the chapters
2. the page with information on a certain topic
3. a list of other books on the same subject
4. definitions of unusual words used in the book
5. the year the book was published

**PRACTICE 2**   Use this textbook for help. Write the answer to each question.

1. What is the title of this book?
2. Who is one of the authors of this book?
3. Which pages have information about nouns?
4. On what pages does Chapter 16 begin?
5. What year was the book written?

**WRITE**   Use a book you have not read before. Choose three chapters from the table of contents. Write a few sentences telling what you would expect to find in each chapter. Then check to see whether you were correct.

INDEX

Acheson, Dean, and
  bureaucratic prose, 90–91
Adler, Renata, and the bitterest
  words a writer can hear, 35
Adverbs, lurching, 109
"Affect" and "effect," their
  correct use illustrated in
  adjacent sentences, 24
Alliteration, to be avoided,
  109
All-of-a-topic-in-one-place rule,
  73–74, 121
"And," "but," and "or," fine
  words to start sentences
  with, 119, 207
Apostrophe, the, 173–74
Aristotle's organizational ideal,
  60
Arnold, Matthew, on style,
  136
Associated Press, the, and
  apostrophes, 174
Assonance, to be avoided, 109

Auden, W. H., on handwriting
  *vs.* typewriting, 137
Audience for informal writing,
  92–95

Bad writing, defined, 8
Baker, Russell, his parody of
  bureaucratic writing, 80, 133
Barth, John, and a rarefied
  point of grammar, 147
Barthes, Roland, on the "I" in
  writing, 95
Bateson, Gregory, on scientific
  truth, 66–67
Benny, Jack, on humility and
  humor, 97
Beyer, Lisa, on word
  processing, 142
Bibliography, 191–92;
  annotated bibliography on
  books about writing, 192–
  98; annotated bibliography
  same as bibliographical

**GO BEYOND**   Work with a partner. In your classroom or library find a book that has an index. In the index find an entry that has three to five pages listed for one topic. Look up those references. See what information is given on the different pages. Are you satisfied with the amount and kind of information you can locate by using the index? What other entries in the index would be helpful for your topic?

*Gathering Facts*

## Practice

**A.** Select from the list the type of reference book you would use to find the information noted in each item below.

atlas                    encyclopedia
almanac                  thesaurus
biographical dictionary

1. the names of President Benjamin Harrison's brothers and sisters
2. the distance from Smolensk to Riga
3. the winners of the National Football League championship for the last three years
4. a synonym for the word *pleasant*
5. how many kinds of turtles there are

**B.** Make up a library catalog card for the book described below. You can make an author card, a title card, or a subject card. The book is *Wild Animals As Pets*. It was written by Seymour Simon and illustrated by Betty Fraser. It has the call number 636.088 and was published in 1975 by Viking Press in New York. It tells how to collect and care for small wild animals.

**C.** Write which source of information, newspapers or people, you would consult to find each piece of information.
1. What happened in yesterday's election?
2. How was gas rationed during World War II?
3. Is Spotcare Cleaners having a special offer this week?
4. What was life in the United States like during the 1950s?
5. What movies are playing at theaters near your home?

**D.** Which part of a book would you use to answer each of the questions?
1. When was the book published?
2. What does *refraction* mean?
3. What is the title of the third chapter?
4. On what page is there information about the Doppler effect?
5. What other books have been written on the same topic?

**E.** Find a more specific word for each numbered word below. If possible, use a thesaurus.
1. beautiful        4. small
2. dark             5. great
3. soft

## Composition

Choose two of the following questions. Consult a source of information that will provide you with answers. Follow the instructions after each question.

1. Who was John Fitch? Summarize his life in a single paragraph.
2. What books in your library offer information about weather forecasting? Make a list of the books. Include the call numbers.
3. Who won the decathlon in the last ten Summer Olympics? Make a list of the winners and the countries they represented.
4. Where is Andorra? Describe the country in a single paragraph.
5. What are the three synonyms for the noun *size*? Use each in a sentence that shows the meaning of the synonym.

## Advanced Challenge

Think of three places you might like to visit but know little about. Which place do you imagine would be your favorite?

Do some research about each of the three places. Decide what you most want to learn about them. Think, too, about where to find the best information. Go to the library if you can.

After you have found the reference books you need, spend ten minutes reading about each of the three places. Then answer these questions.

Did you find the information you wanted about all of the places? About some of them?

Where did you find the best information about each place?

Which of the three places would you call your favorite choice now? Have you changed you mind? If so, what things did you learn that made you change your mind?

343

## DICTIONARY

Suppose you read this sentence: They took it as a fell sign when the queen did not return. To understand the sentence, you probably would have to look up the word *fell*. And if you did, you might first find *fell* described as the past tense of *fall*. This meaning does not fit the sentence. So you would need to look further. *Fell* actually has several different meanings. Read on until you find one that makes sense in the sentence about the fell sign.

**fell** (fel), past tense of **fall.** *Snow fell last night.*
   **fell** (fel) 1. cause to fall; knock down: *The blow felled her to the ground.* 2. cut down (a tree). 3. turn down and stitch one edge of (a seam) over the other.
   **fell** (fel), 1. extremely bad; cruel, fierce; terrible: *a fell blow.* 2. deadly, destructive: *a fell disease.*
   **fell** (fel), skin or hide of an animal.

Which meaning would make the most sense in the sentence about the fell sign?

PRACTICE   Use a dictionary. Write the best definition for each underlined word.
1. Jorge finished in five minutes <u>flat</u>.
2. It took us a long time to <u>compose</u> ourselves.
3. Who is that calf's <u>dam</u>?
4. Did you <u>mat</u> the picture?
5. The envelope had the President's <u>frank</u> instead of a stamp.

# Chapter 24
# Writing a Report

Lesson 1    **Planning a Report**
Lesson 2    **Recording Information**
Lesson 3    **Organizing Information**
Lesson 4    **Outlining Information**
Lesson 5    **Writing from an Outline**
Lesson 6    **Revising a Report**

345

# LESSON 1 Planning a Report

Choosing a topic is the first step in the writing process. To find a suitable topic for a report, first think of a subject that interests you, such as sports or music. Then narrow that general subject to a specific subject, such as softball or the clarinet. Finally, narrow that subject to a topic you can write about in a page or two, such as the beginnings of softball, or how to make a reed for a clarinet.

After you have chosen a topic, list the questions you would like to answer about that topic. These questions will guide your research.

## Example

Marie decided to write a report on the Loch Ness monster. She wrote the following questions to guide her research.

What is Loch Ness?
What could the Loch Ness monster be?
How did it get to Loch Ness?

Where do you think Marie might find answers to her questions?
What other questions could she ask?

**PRACTICE 1**   Marie "brainstormed" while trying to decide on a topic for her report. Below are some of the ideas she had. For each numbered item, write the titles in a different order, going from the most general subject to the narrowest.

1. Exciting Hobbies, Parachuting, Hobbies
2. Exploration of Caves, Caves, Mammoth Cave
3. Dinosaurs, Dinosaur National Monument Park, Dinosaurs in Warm Climates
4. Using Acrylic Paints, Art, Sculpture and Painting
5. The Loch Ness Monster, Monsters Living Today, The Loch Ness Monster and Bigfoot

**PRACTICE 2**   From each pair choose the question that is more useful for doing research. Write the letter of that question.

1. a. Why shouldn't people smoke?
   b. How does smoking affect the lungs?
2. a. What skills are needed to design a bridge?
   b. How are bridges built?
3. a. Where are there water problems?
   b. What regions in the United States need more water?
4. a. Who are some famous explorers?
   b. Who are the important explorers of the Arctic?
5. a. How do banks use computers?
   b. Who uses computers, and how are computers used?

**WRITE**   Choose a topic narrow enough to write about in a one-or two-page research paper. Write five or six questions about it. (If these questions do not lead to enough information, you may add or combine questions later.)

**GO BEYOND**   Find and list sources of information for your topic. Any source you learned about in Chapter 23 might be helpful. Think of every possibility.

**Recording Information**

The following hints will help you take notes on a research topic. Keep a list of the questions you want to answer in your report. As you do your research, write and answer each question on a separate sheet of paper. Later you can find the best order of facts for your report.

To take notes from a written source, first read the entire article or chapter. Then write in your own words only the information you need. Finally, record your source—title, author, publisher, place of publication, date, and page numbers.

## Example

Marie took some notes for her report on the Loch Ness monster.

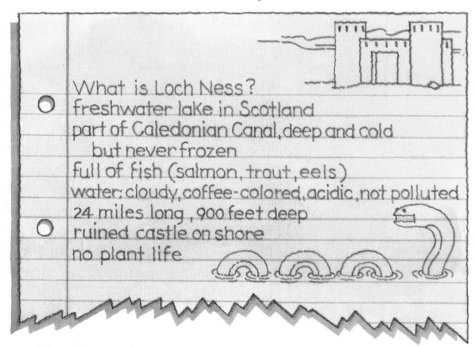

What is Loch Ness?
freshwater lake in Scotland
part of Caledonian Canal, deep and cold
     but never frozen
full of fish (salmon, trout, eels)
water: cloudy, coffee-colored, acidic, not polluted
24 miles long, 900 feet deep
ruined castle on shore
no plant life

How does each note help answer the research question?
Would you like to know other details about Loch Ness?

**PRACTICE 1** Beside each number write *yes* if the detail answers the question What evidence of the Loch Ness monster has been discovered? Write *no* for each detail that does not answer that question.

1. St. Columbus saw Loch Ness monster 1400 years ago.
2. 3000 recorded sightings since 1930
3. estimated weight—2500 pounds
4. photographed by underwater cameras
5. very fast moving animal

**PRACTICE 2** Three of the sentences below tell how the monster supposedly looks. Write that information as notes. Do not write sentences.

1. The Loch Ness monster has many names, but most people call it Nessie.
2. It has a small head and a long slender neck about four or five feet in length.
3. People usually describe Nessie as being gray or black, but some people think it is a greenish color.
4. People have seen the whole body, just the head, or sometimes just an animal moving quickly through the water.
5. In general people agree that Nessie is long and somewhat like an eel.

**WRITE** Read through your sources and take notes for your report. Put each note under its appropriate question. You do not have to write complete sentences.

**GO BEYOND** Work with a partner. Discuss the notes you took to answer one of your questions. Tell what you learned about the subject in answering that question. Did telling the information in your own words help you understand it better? Save your notes for later use.

# Organizing Information

After taking notes, you are ready to **organize** the information you have found. Begin by making sure you have gathered enough information to answer each question you asked. Then, arrange the information in a logical order.

Think of each question and answer as an individual section or paragraph in your report. Decide which question should come first. Then, arrange the questions in the order that they will be answered in your report.

## Example

Marie planned to begin her report with a description of the Loch Ness monster. Here are her notes as she organized them.

QUESTION
What is the Loch Ness monster?

ANSWERS
1. 20 foot long animal
2. shaped somewhat like an eel
3. gray, black, or greenish color
4. small head, long slender neck about four or five feet long
5. like a "monstrous snail" out of water

How does each detail answer the question?
What other details might readers want to know about the monster?

**PRACTICE 1** Here is the next question Marie plans to answer in her report. Write the question. Then write the five answers to that question in an order that makes sense.

QUESTION
What is Loch Ness?

ANSWERS
1. deep and cold but never frozen
2. 3000 recorded sightings since 1930
3. freshwater lake
4. cloudy, coffee-colored water
5. underwater pictures of monster in early 1970s
6. part of Caledonian Canal in Scotland
7. in 1955 banker photographed monster
8. famous photograph of monster taken by surgeon, 1934
9. St. Columbus saw monster 1400 years ago
10. 24 miles long, 900 feet deep

**PRACTICE 2** Here is Marie's third question. Write it. The answers to the question can be found in Practice 1. Write those answers in an order that makes sense.

QUESTION
What evidence of the Loch Ness monster has been discovered?

**WRITE** Review the notes you took during the last lesson. Arrange your questions and their answers in an order that makes sense. Save your work for use in the next lesson.

**GO BEYOND** Discuss the organization of your notes with a partner. Does your partner agree with the order in which you arranged your questions and their answers? Can your partner suggest a better organization?

**Outlining Information**

After organizing your information, you are ready to make an **outline** to guide your writing.

First, turn each question into a main heading. For example, the question, "What is Loch Ness?" can be converted into the heading "Home." Begin each main heading with a capital letter and number it with a Roman numeral and a period (I., II., III., and so on).

Then, turn each answer into a subheading. Begin each subheading with a capital letter. Indent the subheading and mark it with a capital letter and a period (A., B., C., and so on ).

## Example

Here is part of Marie's outline.

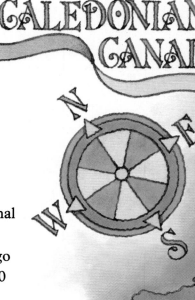

**The Loch Ness Monster**

I. Appearance
   A. About 20 feet long
   B. Shaped a little like an eel
   C. Gray, black, or green
II. Home
   A. Loch Ness, a freshwater lake
   B. Part of Scotland's Caledonian Canal
III. Evidence of monster
   A. St. Columbus saw it 1400 years ago
   B. Seen at least 3000 times since 1930

How does each subheading explain its main heading?
What will Marie number her next main heading?
How will the subheadings be lettered?

*Study Skills*

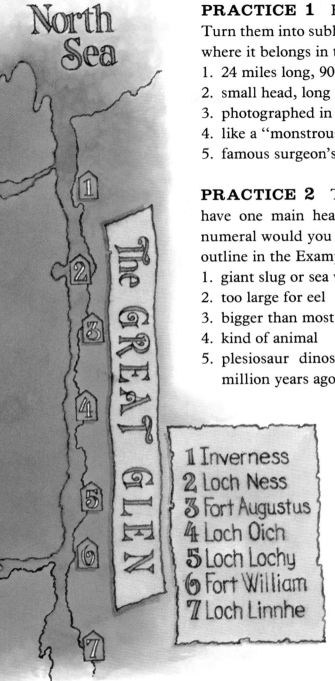

North
Sea

The GREAT GLEN

1 Inverness
2 Loch Ness
3 Fort Augustus
4 Loch Oich
5 Loch Lochy
6 Fort William
7 Loch Linnhe

**PRACTICE 1**   Here are five notes from Marie's research. Turn them into subheadings. Letter each subheading to indicate where it belongs in the outline shown in the Example.

1. 24 miles long, 900 feet deep
2. small head, long slender neck about four or five feet long
3. photographed in 1955 by banker
4. like a "monstrous snail" out of water
5. famous surgeon's photograph taken in 1934

**PRACTICE 2**   Turn these notes into outline form. You will have one main heading and four subheadings. What Roman numeral would you give this information if it were added to the outline in the Example?

1. giant slug or sea worm
2. too large for eel
3. bigger than most fish
4. kind of animal
5. plesiosaur dinosaur—all known ones died about seventy million years ago

**WRITE**   Use the notes you organized during the last lesson. Write an outline for your report. Remember that ideas in the questions become main headings. Answers are in subheadings.

**GO BEYOND**   Exchange outlines with a classmate. Is your partner's outline clear to you? Ask questions if you have trouble understanding (1) what your partner chose as main points or (2) what information goes with those main points. Save your outline.

# LESSON 5  **Writing from an Outline**

It is easy to write a report from an outline. You should have one paragraph for each main heading. The main heading will become the topic sentence. The subheadings will become the supporting sentences of the paragraph. Write your sentences in the order shown in your outline.

## Example

Here is the first part of Marie's outline and her opening paragraph.

**The Loch Ness Monster**

I. Appearance
- A. About 20 feet long
- B. Shaped a little like an eel
- C. Gray, black, or green
- D. Small head, slender neck about 4 or 5 feet long
- E. Like "monstrous snail" out of water

The Loch Ness monster is a sight to remember. It is about 20 feet long and shaped like an eel. Most people who have seen it claim it is gray or black, but others say it is greenish. All agree that its small head is mounted on a slender neck about 4 or 5 feet long. One couple who claim to have seen it out of water describe it as a "monstrous snail."

How well does Marie's paragraph follow her outline?

**PRACTICE 1** Here is the second part of Marie's outline and the paragraph she wrote from it. What facts did she leave out? Which fact is out of order?

II. Home
    A. Loch Ness, a freshwater lake
    B. Part of Caledonian Canal, Scotland
    C. Lake 24 miles long, 900 feet deep
    D. Coffee-colored water
    E. Full of fish, no plants

    Home to the monster is Loch Ness. This coffee-colored body of water is 24 miles long and 900 feet deep. The dark water of Loch Ness supports fish but not plant life.

**PRACTICE 2** Here is the outline for the last paragraph of Marie's report. Use that outline to write her final paragraph.

V. Effects of the monster
    A. Thousands of tourists to Loch Ness
    B. Good for the economy
    C. Food, lodging, souvenirs
    D. Underwater search gives valuable information on lake
    E. People enjoy mysteries

**WRITE** Using your own outline as a guide, write the first draft of your report. It should be one or two pages long. Save your work.

**GO BEYOND** Work with a partner. Give your partner the outline you wrote for your report in Lesson 4, and your first draft. How carefully does your partner follow his or her outline? Discuss any differences your partner finds between your outline and what you wrote in the first draft of your report.

**Revising a Report**

Most writers think of revision as a natural part of the writing process. It's a way to make sure that all the work that went into the research, organization, and writing stages, shows itself in a well written report.

The first step in revising a report is to read over your first draft. Get a sense of whether or not you fully answered all the questions you set out to answer. Look for any places where the report strays from the main idea. Make sure to mark all awkward, unclear, or incomplete sentences that need to be rewritten.

Check what you have written against your outline. The paragraphs in your report should build on one another. If any information needs to be moved, show where it should go.

## Example

Look at the second part of Marie's outline on page 355. Then compare the first and second drafts that she wrote from it.

FIRST DRAFT

Home to the monster is Loch Ness. This coffee-colored body of water is 24 miles long and 900 feet deep. The dark water of Loch Ness supports fish but not plant life.

SECOND DRAFT

Nessie was named after the freshwater lake it calls home— Loch Ness. Part of Scotland's Caledonia Canal, Loch Ness is an ideal hiding place for a water monster. The lake is 24 miles long and 900 feet deep. The murky coffee-colored water makes it difficult to see what's below. No plant life can survive in Loch Ness, but Nessie has plenty of fish to keep it company.

What new information was added to the second draft?
Explain why the second draft is better than the first.

**PRACTICE 1** Read the paragraph below. One of the sentences does not belong. Another is written out of order. Rewrite the paragraph correctly.

For hundreds of years, people have tried different ways to find out about the Loch Ness monster. The earliest description of a monster was recorded over 1400 years ago. Since 1972, scuba divers have tried to take underwater photos of the mysterious monster. These divers must undergo special training from experts who live in the United States and elsewhere. In 1933, the first photos on land where taken. In one picture, the photographer claims to have caught the Loch Ness monster's head and neck sticking up out of the water. In another he claims that the three humps shown rising out of the water are part of the monster's body.

**PRACTICE 2** Read the corrected paragraph you wrote in Practice 1. Revise it to include the following missing information.
1. St. Columbus saw the Loch Ness monster 1400 years ago.
2. 3000 recorded sightings since 1930.
3. Dark waters make it difficult to do underwater photography.

**WRITE** In Lesson 5 you wrote the first draft of your report. Revise your work. If you are missing any information, go to the library and find the facts you need. When you are finished, write a second draft. Make sure you make all the corrections you marked on your first draft.

**GO BEYOND** Work with a partner. Exchange second drafts. Proofread your partner's report. (If you need help remembering the symbols used in proofreading, go back and read Lesson 4 in Chapter 16.) After your report is returned, fix all the errors. Write the final draft of your report.

## Practice

**A.** Write each set of titles in order from the most general to the narrowest.

1. The World of Dance, Dame Margot Fonteyn, Ballet
2. The Name Catherine, A History of Names, Some Popular Names
3. Ivies, English Ivy, House Plants
4. The Common Cold, Contagious Diseases, Health Problems
5. Beethoven's Music, Beethoven's Symphonies, Classical Music

**B.** Take notes as you read the following paragraphs. Notice that the information in the second paragraph seems misplaced. Organize your notes in a logical order.

Wolfgang Amadeus Mozart was born on January 27, 1756, in Salzburg, Austria. His father was a musician, and young Wolfgang grew up in a house of music. At three, Wolfgang tried to play musical instruments on his own. When Wolfgang was four, the elder Mozart began to teach his little boy to play the clavier, a keyboard instrument. After having played for only a year, the child could memorize and play a short piece of music perfectly.

At the age of four, Wolfgang wrote his first piece of music. At five he picked up a violin, on which he had never had a lesson, and played it perfectly the first time.

**C.** Put the following notes on the life of the famous cowgirl, Annie Oakley, in the correct outline form. The outline should have two main headings with four subheadings under each.

1. eight years old—father dies and Annie sent to orphanage
2. wins first sharpshooting contest at 15
3. at 25, joins Buffalo Bill's Wild West show
4. early childhood
5. marries at 17 and begins touring with husband as professional sharpshooter
6. while at orphanage forced to work at nearby farm where she is mistreated
7. start of career
8. after two years at orphanage, runs away and goes to live with mother and mother's new husband
9. at 11 finds old cap-and-ball rifle and begins practicing
10. born 1860 in Ohio—fifth of eight children—real name Phoebe Anne Moses

## Composition

Look over the outline you wrote in Practice C on Annie Oakley. Now imagine that you are writing this report for a popular magazine that is for children ten to twelve years old. The children like the magazine because it is written in a funny manner. Write your report on Annie Oakley as if it is going to be published in this magazine.

## Advanced Challenge

In this chapter you have planned, organized, and written a report. You started by selecting a topic and then framed questions that helped you find information. You took notes on the information you found, organized that information, and made an outline. Finally, you wrote your report.

Make a display showing how you followed the steps for writing your report. Below each item you display—your notes, for example—write a short description of what you did. Show how much time each step took.

Now, for your own information, ask yourself these questions. They are not for the display.

Which part of the project was most difficult? Which took the most time? The next time you write a report, what will you do differently? Why?

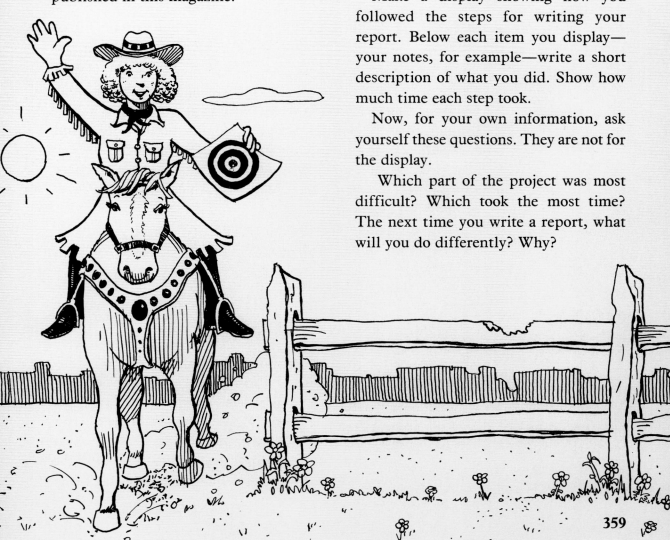

## DICTIONARY

What is your favorite sport or hobby? Most sports and hobbies have special words all their own.

| SOCCER | THEATER | WOODWORKING |
|--------|---------|-------------|
| goal | footlights | vise |
| striker | flats | jigsaw |
| header | greasepaint | wood screws |

Share your sport, hobby, or other interest by making a dictionary of its special terms for your class library. You will need heavy paper for the cover, writing paper for the pages, some scrap paper, index cards, staples or yarn or brass fasteners, a pen, and crayons or colored pencils. You will also need a dictionary, an encyclopedia, one or more books about your subject, scissors, glue, and magazines with pictures of equipment you could cut out.

The first thing to do is to make a list of special terms that are related to your sport or hobby. Write each term from your list on an index card.

Now, using your own dictionary as a guide, add the pronunciation for each term. Then write definitions. Write these on scrap paper first. Try to write the definitions in your own words. Add sentences to show how the terms are used, and tell what part of speech each one is. Write your definitions on your index cards. Make sure your cards are in alphabetical order.

Now copy the terms and definitions on the paper you will use for your dictionary. Write guide words at the top of each page. Draw or glue in illustrations. Add page numbers. Make a cover with a title and your name as author. Fasten the pages and the cover together—and you have a dictionary!

**A.** Complete each sentence by using the correct suffix or prefix from the list. Write your answer.

–en    –ish    mis–    –or    un–

1. Please tight _____ the lid on that jar.
2. Jimmy always needs help _____ locking the door.
3. Who is your favorite act _____ ?
4. We're too early, I _____ read the time on the tickets.
5. When Tom gets that devil _____ look, he always does something unexpected.

**B.** From the list choose the best source of information for each reference problem. Write your answer.

almanac          encyclopedia          card catalog
atlas            thesaurus

1. books that the library has by Paula Fox
2. several synonyms for the word *go*
3. who won the Indianapolis 500 this year
4. general information on the Olympics
5. maps and information on the climate of India

**C.** Imagine that you are writing a report on saving energy. Write an outline using the following six items. There are two main headings and four subheadings. Indent the items correctly. Use roman numerals, capital letters, and periods.

1. when leaving the house
2. when taking a shower or bath
3. when doing the dishes
4. saving heat
5. at night after people go to bed
6. saving hot water

**361**

# More Chapter Practice

## Ways of Communicating (pages 3–15)

**A.** For each activity, write *speaking*, *writing*, *drawing*, or *signaling* to tell the best way to communicate.
1. directing traffic
2. telling a story to a young child
3. mapping your route to school
4. using the telephone to order
5. leaving a message for someone

**B.** Write at least two words to tell how each object might look. Write at least one word to tell how it might sound.
1. airplane
2. record player
3. bus
4. brook
5. dog
6. fireworks
7. television
8. air conditioner
9. cat
10. birds

**C.** Write *true* or *false* for each disussion rule below.
1. Everyone should have the same opinion.
2. Stick to the subject.
3. Let each person give his or her point of view.
4. Discuss at least two topics at once.
5. Respect the opinions of others.

**D.** This is the first paragraph of a report. Write the sentences in order. Begin with the two sentences that make up the introduction.
1. Let me tell you what it is.
2. That is a good name for this African animal.
3. The word *aardvark* comes from Dutch words meaning "earth" and "pig."
4. Did you ever hear of an aardvark?
5. The aardvark looks like a pig and spends its days in a hole in the earth.

**E.** Write these sentences as notes. Remember to be as brief as possible.
1. An abacus is used for counting.
2. The frame of an abacus has eight wires running from top to bottom.
3. A crosspiece divides the frame into an upper and a lower section.
4. There are two beads on each wire in the upper section.
5. There are five beads on each wire in the lower section.

## Expressing Your Ideas (pages 17–31)

**A.** Add words to each word group to form a sentence.

1. Martha and her friend _____ .
2. _____ bought a board game.
3. _____ studied for a test.
4. The big black dog _____ .
5. _____ came home late yesterday.

**B.** Write a paragraph by putting these sentences in order.

1. Then they sank into the tar and died.
2. When it rained, water covered the tar.
3. Today scientists study their bones to learn about Ice Age animals.
4. The tar pits of California are like a history lesson.
5. Animals that waded into the water for a drink got stuck in the tar.

**C.** Write *setting, characters,* or *plot* to describe each note.

1. airplane has crashed
2. pilot, Mark, doesn't like children
3. passengers must walk miles for help
4. hot, steamy jungle
5. eleven-year-old Carlos determined to win Mark's affection

**D.** Turn the following dialogue into play form. Write words in parentheses ( ) to show what the speaker does or feels. Underline those words.

1. "That's odd." The driver scratched his head. "I can't find my car keys."
2. "You left them in your car," the police officer told him brightly.
3. "That's great! Thanks for reminding me," he told him happily.
4. "Not so great." The officer sighed heavily. "Someone just drove off with them."
5. "Oh, no!" The driver grabbed his head. "My brand new car!"

**E.** Write *prewriting, organizing, writing,* or *revising* to identify each item below.

1. improving what you have written
2. choosing a topic to write about
3. arranging information in order
4. gathering information about the topic
5. putting your ideas on paper in a first draft

**F.** Improve the following paragraph by writing the sentences in order and by adding details. You may combine sentences or change words if you wish.

That person was an old man. He walked down the street. I was very interested in the next person who went by. He never reached the corner. Suddenly he disappeared.

# Exchanging Information (pages 33–45)

**A.** Write *tell about, describe,* or *explain* to show what each of these sentences does.

1. Suddenly the ice gave way beneath me, and I plunged into the pond.
2. To protect your feet against the cold, first put on a pair of thin, all-cotton socks; then pull on a pair of woolen socks.
3. The only sound was the steady drumming of the rain on the old tin roof.
4. The ocean was a crystal clear, blue-green color.
5. As soon as Rob hit the ball, I started running for home plate.

**B.** Write in order these steps for making a seashore paperweight.

1. Wash and dry the stone and the items you have collected.
2. Then collect small shells, seaweed, and other items from the beach.
3. Cut a piece of felt the size of the stone and paste it on the bottom of the stone.
4. First, find a pretty stone that has been worn smooth by the waves.
5. Finish by pasting the items from the beach on top of the shell in an attractive pattern.

**C.** After the number of each sentence, write either *fact* or *opinion*.

1. Pots, vases, and dishes made from clay and hardened by heat are called pottery.
2. People who make pottery are called potters.
3. It is great fun to make pottery.
4. The first step in making pottery is selecting and preparing the clay.
5. Modern pottery is prettier than pottery made long ago.

**D.** The following statements are from advertisements. Tell which method is being used in each. Write *statistics, famous person, symbol, expert,* or *image*.

1. Professional race drivers love the way our car handles.
2. Eight-foot-tall "Baskets" Bobble, highest scorer in the NBA, says, "I've been drinking Merry Dairy Milk every since I was seven feet tall."
3. Ducky Dander wouldn't go near the water without Drytoes footwear.
4. Ninety-nine out of every one hundred successful writers use the Smooth Writer word-processing program.
5. Let Crackle Breakfast Cereal start your day with the warm glow of success.

# Nouns (pages 51–63)

**A.** Write each sentence. Underline each noun. Circle each article.
1. The first boat may have been a log.
2. People later made a raft of logs.
3. A hollowed out log became a dugout.
4. Skins and reeds were also used to make boats.
5. Now boats and ships are made of many materials.
6. Canoes are moved with paddles.
7. Rowboats are propelled with oars.
8. Motorboats depend on engines.
9. Motorboats use different types of engines.
10. Some ships can hold as many people as a small city.

**B.** Write each sentence. Capitalize each proper noun. Underline each common noun.
1. My friend lois lived in bunker hill, indiana.
2. Her father, george rawlings, worked for underwater camera, inc.
3. Their family moved to this town last year.
4. Now mr. and mrs. rawlings work together as photographers.
5. I have seen their pictures in the museum of modern photography.

**C.** Write the plural form of each of these singular nouns.
1. girl
2. class
3. birch
4. lighthouse
5. mattress
6. ash
7. search
8. building
9. mix
10. tree

**D.** Write the plural form of each of these singular nouns.
1. monkey
2. leaf
3. enemy
4. trout
5. goose
6. salary
7. fairy
8. holiday
9. woman
10. wife

**E.** Write each sentence. Use the possessive form of the noun in parentheses.
1. The (twins) day was long and busy.
2. They helped to prepare for the (family) trip.
3. They cleaned the (birds) cage.
4. They filled the (cat) dish with fresh water.
5. They took the dog to a (friend) house.
6. They packed the (adults) suitcases.
7. They added a few items to (Mother) shopping list.
8. They recorded the (car) mileage.
9. They set aside some of the (children) games to play while riding.
10. They put new film in (Barry) camera bag.

# Verbs (pages 65–77)

**A.** Write each sentence. Underline the verb. Write *A* after each sentence that contains an action verb and *L* after each sentence with a linking verb.

1. I am a fifth-grade student.
2. My teacher's name is Mr. Wyan.
3. I like spelling and reading.
4. I dislike music.
5. I love recess and lunch.
6. Jean's lunch smells delicious.
7. I brought a peanut butter sandwich for lunch.
8. Each day at this time I become hungry.
9. Fruit tastes good with lunch.
10. The lunch bell just rang.

**B.** Write each sentence. Underline the verb. Write *present, past,* or *future* after the sentence to tell the tense of the verb.

1. I live on Hubert Street.
2. I go to Redd School.
3. Last year I went to Maynard School.
4. Next year I will be in the sixth grade.
5. After that I will go to the junior high school.
6. I studied hard last night for a test.
7. I will take the test this afternoon.
8. I belong to the Scouts.
9. I earned two badges last year.
10. I will camp this summer.

**C.** Rewrite each sentence. Change the form of the verb from present to past tense.

1. Hetty drinks orange juice.
2. Oscar thinks about fishing.
3. That fish fights hard.
4. You sing very well.
5. We buy Zippy shoe polish.
6. We bring books from the library.
7. They come to Scouts every week.
8. Wendall falls on the ice.
9. Herbert and Ming Li run fast.
10. The mail carrier rings the door bell.

**D.** Write these sentences. Draw a line under each present or past participle. Circle the helping verb.

1. My father is planning a garden.
2. He has chosen a spot in the backyard for it.
3. He has drawn a map of the area.
4. Now he is marking the rows of plants on the map.
5. He had bought the seeds already.
6. I am helping him with the garden plan.
7. We are reading gardening books.
8. I have learned a lot about gardens already.
9. Father has been grateful for my help.
10. My sister has promised to help with the weeding and the watering.

*More Chapter Practice*

# Pronouns (pages 79–89)

**A.** Write each sentence. Underline each pronoun. Draw a line from each pronoun to the noun it stands for.

1. Jeremy said, "I got new jeans from my uncle and wore them."
2. Carlos and Arthur held a pet show, and Rubin brought his goat to their show.
3. Agnes has misplaced her hairbrush, Jennifer. Have you seen it?
4. Carlos and Arthur made a sign that told readers, "Bring Your Pet to Our Show."
5. Clara bought a card for Clark and gave it to him.
6. Clark said he liked Clara's card and would thank her for it.
7. Ivan said, "Dad sent me a card."
8. Mindy and Susan said they would buy Ivan a gift on his birthday.
9. Saul and Jenny told the girls, "You can give a gift to us."
10. "You should start a Good Deed Club," Mr. Albert told his students.

**B.** Write each sentence. Draw one line under each subject pronoun. Draw two lines under each object pronoun.

1. I asked her to help with the display.
2. We told them how to bake bread.
3. Last week you entertained us with an interesting story.
4. He asked me to go to the show.
5. She saw him at the football game.
6. They will take you to the circus.
7. We mailed it at the post office.
8. He admires you for your honesty.
9. We watch it on television.
10. He and she will send you to camp.

**C.** Write each sentence. Draw a line under each possessive pronoun used before a noun. Circle each possessive pronoun used alone in place of a noun.

1. That is your book, and this is mine.
2. Peter passed in his homework paper.
3. Is this drawing his or hers?
4. I have my lunch, and they have theirs.
5. Your plan is better than our plan.
6. Is this classroom theirs?
7. The cat went to its dish.
8. Eat your lunch, but don't eat ours.
9. They will get their prize when you get yours.
10. Our dog wags its tail.

**D.** Write each sentence. Underline the demonstrative pronoun. Write *S* above each singular pronoun and *P* above each plural pronoun.

1. This is the way home.
2. That is the bicycle I want.
3. I will buy these.
4. These are the items I need.
5. That was your idea.

## Adjectives (pages 91–99)

**A.** Write these sentences. Underline each adjective. Draw a line from the adjective to the noun it describes.

1. The word *etiquette* comes from a French word meaning "little ticket."
2. Small tickets were given to French people going to a public ceremony.
3. On each ticket were complete directions about how to act.
4. So now *etiquette* means the right way to act with other people.
5. Good manners in one group of people may not be considered acceptable actions in another group.

**B.** Write these sentences. In each blank write an adjective that makes sense.

1. She started the _____ hobby of stamp collecting.
2. A group of _____ Scouts wore uniforms.
3. I have two _____ pairs of gloves.
4. My father wears _____ boots.
5. Three _____ fish swam in the tank.

**C.** Write only the adjectives that compare in each sentence. Write *comparative* or *superlative* beside each adjective.

1. Martin is older than his brother.
2. That was the worst movie I have ever seen.
3. The cobra is one of the most dangerous snakes.
4. My test grade was worse than yours.
5. Danny is the oldest boy in our club.

**D.** Write the correct form of the adjective in parentheses.

1. This is the (ripe) tomato in the garden.
2. Yesterday was the (wonderful) day of my life.
3. Wool cloth is (rough) than nylon.
4. You have given me the (good) present possible.
5. This mystery is (confusing) than the last one I solved.

**E.** Write these sentences. Underline each demonstrative adjective.

1. I like this book better than that book.
2. These papers are ours.
3. Let's walk as far as those houses.
4. These markers are mine.
5. I wish I had earned that badge.

**F.** Write these sentences. Use *this, that, these,* or *those* in each.

1. Look at _____ ring I am holding.
2. It looks as pretty as _____ rings over there.
3. Let's connect _____ wire to _____ wire.
4. Take _____ chairs to the next room.
5. I will give you _____ coins for _____ stamps.

# Adverbs (pages 101–111)

**A.** Write the adverbs from these sentences. Write *how, when,* or *where* beside each adverb to tell how it adds to the meaning of the verb.

1. Yesterday we joyously played outdoors.
2. First we slowly rolled big balls of snow.
3. Then we painstakingly piled the spheres on top of each other.
4. Next we carefully added a hat, button eyes, and a carrot nose.
5. Soon our snowperson was smilingly guarding the front lawn.

**B.** Complete each sentence with an adverb that makes sense. Circle the verb the adverb tells about.

1. Elizabeth awoke _____ on her birthday.
2. She _____ dressed.
3. _____ she raced downstairs.
4. She stopped at the kitchen door and peered _____ .
5. There, by the stove, her new puppy waited _____ for her.

**C.** Write only the adverbs that compare in these sentences. Write *positive, comparative,* or *superlative* beside each adverb to describe its form.

1. Their team pulled harder than ours.
2. You must learn to play more gently.
3. Of all the runners, Becky is fastest.
4. Our friends will arrive soon.
5. We receive mail more regularly now that our friends know our address.

**D.** Write these sentences. Use the correct form of the adverb in parentheses.

1. He ties knots (tight) than I do.
2. The river runs (rapidly) when it is in flood stage.
3. That pilot flies (low) than the captain does.
4. Hank went (willingly) than Arthur did.
5. Of all the baby-sitters, she worked (long).

**E.** Write each sentence. Change the adjective form in the parentheses to the adverb form.

1. The children (hungry) clamored for food.
2. Please leave the room (quiet).
3. I (hard) heard his answer.
4. The lamp (bright) lit the room.
5. The dog crept (cautious) across the thin ice.

**F.** Write an original sentence for each of these adverbs.

1. smoothly
2. unfairly
3. quickly
4. bitterly
5. easily

# Other Parts of Speech (pages 113–123)

**A.** Write each sentence. Underline each prepositional phrase.

1. Galileo is often called the father of modern science.
2. He gave to the world the idea of experimenting.
3. Before Galileo, scholars thought everything had been written about all subjects.
4. During Galileo's day scientists found new truths through testing.
5. Thanks to that man, you will conduct experiments in science class.

**B.** Write only the prepositional phrases from these sentences. Write either *why, when, where, how,* or *which* beside each.

1. A butterfly fluttered across the field.
2. Do not lean against the wall during recess.
3. Down the street rode a tall man on a horse with a silver saddle.
4. We looked under the bed for the puppy.
5. I will go with Kim to the party.

**C.** Complete each sentence with a prepositional phrase. Write the sentences.

1. We saw the bird fly _____ .
2. He was wearing one glove _____ .
3. The boy and the puppy ran _____ .
4. I will meet you _____ .
5. We could see the decorations_____ .

**D.** Write these sentences. Circle the conjunctions.

1. Wisconsin and New York are famous for dairy farming.
2. Good pasture land is needed, but dairy barns are also important.
3. Dairy barns are big and airy.
4. Cows and calves are kept clean and well fed.
5. Chopped cornstalks or other plant food is kept in silos or haylofts.

**E.** Rewrite each pair of sentences, using a conjunction. Be sure to use a comma.

1. Dairy farming is hard work. Farmers enjoy it.
2. Silos must be kept filled. Cows would be hungry in the winter.
3. Milk must be strained and cooled. It is then rushed to the dairy.
4. Most cows give a few quarts of milk a day. The best milkers give more than fifty quarts.
5. Milk is tested for purity and richness. It must be delivered while fresh.

**F.** Add an interjection to each sentence. Write the sentences.

1. _____ The dishes fell and broke.
2. _____ The cat is on the roof.
3. _____ What a beautiful sunset!
4. _____ Here comes the parade.
5. _____ The cardinal is at the feeder.

# Parts of Sentences (pages 129–143)

**A.** Write each sentence and end it with the correct mark. Tell whether the sentence is *declarative, interrogative, imperative, or exclamatory.*
1. Did I tell you about Uncle Alex
2. He was a university scholar
3. Boy, what a man
4. Tell me more about him
5. Would you like to meet him

**B.** Write each sentence. Draw a line between the complete subject and the complete predicate. Underline the simple subject. Circle the simple predicate.
1. Fairs began in the Middle Ages.
2. At that time merchants sold their wares at those gatherings.
3. Certain cities held fairs every year.
4. People came to fairs for entertainment as well as sales.
5. Today state fairs attract many people.

**C.** Write these sentences. Underline each direct object. Circle each indirect object.
1. A male sunfish makes an underwater nest near shore.
2. Then he leaves his mate the nest.
3. She lays eggs in the nest and swims away.
4. The male fertilizes and guards the eggs until they hatch.
5. He gives the new fish no care.

**D.** Write *correct* beside the number of each correct sentence. Rewrite each incorrect sentence to make the subject and verb agree.
1. Little children play well by themselves.
2. They pretends their toys are real.
3. Some children invents playmates.
4. Each imaginary playmate talks to his or her "inventor."
5. A lively imagination help children enjoy their own company.

**E.** Write these sentences. Underline each compound subject, predicate, or object. Write *subject, predicate,* or *object* to tell what kind it is.
1. We gave Pedro and Jean lunch.
2. Then we sat and talked.
3. Later Bruce and I went for a walk.
4. Each person collected leaves, stones, or shells.
5. Tomorrow we will swim and hike.

**F.** Rewrite each statement as a question.
1. People learned farming many years ago.
2. Farming allowed them to settle in one place.
3. *Agriculture* is a name for farming.
4. That word comes from two Latin words meaning "field" and "till."
5. Farmers till, or plow, their fields.

# Writing Sentences (pages 145–159)

**A.** Expand each sentence by adding at least one adjective and one adverb.

1. Harvey played a song on the piano.
2. She buried the treasure behind a tree.
3. He selected one apple and two pears.
4. Lib and Marsha left for the show.
5. Eunice showed us her locket.

**B.** Combine each pair of sentences with a comma and the conjunction *and, but,* or *or.*

1. It is a long hike. I want to do it.
2. Promise to wash the dishes. I will not cook dinner for you.
3. It rained for a week. The river rose.
4. Aunt Gert and Uncle Joe visited us. They only stayed a few days.
5. You must leave now. You will be late.

**C.** Write the number of each word group. If a group is a sentence, write *OK* beside the number. Rewrite each fragment as a sentence.

1. Under the surface of the water.
2. Small fish, large fish, and different kinds of plants.
3. We dived.
4. Saul swam down to the bottom of the lagoon.
5. The rotted hull of a wrecked ship.

**D.** Write the number of each word group. Write *correct* beside the number of each correct sentence. Rewrite each run-on sentence as two sentences or a single compound sentence.

1. The fiery sun steadily climbed the pink sky, slowly erasing the clouds.
2. It was time to go fishing I called Jud.
3. Together we dug worms in his backyard we put a dozen or more worms in a tin can.
4. I had my fishing rod Jud got his rod and our lunch from the house.
5. The lake was deserted when Jud and I arrived.

**E.** Rewrite each sentence. Omit unnecessary words.

1. The idea of using flags is a very old, ancient idea.
2. When soldiers of ancient times went into battle long ago, they wanted to know where their leaders were.
3. Some person thought up the idea of having each one of the leaders carry a tall pole.
4. If the soldiers fighting in the battle could see the pole, they knew that their leader was alive and well.
5. The leader put something like a flag on top of the pole so that the soldiers could tell their leader's pole from the pole of another leader.

**A.** Rewrite this list. Add capitals where they are needed.

1. french cooking
2. dr. dingle
3. you and i
4. red oak road
5. *deadly whispers* (book)
6. flora, oregon 97828
7. austrian trip
8. mrs. akorn
9. "if" (poem)
10. your friend, (letter closing)

**B.** Rewrite these sentences. Add quotation marks and punctuation where they are needed.

1. Who would like to ride the black mare Tex inquired
2. Jenna shouted I would
3. Pauline asked May I ride the little pinto
4. Better put me on a pony Sharon told him
5. Do you need a back that's close to the ground the cowboy asked
6. Yes Sharon agreed as long as it isn't mine
7. You'll be all right the cowboy told her
8. What the frightened girl asked makes you think so
9. Tex told her We'll start at a slow walk
10. Oh, great she said

**C.** Write these sentences. Use commas where needed.

1. Our trip will be on Tuesday February 7 1986.
2. Randolph you can come with us.
3. You will need a pad of paper a pencil and an eraser.
4. We will bring our lunch or we can eat in a restaurant.
5. Well I hope we eat on the bus.

**D.** Write these sentences. Use apostrophes and colons where needed.

1. Its almost 430.
2. Ive done the following homework spelling, math, and science.
3. Shouldnt the greeting of your business letter read "Dear Sir"?
4. I wasnt thinking very well at 1000 last night.
5. Well, lets fix the greeting so it wont be wrong.

**E.** Copy these sentences as they appear. Use proofreading marks to show how they should be corrected.

1. We have juice milk and water.
2. Wendall wants milk and carla is drinking water
3. What kind of juice do do you have?
4. I can give you apple orrange or grapefruit juice.
5. Well I think I'll have milk then

**A.** Rewrite the following paragraph. Leave out any sentence that does not explain or add to the main idea. Be sure to indent.

Dancing began as a way to express feelings. People danced to show they were happy about a good harvest. They danced to celebrate a victory in battle. They should have done more planting and less fighting. They danced to pray to their gods. Now we pray in places of worship.

**B.** Read the following topic sentence. Write the number of each sentence that belongs in a paragraph with that topic sentence.

TOPIC SENTENCE   Some modern dancing is done on the stage for entertainment.

1. Tap dancing is one kind of entertaining dance.
2. I love tap dancing.
3. My cousin Esther Mae took tap dancing lessons for seven years.
4. Various kinds of acrobatic dances are performed on stage.
5. Ballet dancing is done before an audience.
6. Ballet dancing helps keep people on their toes.
7. Some dances are included in operas.
8. Some operas are sung in foreign languages.
9. Musical shows often include dancing.
10. The music in that kind of show is always interrupting the story.

**C.** For each of these topic sentences write at least one supporting sentence.
1. I think we need a few more laws in this country.
2. Some things that people do certainly annoy me.
3. Everyone has at least one very exciting day in his or her life.
4. On some days everything seems to go wrong.
5. It would have been interesting to live in the days of the Wild West.
6. I think that going to school has its rewards.
7. It is a good idea to join a club or a group outside of school.
8. It is not necessary to go very far to have fun on vacation.
9. In my opinion one sport is the best there is.
10. I have learned how to do many things in my life.

# Descriptive Paragraphs (pages 195–207)

**A.** These sentences contain sensory details. Write only those details. There may be more than one in each sentence. Beside each detail write *seeing, hearing, tasting, smelling,* or *touching.*

1. A sharp, disagreeable odor accompanied the black smoke.
2. My bare feet swished across the wet surface of the floor.
3. After the sweet smell of orange, the sour taste of lemon was a surprise.
4. He shivered as the snow washed his overheated face.
5. She fingered the smooth skin of the pepper, then bit into its hot center.

**B.** Read the topic sentence. Write in space order the sentences that follow the topic sentence.

TOPIC SENTENCE It was a house that had seen better days.

1. Black bats zigzagged from the attic.
2. Its stone foundation was crumbling.
3. Its roof was crowned with four chimneys, each tilted at a crazy angle.
4. Every window on the second floor was empty and glassless.
5. A battered bell hung from a wire beside the warped front door.

**C.** Read the topic sentence. Write in time order the sentences that follow.

TOPIC SENTENCE Tom was not expecting what happened next.

1. Trapped, he felt the water rush into the room and climb his legs.
2. He pushed against the door—gently first, then harder.
3. The door banged shut behind him, blowing out his candle.
4. He turned and stumbled back to the door in the dark.
5. It was locked!

**D.** Rewrite each sentence. Improve it by adding good descriptive details.

1. Patricia ran, bouncing the basketball.
2. She stopped and looked for Rena.
3. Patricia's opponent waved her arms and tried to block the throw.
4. Patricia threw the ball to Rena.
5. Rena threw the ball at the hoop.

**E.** Rewrite this paragraph. Put the sentences in order. Leave out those that do not support the topic sentence.

Ben could not believe his eyes. His eyes were blue. "I'll take this," he told the owner. Evidently the owner did not know its value. Yard sales are like garage sales. The man took his money. Here, at a yard sale, was a real Time Machine for only $5! "It's all yours," he told the boy.

# Factual Paragraphs (pages 209–219)

**A.** Write the sentence in each pair that would be the better topic sentence.

1. a. A department store is a special kind of store.
   b. A department store gets its name because it has many shops, or departments.
2. a. One desert in Chile does not get rain for years.
   b. Deserts get very little rain.
3. a. Earthworms live in the ground.
   b. Rain may drive earthworms from their burrows.
4. a. Dinosaurs must have been interesting creatures.
   b. The word *dinosaur* means "terrible lizard."
5. a. Diamond mines are very hot.
   b. Mining diamonds is not easy.

**B.** Write the topic in each pair that is more suitable for development as a single paragraph.

1. a. Diseases
   b. How People Get Measles
2. a. English Compound Words
   b. The English Language
3. a. All About Elephants
   b. The Elephant's Trunk
4. a. Golden Eagle Nests
   b. Eagles
5. a. Atomic Powered Engines
   b. Engines

**C.** Use the following sentences to write a paragraph. Put them in order. Begin with the topic sentence.

1. In 1856 William Perkins got a lavender dye from coal tar.
2. The earliest dyes were probably made from berry juice.
3. The Phoenicians made dye from sea snails 3000 years ago.
4. People have used dyes to color cloth for many years.
5. Most dyes that we use today are based on Perkins's discovery.

**D.** Revise this paragraph. Put the sentences in order. Leave out sentences that do not develop the topic sentence.

Our ears have three parts. Some ears are large and some ears are small. The inner ear sends sound messages to the brain. The outer ear sends sounds to the middle ear. These parts are (1) the outer ear, (2) the middle ear, and (3) the inner ear. Mom insists that we wash our ears. The middle ear sends sounds to the inner ear.

**E.** Write a factual paragraph about a friend, a pet, or a favorite or sport. Begin your paragraph with a topic sentence. Remember to indent. Write three or more sentences that add to the main idea.

# Building Paragraphs (pages 221–231)

**A.** Write the letter of the topic in each pair that is narrow enough to tell about in one or two paragraphs.

1. a. hiking
   b. my favorite hike
2. a. a great bargain
   b. shopping
3. a. people in our neighborhood
   b. one person I know
4. a. all about television
   b. a television show I like
5. a. the camel
   b. zoo animals

**B.** Read this first draft. Answer the questions that follow.

I wanted to impress someone. I told her I played the piano. Later she invited me to her party. "We're having a surprise," she told me. "You'll love it." At the party I learned that someone was going to play the piano—me! Was I embarrassed!

1. What is the topic of the paragraph?
2. How could you make the opening sentence more interesting?
3. Are the events presented in the order in which they took place?
4. What details could you add to improve the paragraph?
5. Could the ending be improved?

**C.** Rewrite the paragraph in Exercise B. Use your answers to the questions in that exercise as a revision guide. Add more details if you wish, but be sure that each sentence you write supports the topic sentence.

**D.** Select one of the following topics. Write one or two paragraphs about it. Save your paper for the next exercise.

1. My Most Embarrassing Experience
2. My Most Satisfying Experience
3. The Saddest Day of My Life
4. My Favorite Place
5. What I Am Most Proud Of

**E.** Revise and proofread the paper you wrote for Exercise D. Use proofreading marks to show where you should make corrections. Write a final draft.

**F.** Copy these sentences just as they appear. Use proofreading marks to show what corrections are needed.

1. This year jenny is in a new school and she likes it.
2. She said likes her teacher
3. She tells me it is called Haywood elementary school.
4. "We have a lot of hoomework, though," she said
5. "I think I will learn lot at my new school," Jeny told me.

## Narrative Writing (pages 239–255)

**A.** Use one of the following as the first sentence of a one-paragraph story summary. Write the summary.

1. I will die, Maggie thought, if I do not get that horse!
2. David's father was injured.
3. The river burst over its banks.
4. Why would a spy steal gum?
5. Lisa and Morgan were missing.

**B.** Rewrite each sentence, or add other sentences to create the setting for a story. Add descriptive details that will give the reader a clear picture of the setting.

1. It was evening in the swamp.
2. The house was spooky.
3. By morning we had reached the mountaintop.
4. She looked around the cave.
5. It was an unusual room.
6. Barnaby was sitting behind the wheel of a new automobile.
7. We started up the trail.
8. I looked around the barn.
9. Inside, by the fire, it was warm.
10. Water from a spring ran into the pool.

**C.** Choose one of these characters. Write a description of that character.

1. a boy or girl about your age
2. sports figure
3. a visitor from another planet
4. an important world leader
5. a woman with supernatural powers

**D.** Write the plot for a story. You may use the character and a setting you wrote about in Exercises B and C, or you may invent another person and place. Write your plot in note form, answering these questions.

1. What problem does your main character have?
2. How does he or she try to solve that problem?
3. What happens?
4. How is the problem finally solved?
5. How does the story end?

**E.** Write the story you plotted in Exercise D. Be sure it contains the following.

1. an interesting setting
2. characters that act predictably
3. a problem to be solved
4. a reasonable solution to that problem
5. a satisfying ending

**F.** Exchange the story you wrote for Exercise E with a classmate. Ask how he or she thinks it could be improved. Make those changes with which you agree. Proofread your final copy of the story for errors.

# Writing a Mystery (pages 257–265)

**A.** A valuable painting has been stolen from the third-floor library of Oscar Van Frump's home. Some of these clues might be given in a mystery story about that event. Others are not appropriate. Write the number of each good clue. Explain your choice.

1. A window in the library is open.
2. The Van Frumps have owned the painting for two years.
3. A ladder is still leaning against the house beneath the open window.
4. Mrs. Van Frump is fifty-five years old.
5. Oscar Van Frump was very fond of the missing painting.
6. Footprints near the ladder were made by Colonel Crowe's shoes.
7. Mrs. Van Frump was given the painting as a gift by Oscar.
8. Colonel Crowe was once tried for theft but was not convicted.
9. Only Miss Meek, a retired art dealer, and the Van Frumps know the value of the painting.
10. Colonel Crowe is afraid of heights.

**B.** Choose one of the following as the main character in a mystery story. Write notes about the personality of that character. How does he or she act?

1. a boy or girl who is thought to be stupid but is really very clever
2. a world-famous detective
3. a boy or girl who pretends to be interested only in animals
4. a timid tourist who is mistaken for an internationally-known jewel thief
5. a boy or girl who loves mysteries

**C.** Choose a main character for a mystery story. Write notes about the plot of a mystery story. Try to answer these questions in your notes.

1. What is the mystery?
2. How did the main character investigate the mystery?
3. Who is the guilty person?
4. What clues gave the guilty person away?
5. What other people are involved in the mystery?

**D.** Rewrite the ending of the following mystery story. Show, rather than tell, what the characters say and do. Use dialogue where it is needed.

Lester said he thought at first that Bruiser Barnes had stolen the money. Then he decided that Bruiser was innocent. When he said that, Bruiser was happy. Lester said Mrs. Marsh was guilty. She had worn Bruiser's clothes the night of the crime. Mrs. Marsh admitted her guilt.

**A.** Write the number of each sentence that would be a good beginning of a mystery story. A good beginning should get the reader interested and provide information.

1. "Help!" the wealthy widow shouted, "I've been robbed."
2. I'm going to tell an interesting story.
3. "Why would anyone steal a lion?" the detective asked himself.
4. This story takes place in Miami.
5. A dark figure in a cape darted across the lawn.
6. Henrietta turned quickly at the sound of the door closing.
7. "Stop!" the police officer shouted, pointing his gun at the running figures.
8. "I'm trapped," thought Kurt, "and no one will know I'm in here."
9. The main character in this mystery is a girl named Rose.
10. "It's gone," cried Mrs. Van Frump. "My painting has disappeared."

**B.** Write a more precise word or phrase for each item below.

1. (he or she) said
2. a room
3. a city
4. moved quickly
5. an animal
6. a strange sound
7. a building
8. a fast car
9. looked happy
10. a party

**C.** Rewrite this paragraph. Correct every error. Remember to start a new paragraph each time the speaker changes.

It was john who came up with the first spanish coin. The ship must have gone down here he told the others. Linda's head popped out of the water. "Look at this! she shouted, holding up a gold statue. I do believe we've found the pirate treasure.

**D.** Write the number of each good way to share your mystery story.

1. Write a summary of the story to interest others in reading it.
2. First tell how the story ends.
3. Have boys and girls play the parts of the characters.
4. Tell what you do not like about the story.
5. Read the story aloud.
6. Draw pictures of some of the exciting parts of the story.
7. Record the story on tape, and play the tape for an audience.
8. Tell another story that is like the one you wrote.
9. Make a book out of the story you wrote and place it in your classroom library.
10. Draw pictures of your classmates as they read the story silently.

# Descriptive Writing (pages 285–297)

**A.** Write the number of each sentence. Beside the number write the sense or senses appealed to by that sentence.

1. He slid the wooden crate of sweet-smelling melons onto the truck.
2. She poured a ruby spoonful of the bitter medicine into her mouth.
3. The ice creaked and groaned in the frigid air.
4. The fragrance of roasted turkey filled the kitchen.
5. A door banged shut in the old house.

**B.** Write the two things that are being compared in each sentence. Beside those words write *simile* or *metaphor* to identify the comparison.

1. The guide was an eagle: big, strong, and fearless.
2. The full moon, a spotlight in the sky, lit up the field.
3. He handed me a package as cold as chilled metal.
4. The frightened cat sprang like an arrow through the open window.

**C.** Write the number of each sentence. Write *T* or *F* beside each number to tell whether that sentence is true or false.

1. Words that rhyme end with the same sound.
2. Some poems contain no rhyming words.
3. A group of lines in a poem is called a stanza.
4. Similes and metaphors help a writer create powerful descriptions.
5. Poetry does not have rhythm.
6. A lyric poem may have more than one stanza.
7. Poetry often uses similes and metaphors to create mental pictures.
8. A narrative poem tells a story.
9. A lyric poem often describes the writer's feelings.
10. The words *rain* and *ran* rhyme.

**D.** Write the number of each topic. Decide which topics would be good subjects for a lyric poem. Write *lyric* beside those numbers.

1. the discovery of the New World
2. the loneliness of being snowbound
3. the joy of finding a new friend
4. the accomplishments of a great person
5. the fear of trying something new

**E.** Complete these comparisons with new ideas, something you have not heard or read before.

1. as warm as _____
2. as quiet as _____
3. _____ blue, like _____
4. a _____ of a player
5. fingers like _____

**A.** Write the number of each statement. Then write *true* or *false* beside that number.

1. A book report lets you share your opinions about a book with others.
2. Always begin a book report by telling how the book ends.
3. You should not tell what the book is about.
4. A book report helps others decide whether they would like to read that book.
5. A book report should tell whether the book is fiction or nonfiction.
6. All books have characters.
7. If the book has characters, you should tell something about them.
8. You do not need to include the title and author in a book report.
9. Do not try to guess what type of reader would like the book.
10. Tell something about the book, but do not tell your favorite part.

**B.** Here are reasons for writing a letter. Beside the number of each reason write *friendly* or *business* to tell what kind of letter would be better.

1. to invite a friend to stay with you
2. to ask a company about one of its products
3. to complain about poor service
4. to ask for a catalog
5. to thank your aunt for a gift

**C.** Here are descriptions of parts you might write in a business letter. Beside the number of each description write *heading, inside address, greeting, body, closing,* or *signature.*

1. the main part of the letter
2. your address and the date
3. your name
4. the word *Sincerely*
5. the name of the person to whom you are writing, followed by a colon
6. the name and address of the company to which you are writing

**D.** Write a message after taking the following call. Include all the important information.

Caller: I'm sorry your brother Herman isn't home. He's always out, isn't he? I'm Mrs. Welch. Do you remember me? I work in One Stop Shopping at Lincoln Mall. We're having a big sale this week. Herman lost his wallet in the store. He's sure forgetful! I'll hold it for him. If he can't get here before five o'clock—that's when I go home— I'll turn it into Lost and Found.

## More About Words (pages 315–325)

**A.** Write the number of each pair of words. Write *synonyms, antonyms,* or *homophones* to describe each pair.

1. road, street
2. break, brake
3. brave, cowardly
4. reveal, tell
5. miner, minor
6. strong, weak
7. passed, past
8. quickly, slowly
9. laugh, giggle
10. peace, piece
11. useful, worthless
12. save, spend
13. principal, principle
14. automobile, car
15. permanent, temporary

**B.** Write a contraction for each word group.

1. are not
2. we have
3. had not
4. were not
5. it will
6. was not
7. is not
8. I am
9. she is
10. do not

**C.** Complete the following chart.

| PREFIX | MEANING | EXAMPLE |
|--------|---------|---------|
| 1. bi- | two | _____ |
| 2. _____ | _____ | disloyal |
| 3. in- | not | _____ |
| 4. mis- | wrongly | _____ |
| 5. _____ | again | _____ |
| 6. _____ | _____ | semifinal |
| 7. sub- | _____ | _____ |
| 8. tri- | _____ | triangle |
| 9. un- | not | _____ |
| 10. _____ | _____ | unicycle |

**D.** Beside the number of each word write the letter of its meaning.

1. monthly
2. stiffen
3. fascination
4. boyish
5. personalize
6. botanist
7. strengthen
8. sailor
9. smoothly
10. joyous

a. like a boy
b. in a smooth way
c. make personal
d. one who studies botany
e. one who sails
f. strong attraction
g. full of joy
h. every month
i. make stronger
j. make stiff

**E.** Rewrite the following sentences. Correct each error.

1. He cant brake that stick
2. Arent those flours in the garden pretty?
3. He road a unicycle, which has two wheels.
4. The conductist led led the orchestra.
5. Ill buy a very unexpensive gift for him.

# Gathering Facts (pages 327–343)

**A.** Beside the number of each question write *newspaper, person,* or *dictionary* to tell the best source of that information.

1. How many syllables are there in *aeration?*
2. What should I do for a broken arm?
3. Does *pinnacle* have anything to do with *pins?*
4. Who lost this cute little puppy?
5. What movies are playing near me?
6. Why does the drinking water in our town taste rusty?
7. Which stores have the best sales on children's clothing?
8. Is the word *figure* accented on the first or second syllable?
9. How many people ride the train to the city each day?
10. What does *pronunciation* mean?

**B.** Write the number of each encyclopedia part. Beside each number write the letter of its description.

1. cross-reference
2. volume
3. letter or number
4. guide words
5. article

a. words at top of page that tell what topics are included on the page
b. information about one topic
c. one book in a set
d. way of marking each volume
e. titles of articles related to the topic

**C.** Beside the number of each description write *atlas, encyclopedia, almanac, biographical dictionary,* or *thesaurus.*

1. a book containing information about famous people
2. one volume containing brief facts on many subjects
3. a set of volumes containing articles about many topics
4. a dictionary of synonyms
5. a book of maps
6. tells much about the events of the year in which it was printed
7. has information about well-known people in sports
8. groups synonyms by ideas
9. has information about crops and climate
10. has its index in a separate volume

**D.** Write the number of each question. Beside it write the letter of the place that contains the answer.

1. When was the book published?
2. What does *lexicographer* mean?
3. Does the library have the book?
4. Where does the book tell about world fairs?
5. What is the title of Chapter 3?

a. card catalog
b. index
c. copyright page
d. glossary
e. table of contents

## Writing a Report (pages 345–359)

**A.** Select and write the narrowest topic in each group.

1. Animals, Animals from China, The Giant Panda
2. House Plants, Plants, Raising Christmas Cactus
3. The Story of Icarus, Greek Myths, Myths of the World
4. Natural Wonders, Places to Visit in the United States, Grand Canyon
5. Trees, Needle-bearing Trees, The White Pine

**B.** Choose one of the narrow topics in Exercise A. Write five questions you would like to answer about that topic.

**C.** Read the paragraph below. Take five notes. Each note should list a fact you learned from reading the paragraph.

Harun al-Rashid was a real person who appeared in many of the stories in the *Arabian Nights*. He ruled the city of Bagdad and the eastern Moslem empire about 1200 years ago. In some *Arabian Nights* stories al-Rashid disguised himself and went out among his people. By doing this he learned what his people were doing and saying. In other stories, al-Rashid invited poets, musicians, and storytellers to his court.

**D.** Complete this outline by writing the notes numbered 1–5 where they belong.

### Lions

I. Appearance
   A.
   B.
II. Diet
   A.
   B.
III. Habits
   A. usually hunt at night
   B.

1. eat mostly zebras and antelopes
2. young cubs look like cats
3. wait for their prey at water holes
4. male has heavy mane on neck
5. sometimes eat humans

**E.** Rewrite this paragraph. Put the sentences in order. Leave out any sentences that do not belong.

Did you know there was more than one kind of magnet? It's true. Manufactured magnets are usually steel. There are natural magnets and manufactured magnets. I had three magnets once. Natural magnets are magnetite, which is ferro-ferric oxide. Manufactured magnets can be found in the small electric motors that run drills, blenders, and stereos.

# More Lesson Practice

## Understanding Nouns
### (pages 52–53)

Write each sentence. Underline each noun and circle each article.
1. The train entered the dark tunnel.
2. Sara returned a book to the library.
3. May my friend have an apple?
4. My bicycle needs a new tire.
5. Did the caller leave a message?

## Common and Proper Nouns
### (pages 54–55)

Write each sentence. Underline each common noun once and each proper noun twice.
1. Vancouver is a beautiful city.
2. Dr. Ames lives in an unusual home.
3. Davis Stadium is a large place.
4. The road crosses the Rogue River.
5. Henry has several chores to do.

## Singular and Plural Nouns
### (pages 56–57)

Write the plural forms of the first five nouns. Write the singular forms of the last five nouns.

1. pass
2. birch
3. crash
4. dish
5. desk
6. boxes
7. glasses
8. lunches
9. ashes
10. gases

## More Ways of Forming Plurals
### (pages 58–59)

Write each sentence. Use the plural form of the noun in parentheses.
1. My brother said he heard (wolf).
2. A shepherd watches the (sheep).
3. The United States has many (ally).
4. The (life) of athletes interest me.
5. The (child) took these pictures.
6. The (mouse) were in the field.
7. Our state has twenty-four (county).
8. The (shelf) are full of merchandise.

## Possessive Forms of Nouns
### (pages 60–61)

Write each sentence. Use the possessive form of the noun in parentheses.
1. Trees grow all along the (river) banks.
2. I work in my (parents) store.
3. (Mr. James) hat is in the closet.
4. The (citizens) rights must be protected.
5. (Ms. Sims) brother lives in Ohio.
6. Our (country) history is fascinating.
7. The (horses) stalls are cleaned.
8. The (families) names were listed in alphabetical order.

## Understanding Verbs
## (pages 66–67)

Write each sentence. Draw one line under each action verb and two lines under each linking verb.

1. This old car is in good condition.
2. We pick fresh flowers every day.
3. I always count my change.
4. This soup smells delicious.
5. Tom looks very restless.

## Verb Tenses
## (pages 68–69)

Write each sentence and underline the verb. Write *present, past,* or *future* to tell the tense of the verb.

1. My uncle collected stamps for years.
2. Ruth enjoys a fast game of tennis.
3. I will finish this job tomorrow.
4. The train arrived at noon.
5. The workers need some rest.

## Irregular Verbs
## (pages 70–71)

Write each sentence. Use the correct past tense form of the verb in parentheses.

1. Fran (draw) a beautiful picture.
2. The boys (think) the book was interesting.
3. Several boxes (fall) from the shelf.
4. Henry (sing) a folk song.
5. Nancy (run) around the block.

6. Karen (choose) new curtains for her room.
7. Each person (bring) some food to the picnic.
8. Mr. Sheehan (catch) the early train.

## Other Forms of Regular Verbs
## (pages 72–73)

Write these sentences. Underline each two-word verb. Circle the helping verb.

1. We had finished practice early.
2. George was examining the coin.
3. The boys have replaced the old tile floor.
4. I am visiting my cousins this week.
5. My friends were complaining about the test.

## Other Forms of Irregular Verbs
## (pages 74–75)

Complete each sentence with the past participle of the verb in parentheses. Write each sentence.

1. The temperature has _____ in the last hour. (fall)
2. My Aunt Alice had _____ in India before. (be)
3. The visitors have _____ home. (go)
4. Charley had _____ a dozen fish in an hour. (catch)
5. Sheila has _____ a partner already. (choose)

## Understanding Pronouns
### (pages 80–81)

Write each sentence. Underline each pronoun. Draw a line from each pronoun to the noun it takes the place of.

1. Sam flew his model glider, but it crashed.
2. Andrea changed her mind and called her mother.
3. Noriko bought fresh oranges and squeezed them.
4. Mrs. Stevens found her purse, but she has lost it again.
5. The girls left their books on the bus.

## Personal Pronouns
### (pages 82–83)

Write each sentence. Underline the subject pronoun once and the object pronoun twice.

1. We met him at the bus station.
2. I found it on the lawn.
3. She saw him last night.
4. He drove her to school.
5. She told us about the movie.
6. You resemble her very much.
7. He told me about the book.
8. I will see them tomorrow.

## Possessive Forms of Pronouns
### (pages 84–85)

Write each sentence. Draw one line under possessive pronouns used before nouns. Draw two lines under possessive pronouns used alone in place of nouns.

1. My brother needs your advice.
2. Karen forgot her book, but I brought mine.
3. John made his decision right away.
4. They hung their coats in the closet.
5. Kim bought her costume, but Al made his.
6. Our dog often chases its tail.
7. The money is theirs.
8. The gloves on the table are yours.

## Demonstrative Pronouns
### (pages 86–87)

Write each sentence. Underline the demonstrative pronouns. Circle the verb that each demonstrative pronoun comes before or follows.

1. This is my favorite stamp.
2. Put these in a safe place.
3. I will do that tomorrow.
4. Diane will take these home.
5. Will you wrap this for me?

## Understanding Adjectives
### (pages 92–93)

Write the following sentences. Underline each adjective. Draw two lines under the noun that the adjective describes.

1. A steady rainfall watered the dry ground.

2. The nasty weather lasted two days.
3. Lofty mountains towered over the peaceful valley.
4. The tiny children enjoyed the shallow pool.
5. The young man carried a thick notebook.

1. I visited _____ city last year.
2. _____ library books on the table are overdue.
3. Mr. Carpenter read _____ reports last week.
4. _____ dog seems lost.
5. _____ photographs are really fabulous.

## Comparing with Adjectives (pages 94–95)

Write each sentence. Use the correct form of the adjective in parentheses.
1. Last night's game was the (strange) I have ever seen.
2. This is the (high) bridge in the country.
3. The first question is (easy) than the second.
4. Ms. Janna is the (wise) person I know.
5. That story is (unbelievable) than the last one.
6. Hiram was (clever) than Jed.
7. This is the (recent) issue of the magazine.
8. A river is usually (wide) than a brook.

## Demonstrative Adjectives (pages 96–97)

Use the demonstrative adjective *this, that, these,* or *those* to complete each sentence. Write each sentence.

## Understanding Adverbs (pages 102–103)

Write the adverb that appears in each of the following sentences. Next to each adverb, write the verb that the adverb tells about.
1. We often walk along the beach.
2. It rained continuously throughout the night.
3. Johnson has never caught a fish.
4. The road went nowhere.
5. The old car runs well.
6. The holiday weekend begins tomorrow.
7. I always read the daily newspaper.
8. We went outside to play.

## Comparing with Adverbs (pages 104–105)

Write each sentence. Use the correct form of the adverb in parentheses.
1. Jeffrey arrived (late) than John.
2. The trains run (frequently) during the week.

3. Karen works (carefully) than her sister.
4. Of all the team members, Jack practices (faithfully).
5. Is the antelope the (fast) of all the animals?

## More About Adverbs (pages 108–109)

Write each of the following sentences. Use the correct adverb form in place of the adjective form in parentheses.
1. It was (near) six o'clock when we left the party.
2. The handle should turn (easy).
3. Benita moved very (quick) to take the lead.
4. Watch (close) what I do.
5. It snowed (steady) for three days.

## Understanding Prepositions (pages 114–115)

Write each sentence. Underline the prepositional phrase or phrases in each.
1. We rowed the boat to the middle of the lake.
2. We walked across the snowy fields after the storm.
3. The fire started in the evening and burned throughout the night.
4. We can't leave without them.
5. Tom took a picture of the polar bears.

## Using Prepositional Phrases (pages 116–117)

Write each sentence. Underline each prepositional phrase in the sentence. Circle the preposition.
1. She walked down the center of the path.
2. I will be at the Shady Pines hotel until Thursday afternoon.
3. Wildflowers grew along the sides of the road.
4. Turtles sunned themselves by the edge of the pond.
5. After the parade we attended a picnic in the park.

## Understanding Conjunctions (pages 118–119)

Rewrite each pair of sentences to make one new sentence. Join the sentences with *and, but,* or *or.* Use a comma before the conjunction.
1. We can go to the post office now. We can wait until this afternoon.
2. It rained for four straight days. The rivers and streams began to overflow.
3. I called this number several times. No one answered the phone.
4. The nights became colder. Some kinds of birds flew south.
5. The car's body is in good condition. The engine needs a lot of work.

## Understanding Interjections
## (pages 120–121)

Write the interjection in each of the following.
1. Wow! This water is icy cold.
2. Whew! This package is heavy.
3. Wait! I thought I saw something.
4. Finally! The sun is coming out.
5. Ouch! Those flies can bite.

## Four Kinds of Sentences
## (pages 130–131)

After the number of each sentence, write which kind of sentence it is: *declarative, interrogative, imperative,* or *exclamatory.*
1. The travel time to Cincinnati is six hours.
2. Put this card in your wallet.
3. The elevator is falling!
4. Where are the spoons?
5. Read the passage on page 342.

## Subjects and Predicates
## (pages 132–133)

Write each sentence. Draw a line between the complete subject and the complete predicate. Then underline each simple subject once and each simple predicate twice.
1. My brother's car needs new tires.
2. The captain of the team called a meeting.

3. We worked throughout the entire two days.
4. Several of the boys and girls were late.
5. Brad explained the problem to me.

## Objects in Sentences
## (pages 134–135)

Write each sentence. Underline each direct object once and each indirect object twice.
1. I returned the overdue books to the library.
2. Jim sent Margaret a long letter.
3. Geraldine borrowed two eggs from Mrs. Stone.
4. Donald gave his mother the message.
5. I told her that story yesterday.
6. The hikers bought supplies at a small store.
7. John taught Marie the code.
8. The carpenters built the house in four days.

## Subject-Verb Agreement
## (pages 136–137)

Write each sentence, using the correct word in parentheses.
1. John (prefers, prefer) fresh fruit.
2. We (gathers, gather) every year.
3. This mechanic (understands, understand) the problem.

4. Our coaches always (watches, watch) each play.
5. A clerk (keeps, keep) the files in order.

## Compound Sentence Parts
## (pages 138–139)

Write each sentence. Underline the compound part in each. Identify it as subject, predicate, or object.
1. Danny and Ron practice every afternoon.
2. One worker sorts and inspects the parts.
3. My brother collects stamps and coins.
4. The teacher asked Carl and Philip a difficult question.
5. We will fix or replace this television.

## Statements and Questions
## (pages 140–141)

Change the statements that follow to questions. Change the questions to statements. Write each sentence.
1. Fresh fruit is healthy and delicious.
2. The town has appointed a new police chief.
3. The new express train stops at this station.
4. Does your friend's mother know the address?
5. Was the party a great success?

## Adding Words to Sentences
## (pages 146–147)

Complete each sentence by adding an adjective and an adverb. Write each sentence. Draw one line under the adjective you add and two lines under the adverb.
1. The ship _____ disappeared into the _____ fog.
2. Jason _____ completed the _____ assignment.
3. The _____ waves crashed _____ against the shore.
4. The car bounced _____ over the _____ road.
5. The _____ cat sat _____ on a sofa.

## Combining Sentences
## (pages 148–149)

Combine each pair of simple sentences into a compound sentence by using *and*, *but*, or *or*. Write each sentence, and remember to put a comma before the conjunction.
1. The dam must hold. The valley will flood.
2. I want to go to the game. I am going to a play tonight.
3. The passengers boarded. The train departed.
4. We can set up camp here. We can move farther up the mountain.
5. The sun was nice and warm. The wind had a chill in it.

## Avoiding Sentence Fragments (pages 152–153)

After the number of each item, write whether the group of words is a sentence or a sentence fragment. Make each sentence fragment into a complete sentence. Write the new sentence.

1. In the front of the room.
2. The contest officials announced the winner.
3. The main river in the eastern part of the state.
4. During a break in the game's action.
5. Julio remembered the combination of the safe.

## Avoiding Run-On Sentences (pages 154–155)

After the number of each sentence, write either *correct* or *run-on*. Correct each run-on sentence. Write separate sentences or a compound sentence. Remember to place a comma before the conjunction in a compound sentence.

1. We got to the bank on time we forgot it was Sunday.
2. I admire my older brother and try to learn from him.
3. Many onlookers gathered on the beach and watched the rescuers.
4. Mario plays in the band and sings.
5. The farmer plowed the field then he seeded it.

## Avoiding Wordiness in Sentences (pages 156–157)

Rewrite each sentence. Omit any unnecessary words.

1. Our cat that is called Samantha has two black and white baby kittens.
2. The car moved along very slowly down the street.
3. In my opinion, I think we ought to go home.
4. At the final end of the story, the detective solves the mystery.
5. I run my daily mile every day.

## Capitalization (pages 162–163)

Rewrite each sentence. Capitalize correctly.

1. the flight to houston was late.
2. fred speaks spanish in madrid.
3. ms. juarez asked louise to read a book called *voyage to the stars*.
4. phil and i work each summer for the federated corporation.
5. mr. po recommended a chinese restaurant to us.
6. the mississippi river flows into the gulf of mexico.
7. my high school tennis team is called the netters.
8. professor reuben teaches at morningside college.

## Capitalization in Letter Writing (pages 164–165)

Rewrite the following letter. Correct the capitalization errors.

318 Fulton Lane

dallas, TX 75207

september 4, 19--

dear uncle ed,

Thank you for sending the notebook that I left at your house. It had some important homework in it, and I really needed it by Wednesday. Thanks to you I got it.

Once again, I thank you and Aunt Dorothy for inviting me to visit.

your niece,

Martha

## Using Quotation Marks (pages 166–167)

Write each sentence correctly. Add whatever punctuation marks are necessary.

1. Please turn off the water said Andrea
2. Which road leads to Nashville the last traveler asked
3. Did Benjamin Franklin say A penny saved is a penny earned
4. Glen, please give me the answer to the first problem said the teacher
5. The principal asked Who would like to enter the contest

## More About Writing Quotations (pages 168–169)

Rewrite the following sentences. Add quotation marks, commas, and capital letters where necessary.

1. We will begin the guide said in the room on the right.
2. General McClellan marched for two days the teacher said. he then set up camp.
3. The first thing we must do explained Harry is apologize to them.
4. The problem is clear Captain Anderson explained. we don't have enough officers to patrol the entire town.
5. These flowers said Sheila need direct sunlight.

## Commas in Sentences (pages 170–171)

Write each sentence. Add commas where they are needed.

1. My youngest sister was born on September 15 1976 in Tampa Florida.
2. Tom please wash your hands.
3. Yes the student with the highest grade will receive a special prize.
4. The weather will turn colder but no storms are expected.
5. The play will be starring Cara Greg and Eileen.

## Using Apostrophes
## (pages 172-173)

Complete each sentence by forming a contraction that uses the word in parentheses. Write each sentence.

1. We _____ use the field this afternoon. (can)
2. _____ the best soccer player on our team. (he)
3. I _____ met Tony yet. (have)
4. Wilma, _____ the fastest runner we have. (you)
5. The plane from New York _____ arrived yet. (has)
6. _____ the strangest story I have ever heard. (it)
7. Francis said _____ prefer to wait for the next bus. (he)
8. _____ the boy in the light tan jacket? (who)

## Using Colons
## (pages 174-175)

Rewrite each of the following items, adding colons where they are needed.

1. These streets will be paved Gould Street, Ray Street, and Deer Drive.
2. I will meet you tonight at 645.
3. Dear Ms. Wainwright
4. Does every night game begin at 730?
5. These jobs are the hardest for me walking the dog, taking out the trash, and dusting the furniture.

## Proofreading Sentences
## (pages 176-177)

Copy each sentence. Then use proofreading marks to show the correction asked for in parentheses.

1. Take care of your shoes They are expensive. (Use a period.)
2. Janice is the president our class. (Add a word.)
3. Lemons oranges and limes are citrus fruits. (Add commas.)
4. I am interested in american history. (Use a capital letter.)
5. The first question was was easy. (Take out a word.)
6. The car was moving to fast. (Add a letter.)
7. "The world is getting smaller," said the teacher. "the jet plane has done that." (Use a capital letter.)
8. "Do you know who the thieves are?" asked Captain Washington. "I have no idea," replied Tom. (Begin a new paragraph.)
9. I ran too the grocery store this morning. (Take out a letter.)
10. Tim please give me a hand. (Use a comma.)

# Handbook

## I. Capital Letters

**first words**
Begin the first word in a sentence with a capital letter.
> **T**he waves crashed against the rocky shore.
> **W**hat time is it?

**proper nouns**
Begin proper nouns with capital letters.
> **L**abor **D**ay       **J**ulius **I**rving       **W**ednesday

**proper adjectives**
Begin proper adjectives with capital letters.
> **S**panish explorer     **J**apanese camera     **R**oman numerals

**I**
Write the pronoun *I* as a capital letter.
> She thought **I** would be late.

**letters**
Begin the greeting and the closing of a letter with a capital letter.
> **D**ear Mrs. Kwan,        **D**ear Julio,       **Y**ours truly,

**titles of people**
Begin the titles that people have with a capital letter.
> **D**octor Brown        **A**unt Nancy      **S**enator Brooks

**book titles**
Use capital letters to begin the first word, the last word, and all the important words in the title of a book, play, story, or poem.
> *Call **I**t Courage*        *The **W**ind in the **W**illows*

3. dr. lee moved her office to cityside plaza.
4. did you read the book *the secret garden*?
5. my uncle john climbed glacier peak in washington.

## II. Punctuation

### END MARKS

**period**

Use a period after declarative and imperative sentences.
My brother likes to swim.
Watch the magician's clever trick.

Use a period at the end of an abbreviation.

| | | | |
|---|---|---|---|
| Tues. | Mr. | Dr. | Chestnut St. |
| U.S. | Ms. | Jan. | dept. |

**question mark**

Use a question mark after an interrogative sentence.
May I borrow your eraser? Are you ready to go?

**exclamation mark**

Use an exclamation mark after an exclamatory sentence.
You won first prize! I can't wait!

**PRACTICE**

Write each sentence. Use the correct end mark.
1. Does your dog do tricks
2. The river flows through the valley
3. Please turn down the music
4. Oh no, I lost all of my money
5. Try to be on time

### COMMAS

**dates and addresses**

Use a comma to set off items in dates and addresses.
The art museum is at 4 Kurt Street, Salem, Oregon.
On Thursday, October 11, 1984, a woman astronaut walked in space.

---

*Handbook*

| | |
|---|---|
| **series** | Use commas to separate three or more words or groups of words in a series. |
| | Jack put grapes, oranges, and bananas in the fruit salad. |
| | I jumped out of bed, got dressed, and left for school. |
| **letters** | Use a comma after the greeting and the closing of a friendly letter. |
| | Dear Robert,  Dear Uncle Ben,  Your pal, |
| **direct quotation** | Use a comma to separate a direct quotation from the rest of the sentence. |
| | Sonja said, "It is my turn now." |
| | Tom asked, "Will the bus leave on time?" |
| | "The meeting will start at eight," said Diana. |
| **names of people spoken to and introductory words** | Use commas to set off the names of persons spoken to. |
| | Lucy, please answer the telephone. |
| | Please fold the napkins, Luke, before you set the table. |
| | Use commas to set off introductory words. |
| | No, the mail has not arrived. |
| | Well, this is a pleasant surprise! |
| **compound sentence** | Use a comma before the conjunction in a compound sentence. |
| | We raked the leaves, but the wind blew them away. |
| | The thick fog lifted, and the sun began to shine. |

**PRACTICE**  Write each sentence. Use commas correctly.

1. Yes this train stops in Cleveland Ohio.
2. The new store opened on Monday April 12 1982.
3. Mary said "No I am not hungry yet."
4. Jake runs very fast but Mark runs faster.
5. He finished his homework wrote a letter and read a magazine.

# QUOTATION MARKS

**direct quotation**

Use quotation marks before and after someone's exact words. Begin the first word of a quotation within a sentence with a capital letter.

> "Let's play a game," said Ellen.
> Carl shouted, "What a wonderful gift!"

Put the end mark inside the closing quotation mark if it is part of the quotation. Otherwise put the end mark outside the closing quotation mark.

> Mr. Fernandez asked, "Who is the captain of the team?"
> Did the team captain say, "I know we'll win this game"?

**divided quotation**

Use quotation marks before and after each part of a divided quotation. Begin the second part of a divided quotation with a capital letter only if it begins a new sentence.

> "Come in," said Eli, "and make yourself at home."
> "Who should we invite?" asked Mike. "Let's make a list."

**PRACTICE**

Write each sentence correctly. Add quotation marks, commas, and capital letters where necessary.

1. Yes, I enjoy gymnastics he said.
2. Was it Yoshi who said I will make the salad?
3. I must leave right now! Carlos exclaimed.
4. I want to join the team Ted said. when is practice?
5. Let's leave now said Pam so we will be on time.

# APOSTROPHE

**possessives**

Use an apostrophe in the possessive form of a noun.

> The dog's bone was buried in the snow.
> The monkeys' cages were cleaned this morning.
> Charles's bicycle is red.
> The Jameses' garden was in bloom.

---

| | |
|---|---|
| **contractions** | Use an apostrophe in a contraction.<br>We can't leave right away.<br>Kim thought that she'd turned off the light. |

**PRACTICE**  Add apostrophes to the following sentences.
1. They arent moving until December.
2. We heard womens voices.
3. Johns desk is well organized.
4. Its too early to leave.
5. The horses coats were sleek and smooth.

## COLON

| | |
|---|---|
| **business letter** | Use a colon after the greeting in a business letter.<br>Dear Sir or Madam:        Gentlemen: |
| **list** | Use a colon to introduce a series or a list of items.<br>On Saturday, Rick did these chores: washed the floor, cut the grass, shopped for groceries.<br>Bring these things to school: paper, pencils, and a ruler. |
| **time of day** | Use a colon to separate the numbers for hours and minutes in writing the time of day.<br>12:30 P.M.     6:13 A.M.     4:46 P.M.     11:01 A.M. |

**PRACTICE**  Write each sentence. Add colons where needed.
1. I needed many items at the store milk, eggs, peanuts, and apples.
2. The birds began to sing at 503 A.M.
3. This paint comes in these colors tan, yellow, and brown.
4. Marianne always goes to sleep at 830 P.M.
5. By 1115 A.M., the students had had four subjects reading, math, social studies, spelling.

# III. Usage

## USING VERBS

**is**
**are**

Use *is* for subjects that name one person or thing, except for *I* and *you*.

> The road **is** rocky.

Use *are* for subjects that name more than one.

> The leaves **are** falling from the trees.

**PRACTICE**

Use *is* or *are* to complete each sentence. Write each sentence.
1. My mother _____ a lawyer.
2. Those children _____ always friendly.
3. _____ that your sister?
4. Small cars _____ popular now.
5. _____ those your books?

**was**
**were**

Use *was* for subjects that name one person or thing, except for *you*.

> Penny **was** last in line.

Use *were* for the subjects that name more than one.

> The horse and the dog **were** in the barn.

**PRACTICE**

Use *was* or *were* to complete each sentence.
1. _____ my cousin here earlier?
2. Phil _____ the one who helped me.
3. Several cars _____ in the parking lot.
4. _____ they planning to go to the movies?
5. Sally Ride _____ the first American woman in space.

**does**
**do**

Use *does* for subjects that name one person, except for *I* and *you*.

> Brian **does** the laundry for the family.

Use *do* for subjects that name more than one.
Becky and Kim **do** the cleaning.

**PRACTICE**  Use *does* or *do* to complete each sentence.
1. Vinnie _____ the dishes quickly.
2. _____ your friends like to go camping?
3. The two brothers _____ projects together.
4. Lee _____ her paper route in an hour.
5. _____ Bill like broccoli?

**has**
**have**
**had**

Use *has* for subjects that name one person or thing, except for *I* and *you*.
The dog **has** a collar on.

Use *have* when the subject names more than one.
The students **have** free time at one o'clock.

Use *had* for both singular and plural subjects to show that the action happened in the past.
I **had** three dimes before I lost one.
They **had** five dollars to spend.

**PRACTICE**  Use *has, have,* or *had* to complete each sentence.
1. We _____ guests last night.
2. Heidi now _____ a nice singing voice.
3. Scott and Mario _____ the same teacher now.
4. My mother now _____ an office at home.
5. He _____ a cold last week.

**eat**
**ate**
**eaten**

Use *eat (eats)* to show that the action is happening now.
Sandy **eats** breakfast early.
Those children **eat** good food.

Use *ate* to show that the action happened in the past.
Rick **ate** an apple for dessert.

Use *eaten* after *has, have,* or *had.*

> The mouse has already **eaten** the sausage.
> The guests have **eaten** their salads.
> We had **eaten** before Mark arrived.

**PRACTICE**

Use *eat (eats), ate,* or *eaten* to complete each sentence.
1. Cathy _____ dinner late today.
2. The moths have _____ through the cloth.
3. Sy _____ his lunch with his friends yesterday.
4. Gabe now _____ more quickly than her sister.
5. Adam has _____ the fish he caught today.

**come**
**came**
**come**

Use *come (comes)* to show that the action is happening now.

> My cat **comes** when I call her.
> The children **come** in early when it is cold out.

Use *came* to show that the action happened in the past.

> The sun **came** out after the rain.

Use *come* after *has, have,* or *had.*

> Roger has **come** to get his math book.
> Our neighbors have **come** to visit.
> They had **come** to see Jenny.

**PRACTICE**

Use *come (comes), came,* or *come* to complete each sentence.
1. My cousin _____ here for the holiday.
2. That train _____ at 6:30 sharp each day.
3. These ten people have _____ to help.
4. Yesterday your mail _____ late.
5. Sam and Ellen always _____ to school early.

**do**
**did**
**done**

Use *do (does)* to show that action is happening now.

> Sarah **does** her work in the library.
> Mom and Dad **do** the waltz very gracefully.

Use *did* to show that the action happened in the past.
Ellen **did** her report on clouds.

Use *done* after *has, have,* or *had.*
Rhonda has **done** neat work on this assignment.
Lance and Missy have **done** all the shoveling.
I had **done** my homework before dinner.

**PRACTICE**

Use *do (does), did,* or *done* to complete each sentence.
1. Eric _____ that puzzle quickly yesterday.
2. The governor has _____ all she can to lower taxes.
3. The teachers _____ the attendance first.
4. They have _____ a good test on the equipment.
5. Stu now _____ his errands in the morning.

**run**
**ran**
**run**

Use *run (runs)* to show that the action is happening now.
Leah **runs** to school when she is late.
I **run** the rehearsal when Mrs. Ross is busy.

Use *ran* to show that the action happened in the past.
One hundred people **ran** in today's road race.

Use *run* after *has, have,* or *had.*
Becky has **run** more than a mile.
The workers have **run** telephone wires to the new house.
She had **run** into difficulty after the first problem.

**PRACTICE**

Use *run (runs), ran,* or *run* to complete each sentence.
1. Jess had _____ in this race before.
2. The heater _____ automatically.
3. The students _____ their own store last year.
4. I _____ a mile each day.
5. Have you _____ out of milk?

**see**
**saw**
**seen**

Use *see (sees)* to show that the action is happening now.

> I **see** better with glasses.
> The baby smiles when he **sees** his mother.

Use *saw* to show that the action happened in the past.

> I **saw** the play the sixth graders produced.

Use *seen* after *has, have,* or *had.*

> Glen has **seen** this painting in the museum.
> The students have **seen** this movie before.
> We had **seen** Ken earlier in the day.

**PRACTICE**

Use *see (sees), saw,* or *seen* to complete each sentence.
1. I can _____ the ocean from my window.
2. The dentist _____ twenty patients a day.
3. Sue has just _____ the new ad.
4. I _____ an old friend last night.
5. Have you _____ my coat?

**go**
**went**
**gone**

Use *go (goes)* to show that the action is happening now.

> George **goes** to college in Oklahoma.
> People **go** into the city everyday.

Use *went* to show that the action has happened in the past.

> The bus just **went** by.

Use *gone* after *has, have,* or *had.*

> My brother has **gone** to work.
> My friends have **gone** to the beach.
> The sun had **gone** down.

**PRACTICE**

Use *go (goes), went,* or *gone* to complete each sentence.
1. We _____ roller-skating every Saturday.
2. Last summer _____ by quickly.
3. Had Amy ever _____ to a rodeo?

4. Ryan _____ to his friend's house every afternoon.
5. Pedro and Steven have _____ fishing.

**know**
**knew**
**known**

Use *know (knows)* to show that the action is happening now.
　Eric **knows** the answer.
　Stacy and Linda **know** the way to my house.

Use *knew* to show that the action happened in the past.
　Charles **knew** how to paddle a canoe.

Use *known* after *has, have,* or *had.*
　Kim has **known** Darla since first grade.
　We have **known** our neighbors for many years.
　They had **known** the secret all along.

**PRACTICE**

Use *know, (knows), knew,* or *known* to complete each sentence.
1. We have _____ the store owner since he bought the store.
2. Sandy had _____ about the party before we told her.
3. Do you _____ how to get there?
4. Bill _____ the rules of the game.
5. I _____ the answer, but I forgot it.

**throw**
**threw**
**thrown**

Use *throw (throws)* to tell about an action that is happening now.
　Please do not **throw** these papers away.
　This pitcher always **throws** a curve ball.

Use *threw* to tell about an action that happened in the past.
　Gary **threw** the anchor into the water.

Use *thrown* after *has, have,* or *had.*
　Louise has **thrown** the trash away.
　People have **thrown** pennies into the wishing well.
　Dad had **thrown** away the directions.

**write**
**wrote**
**written**

Use *write (writes)* to tell about an action that is happening now.
  Mom **writes** a column in the local newspaper.
  The pen pals **write** letters every week.

Use *wrote* to tell about an action that happened in the past.
  We **wrote** the invitations in pen.

Use *written* after *has*, *have*, or *had*.
  Sara has **written** a thank-you note.
  They have **written** their ideas on the board.
  She had already **written** her name on the board.

**bring**
**brought**

Use *bring (brings)* to tell about an action that is happening now.
  The puppies **bring** me my slippers.
  Gail **brings** the cows in from the pasture.

Use *brought* to tell about an action that happened in the past.
  We **brought** you some flowers.

Use *brought* with *has*, *have*, or *had*.
  The waiter has **brought** our dinner.

---

We have **brought** our favorite game from home.

Joe had **brought** his own sleeping bag.

**PRACTICE**

Use *bring (brings)* or *brought* to complete each sentence.

1. The papergirl always _____ the paper at 7:00 A.M.
2. Aunt Lois _____ us gifts from Europe last week.
3. The children have _____ their lunches to the lunchroom.
4. Nick has _____ slides for us to see.
5. Please _____ the clothes in from the line.

**choose**
**chose**
**chosen**

Use *choose (chooses)* to tell about an action that is happening now.

Sam always **chooses** to read in his free time.

Let's **choose** a movie to watch.

Use *chose* to tell about an action that happened in the past.

I **chose** a sweater to wear that day.

Use *chosen* after *has, have,* or *had.*

Uncle Saul has **chosen** to take the train.

The children have **chosen** a bedtime story.

The coach had **chosen** Yoshi to pitch.

**PRACTICE**

Use *choose (chooses), chose,* or *chosen* in each sentence.

1. Yesterday the students _____ partners for their projects.
2. Has your family _____ a place for vacation?
3. Voters _____ between candidates in each election.
4. The taxi driver often _____ the shortest routes.
5. Both teams have _____ captains.

**fall**
**fell**
**fallen**

Use *fall (falls)* to tell about an action that is happening now.

Carl's pencil **falls** when he opens his desk.

I **fall** asleep easily at night.

Use *fell* to tell about an action that happened in the past.

The rock **fell** from the cliff.

Use *fallen* after *has, have,* or *had.*
> The beginning skater has **fallen** many times.
> Those books have **fallen** over.
> Snow had **fallen** during the night.

**PRACTICE**     Use *fall (falls), fell,* or *fallen* to complete each sentence.
1. Leaves _____ from the trees in autumn.
2. The picture just _____ off the wall.
3. The dime has _____ out of my pocket.
4. Thanksgiving always _____ on a Thursday.
5. The petals have _____ off this rose.

**ring**
**rang**
**rung**

Use *ring (rings)* to tell about an action that is happening now.
> You can **ring** this bell for room service.
> The school bell **rings** at 8:00.

Use *rang* to tell about an action that happened in the past.
> The chimes **rang** when the wind blew.

Use *rung* after *has, have,* or *had.*
> The school bell has already **rung.**
> Sailors have always **rung** the ship's bells on foggy nights.
> Makiba had **rung** the bell on her bicycle three times.

**PRACTICE**     Use *ring (rings), rang,* or *rung* to complete each sentence.
1. The bell _____ twelve times each day at noon.
2. Greg just _____ his neighbor's doorbell.
3. The phone had _____ four times before she answered it.
4. Customers always _____ the bell for service here.
5. We have _____ their doorbell three times.

**think**
**thought**

Use *think (thinks)* to tell about an action that is happening now.
> I **think** I know the answer.
> Bruce **thinks** of songs in his head.

Use *thought* to tell about an action that happened in the past.
> We **thought** we heard voices outside.

Use *thought* after *has, have,* or *had.*
> Linda has **thought** of a good plan.
> The scientists have **thought** of a solution.
> Finally, Joe had **thought** of an answer.

**PRACTICE**

Use *think (thinks)* or *thought* to complete each sentence.
1. I _____ that we are lost now.
2. Rose _____ of ideas before she writes stories.
3. Have you _____ of the answer to the question yet?
4. Marty has _____ of the gift that he wants to buy.
5. Yesterday I _____ of a new idea for our project.

**give**
**gave**
**given**

Use *give (gives)* to tell about an action that is happening now.
> Cathy **gives** her dog a bath.
> Teachers **give** students help on their work.

Use *gave* to tell about an action that happened in the past.
> Greg **gave** his brother a baseball mitt.

Use *given* after *has, have,* or *had.*
> Margo has **given** the correct answer.
> We have **given** you all the clues to the puzzle.
> Ms. Scott had already **given** us homework for tonight.

**PRACTICE**

Use *give (gives), gave,* or *given* to complete each sentence.
1. Mom _____ us a ride to school when it rains.
2. Chapter two just _____ me a clue to the mystery.
3. They always _____ prizes for the best costume.
4. Had he _____ away all his old toys?
5. I have _____ away the secret by mistake.

## USING PRONOUNS

**I, me, we,**
**us, he, him,**
**she, her,**
**they, them**

Use *I, we, she, he,* and *they* as subject pronouns. Subject pronouns come before the verb in a sentence.

**I** like fruit.

**We** walk to school.

**He** made a kite.

**She** and her friends went on a bike ride.

**They** wrote articles for the school newspaper.

Use *me, us, him, her,* and *them* as object pronouns. Object pronouns come after the verb in a sentence.

Lucy called **me**.

Evan invited **us** to the party.

Diane reminded **him** about the meeting.

The judges gave **her** first prize.

The writer sold **them** copies of her book.

**PRACTICE**

Write each sentence. Use the correct word in parentheses.

1. Doug gave (they, them) pictures of the trip.
2. (We, Us) held the doors for the class.
3. Carl and (she, her) will be team captains.
4. The author will tell (they, them) how he writes.
5. (He, Him) and Mary sit in the first row.
6. Please tell (I, me) how to get to that store.
7. My parents took (he, him) to the circus.
8. Margaret and (I, me) like to roller-skate.
9. (She, Her) and Bruce are the fastest runners in the class.
10. Lisa helped (we, us) paint the mural.

## USING OTHER WORDS

**a**

**an**

Use *a* before any word that begins with a consonant sound.

**A** yellow coat was left here.

Use *an* before any word that begins with a vowel sound.
There is **an** opening in the cave.
That is **an** honorable thing to do.

**PRACTICE**

Write each sentence. Use *a* or *an* to complete each sentence.
1. Ilene has _____ office in _____ large building.
2. _____ honest answer is always the best.
3. That was _____ happy ending.
4. Try to take _____ morning or _____ afternoon plane.
5. Do you have _____ question?

**between**
**among**

Use *between* to refer to two people, places, or things.
Judy was seated **between** Luke and Yoshi.

Use *among* to refer to more than two people, places, or things.
Judy was seated **among** the sixth-grade students.

**PRACTICE**

Use *between* or *among* to complete each sentence.
1. My bicycle is parked _____ the racer and the dirt bike.
2. Kareem is _____ that team of boys wearing green uniforms.
3. Please stand _____ Sue Ellen and Jacob.
4. It took _____ five and six minutes for us to stop laughing.
5. Karen's coat was _____ that group piled on the bed.

**its**
**it's**

Use the pronoun *its* to mean "belonging to it."
The old piano had lost **its** tune.

Use the contraction *it's* to mean "it is."
**It's** time for school.

**PRACTICE**

Use *its* or *it's* to complete each sentence. Write each sentence.
1. The cat hurt _____ paw.
2. _____ going to rain this afternoon.

3. The boat lost _____ sail in the storm.
4. I know that _____ not noon yet.
5. The team won _____ last game.

**let**
**leave**

Use *let* when you mean "to give permission."
   **Let** me help you.

Use *leave* when you mean "to allow to stay" or "to go away."
   May I **leave** my bicycle here?
   We **leave** at noon on Friday.

**PRACTICE**

Use *let* or *leave* to complete each sentence.
1. _____ Doug have a turn.
2. _____ your hat and coat here.
3. Will your parents _____ you go camping?
4. We will _____ right after school.
5. Please _____ me use your pen.

**their**
**there**
**they're**

*Their* is a possessive pronoun that comes before a noun.
   **Their** desks are in rows.

*There* is an adverb.
   We will go **there** for the picnic.

*They're* is a contraction that means "they are."
   I hope **they're** having fun.

**PRACTICE**

Use *their*, *there*, or *they're* to complete each sentence.
1. We want to go _____ first.
2. _____ team plays well together.
3. _____ is your umbrella.
4. I like _____ recipe the best.
5. Do you think that _____ the best artists?

| to | Use *to* to mean "towards." |
| too | Please hand it **to** me. |
| two | I walk **to** the beach in the summer. |

Use *too* to mean "also" or "to an excessive degree."

I will volunteer, **too.**

My pants are **too** short now.

Use *two* to mean "more than one."

I have **two** cousins.

I read **two** books by that author.

**PRACTICE**     Use *to, too,* or *two* to complete each sentence.

1. We walked _____ the baseball field.
2. The poem is _____ long for me to remember.
3. George will hand out the papers and collect them _____ .
4. You gave me _____ copies of the newspaper.
5. Dave went _____ the refrigerator to get the milk.

| your | Use *your* to mean "belonging to you." |
| you're | This is **your** yard. |
| | Is this **your** ticket? |

Use the contraction *you're* to mean "you are."

If **you're** the last one, please close the door.

**You're** the representative from this class.

**PRACTICE**     Use *your* or *you're* to complete each sentence.

1. _____ letter arrived yesterday.
2. _____ the first one to think of the answer.
3. You left on _____ radio.
4. I hope that _____ coming home soon.
5. Please tell me if _____ not warm enough.

# Glossary

**action verb**        A word that tells what the subject of a sentence does (page 66).

**adjective**        A word that describes a noun or pronoun (page 92).
        **last** year                **some** students

**adverb**        A word that tells how, when, or where about an action verb (page 102).
        **quickly**        **often**        **here**

**agreement**        The subject and verb in a sentence must both be singular or must both be plural (page 136).

**almanac**        A book that contains facts on many subjects (page 334).

**antonym**        One of two words with an opposite meaning (page 316).

**apostrophe (')**        A punctuation mark used in forming contractions and with nouns to indicate possession (pages 172 and 318).

**article**        A word that is always followed by a noun (page 52).
        **a** pencil        **an** apple        **the** teacher

**atlas**        A book of maps (page 334).

**bibliography**        A list of books an author used to research a topic (page 340).

**biographical dictionary**        A book or books containing information about well-known people (page 334).

**body of a letter**        The main content of a letter (page 302).

| | |
|---|---|
| **brainstorming** | Quickly listing all the ideas you have on a topic (page 222). |
| **card catalog** | A cabinet containing alphabetically arranged cards for each book in the library (page 338). |
| **characters** | The people in a story or play (pages 22 and 242). |
| **closing of a letter** | The part of a letter that comes immediately above the signature (page 302). |
| **colon (:)** | A punctuation mark that separates the hours and minutes in the time of day, follows the greeting in a business letter, or introduces a list of items (page 174). |
| **comma (,)** | A punctuation mark used to separate words, groups of words, and numbers from each other (page 170). |
| **common noun** | A noun that names any person, place, thing, or idea (page 54). **neighbor    city        tree        democracy** |
| **comparative form (adjective)** | The form of an adjective that compares two things. It usually ends in *-er* or is preceded by the word *more* (page 94). **wider                        more crowded** |
| **comparative form (adverb)** | The form of an adverb that compares two things. It usually ends in *-er* or is preceded by the word *more* (page 104). **slower                      more loudly** |
| **complete predicate** | The verb and all the other words that tell what the subject of a sentence does or is (page 132). |
| **complete subject** | The noun and all the other words that tell who or what the sentence is about (page 132). |

| | |
|---|---|
| **compound object** | Two or more nouns or pronouns joined by a conjunction that follow an action verb. Both direct and indirect objects may be compounded (page 138).<br>    Beth teaches **French** and **Spanish**. (direct objects)<br>    Lee gave **Dave** and **me** directions. (indirect objects) |
| **compound predicate** | Two or more verbs joined by a conjunction (page 138).<br>    Robert **sang** and **danced** to the music. |
| **compound sentence** | A sentence made up of two simple sentences joined by a conjunction (page 148). |
| **compound subject** | Two or more nouns or pronouns joined by a conjunction and used as the subject of a sentence (page 138).<br>    **Dorthea** and **Jarred** mowed the lawn. |
| **compound word** | A word made by combining two other words (page 232). |
| **conjunction** | A word that connects similar words, word groups, or sentences (page 118). |
| **connotation** | The feelings, pleasant or unpleasant, that a word suggests (page 32). |
| **contraction** | Two words joined to make one shorter word (pages 172 and 318). |
| **copyright page** | A page that follows the title page and tells the year when the book was published (page 340). |
| **cross-reference** | A different heading or title where you can find more information on a topic (page 332). |
| **declarative sentence** | A sentence that makes a statement about something and has a period as an end mark (page 130). |

| | |
|---|---|
| **demonstrative adjective** | An adjective that points out something or someone (page 96). |
| | **this** puzzle         **those** flowers |
| **demonstrative pronoun** | A pronoun that points out people or things. Demonstrative pronouns serve as subjects and objects (page 86). |
| | **That** is yours.         I'll carry **those**. |
| **denotation** | The exact meaning of a word (page 32). |
| **descriptive paragraph** | A paragraph that describes a person, place, object, or event (page 196). |
| **dialogue** | Words spoken in a play or story (pages 24 and 262). |
| **dictionary** | A reference book that defines words (pages 330 and 334). |
| **direct object** | A noun or pronoun that follows an action verb and answers the question *what* or *whom* (page 134). |
| | Anne liked **math**.   Jim saw **Jerry**. |
| **divided quotation** | A quotation that is broken into two parts (page 168). |
| | **"Go upstairs,"** Sal said, **"and close the door."** |
| **encyclopedia** | A set of books with information about many topics (page 332). |
| **entry words** | The words listed and defined in a dictionary (page 330). |
| **exclamatory sentence** | A sentence that shows strong feeling and ends with an exclamation mark (page 130). |
| **factual paragraph** | A paragraph that informs or explains (page 210). |
| **first draft** | A first attempt at writing a report, story, or play (page 224). |

| | |
|---|---|
| **future tense** | The verb form that uses the word *will* and tells that something will happen sometime after the present (page 68). <br> We **will leave** tomorrow. |
| **glossary** | A small dictionary of special words and phrases that appears at the back of a book (page 340). |
| **greeting of a letter** | The part of a letter that tells to whom the letter is written (page 302). <br> **Dear Cara,** **Dear Sir or Madam:** |
| **guide words** | The words at the top of an encyclopedia or a dictionary that tell you the first and last word or topic on the page (pages 144 and 332). |
| **heading of a letter** | The part of a letter that tells the writer's address and the date (page 302). |
| **helping verb** | A verb that combines with the present and past participles to form two-word verbs (page 72). <br> **is** waving **had** played |
| **homophone** | A word that has the same sound as another word but a different spelling and meaning (page 316). |
| **idiom** | A group of words that has an unexpected meaning (page 208). <br> **hot potato**—a controversial issue |
| **imperative sentence** | A sentence that tells or asks someone to do something. It usually ends with a period (page 130). <br> **Don't forget your gloves. Please close the window.** |
| **index** | An alphabetized list of the topics and names mentioned in a book and their page numbers (page 340). |

| | |
|---|---|
| **indirect object** | A noun or pronoun that appears after the verb and before the direct object (page 134). |
| | Tony threw the **dog** a ball. |
| **inside address** | The part of a business letter that tells to whom and where the letter is going. It appears above the greeting (page 304). |
| **interjection** | A word or phrase that shows strong feeling and is followed by an exclamation mark (page 120). |
| | **Help!**        **Pow!**        **Oh, no!** |
| **interrogative sentence** | A sentence that asks a question (page 130). |
| **irregular verb** | A verb that does not form the past tense by adding *-d* or *-ed* to its present tense form (page 70). |
| **linking verb** | A verb that joins the subject of a sentence with a word or words after the verb that name or describe the subject (page 66). |
| **lyric poem** | A poem that expresses the writer's feelings (pages 290 and 292). |
| **metaphor** | A figure of speech that describes one thing by calling it something else (page 288). |
| | She was a **tiger** at volleyball. |
| **narrative poem** | A poem that tells a story (page 290). |
| **noun** | A word that names a person, place, thing, or idea (page 52). |
| **outline** | A plan that lists the main topics and subtopics that will be covered in a report (page 352). |
| **paragraph** | A group of sentences about one main idea (pages 20 and 186). |

| | |
|---|---|
| **past participle** | Regular verbs form the past participle by adding *-ed* to the present tense form. Irregular verbs form the past participle in different ways and must be remembered (pages 72 and 74).<br>  jump/**jumped**           see/**seen** |
| **past tense** | The verb form that tells that something happened some time before the present (page 68).<br>  I **played** on the soccer team last year. |
| **personal pronoun** | A pronoun that stands for one or more persons or things. *I, you, he, she, it, we,* and *us* are some personal pronouns (page 82). |
| **positive form (adjective)** | The regular form of an adjective (page 94).<br>  **small**      **damp**      **few**          **pretty** |
| **positive form (adverb)** | The regular form of an adverb (page 104).<br>  **smoothly**           **loudly** |
| **possessive noun** | A noun that shows ownership (page 60).<br>  the **girls'** bike           **Val's** dog |
| **possessive pronoun** | A pronoun that shows ownership (page 84).<br>  **their** books      **his** pen           **our** paper |
| **prefix** | A group of letters added to the beginning of a word to form a new word (page 320). |
| **prepositional phrase** | A group of words that begins with a preposition and ends with a noun or a pronoun (pages 114 and 116).<br>  **through the door**           **after the dance** |
| **present participle** | The verb form made by adding *-ing* to the present tense (page 72).<br>  **blinking**           **thinking**           **smiling** |

| | |
|---|---|
| **present tense** | The verb form that tells something is happening in the present time (page 68). |
| **pronoun** | A word that can take the place of a noun (page 80). |
| **proofread** | To read for errors (pages 176 and 228). |
| **proper noun** | A noun that begins with a capital letter and names a particular person, place, thing, or idea (page 54). |
| **quotation marks (" ")** | Marks that set off a speaker's exact words (page 166). |
| **regular verb** | A verb that forms the past tense by adding -d or -ed to its present tense form (page 70). |
| **revise** | To improve what was written previously (page 216). |
| **rhyme** | Repeated sounds at the end of words (page 290). |
| **rhythm** | The beat in a line of poetry (page 290). |
| **run-on sentence** | Two or more sentences that are not correctly separated from each other (page 154). |
| **sentence** | A group of words that expresses a complete thought (pages 18 and 130). |
| **sentence fragment** | A group of words that is punctuated like a sentence but does not express a complete thought. Often it is missing a subject and/or a verb (page 152). |
| **setting** | Where and when the action of a story takes place (pages 22 and 242). |

| | |
|---|---|
| **signature of a letter** | Handwritten name that is at the end of a letter (page 302). |
| **simile** | A comparison made between two different things using the word *like* or *as* (page 288).<br>His cough sounded **like** the backfire of an old car. |
| **simple predicate** | The verb in the complete predicate (page 132). |
| **simple sentence** | A sentence that has only one single or compound subject and one single or compound predicate (page 148). |
| **simple subject** | The most important noun or pronoun in the complete subject (page 132). |
| **singular noun** | A noun that names one person, place, thing, or idea (page 56). |
| **space order** | An arrangement of details according to the way they are observed, for example, from top to bottom, from left to right, or from near to far (page 198). |
| **stanza** | A group of lines in a poem (page 290). |
| **statistics** | Facts stated in terms of numbers (page 42). |
| **subject card** | A card in the card catalog that names the subject of a nonfiction book (page 336). |
| **suffix** | A group of letters added to the end of a word to form a new word (page 322). |
| **superlative form (adjective)** | The form of an adjective that compares more than two things. It usually ends in *-est* or is preceded by the word *most* (page 94).<br>**hottest**          **most ragged** |

| | |
|---|---|
| **superlative form (adverb)** | An adverb that compares more than two things. It ends in -*est* or is preceded by the word *most* (page 104). |
| | **earliest**　　　　　**most thoroughly** |
| **supporting sentences** | Sentences that provide details and examples to explain the topic sentence of a paragraph (page 190). |
| **syllables** | Units of sound in a word (page 330). |
| **synonym** | One of two or more words that have similar meanings (page 316). |
| | **smiling/grinning**　　　　**jog/trot** |
| **table of contents** | A listing of chapter titles and their page numbers in the front of the book (page 340). |
| **thesaurus** | A dictionary of synonyms, usually grouped according to ideas (page 334). |
| **time order** | The arrangement of details according to what happened first, second, and so on (page 200). |
| **title page** | The page in the front of a book that gives the book's title, author, publisher, and place of publication (page 340). |
| **topic sentence** | The sentence that states the main idea of a paragraph (page 188). |
| **writing process** | The four steps to follow in writing (pages 26, 236, 237, and 238). |
| | Prewriting—gathering ideas |
| | Organizing—planning the order to use |
| | Writing—putting ideas on paper |
| | Revising—improving what has been written |

# Index

*A, an,* 411
Abbreviations, 162–163
Accent marks in dictionaries, 16, 330–331
Action verbs, 66–67, 415
Adjectives
  adverbs and, 108–109
  for clear description, 92–93, 100, 146–147
  defined, 92, 415
  demonstrative, 96–97, 418
  forms of, 94–95, 416, 424
  proper, 162–163, 396
Adverbs
  adjectives and, 108–109
  for clear description, 102–103, 112, 146–147
  defined, 102, 415
  forms of, 104–105, 416, 424
Advertising methods
  use of experts, 42–43
  use of famous person, 42–43
  use of statistics, 42–43
  use of symbols, 42–43
Agreement, subject-verb, 136–137, 415
Almanacs, 334–335, 415
Antonyms, 316–317, 415
Apostrophes
  in contractions, 172–173, 318–319, 400
  defined, 415
  in possessive nouns, 60–61, 172–173, 399
Articles, 52–53, 411–412, 415
Atlases, 334–335, 415

*Be*
  in contractions, 318–319

  to form questions, 140–141
  forms of, 66–67
  as helping verb with present participle, 72–73, 74–75
  as linking verb, 66–67
*Between, among,* 412
Bibliographies, 340, 415
Biographical dictionaries, 334–335, 415
Book reports, 300–301
Books
  capital letters in titles of, 162–163, 396
  finding in library, 338–339
  parts of
    bibliography, 340–341, 415
    copyright page, 340–341, 417
    glossary, 340–341, 419
    index, 340–341, 419
    table of contents, 340–341, 424
Brainstorming, 222, 416
*Bring, brought,* 407
Business letters, 304–305

Call numbers, 338–339
Capital letters
  in abbreviations, 162–163, 396
  in book titles, 162–163
  in divided quotations, 168–169
  in first word in sentence, 162–163, 396
  for *I,* 162, 396
  in letters, 164–165, 302–305
  in outlines, 352–353
  in proper adjectives, 162–163, 396
  in proper nouns, 54–55, 162–163, 396

in quotations, 168–169, 399
in titles of people, 162–163, 396
Card catalog
  author card, 338–339
  call number, 338–339
  defined, 338, 416
  subject card, 338–339, 423
  title card, 338–339
Characters, in stories, 22, 242–245, 416
*Choose, chose, chosen,* 408
Colons
  in business letters, 174–175,
    304–305, 400
  defined, 174, 416
  to introduce series of items,
    174–175, 400
  in time of day, 174–175, 400
Combining sentences, 148–149
*Come, came, come,* 403
Commas
  in compound sentences, 148–149,
    170, 398
  in dates and addresses, 170–171, 397
  defined, 416
  in direct quotations, 166–169, 398
  after introductory words, 170, 398
  in letters, 164–165, 304–305, 398
  after names of people spoken to,
    170–171, 398
  with quotation marks, 166, 168
  in series of items, 170–171, 398
Common nouns, 54–55, 416
Communicating, 4–5
Comparative forms of adjectives, 94–95,
  416
Comparative forms of adverbs, 104–105,
  416
Complete predicates, 132–133, 416
Complete subjects, 132–133, 416
Compound objects, 138–139, 417
Compound predicates, 138–139, 417
Compound sentences, 148, 170, 398, 417

Compound subjects, 138–139, 417
Compound words, 232, 417
Conjunctions, 118–119, 148–149, 417
Connotation, 32, 46, 417
Contractions, 172–173, 318–319, 417
Copyright page, 340–341, 417
Cross-curriculum activities,
    introduction of
  art, 43
  health, 71
  music, 358
  physical education, 85
  science, 12
  social science, 10
Cross references, 332–333, 417

Declarative sentences, 130, 140, 417
Definitions of words, 330–331
Demonstrative adjectives, 96–97, 418
Demonstrative pronouns, 86–87, 418
Denotation, 32, 418
Description, writing
  of event, 200–201
  of person, 198–199, 286–287
  of place or object, 198–199, 286–287
Descriptive paragraphs, 196–197,
    198–199, 200–201, 202–203, 418
Dialogue
  defined, 24–25, 418
  in plays, 24–25
  in stories, 262–263
  writing, 24–25
Dictionaries
  accent marks, 16, 330–331
  alphabetical order in, 160, 194, 330
  defined, 330–331, 418
  definitions in, 220, 330–331, 344
  entry words in, 330–331, 418
  guide words in, 144, 419
  idioms in, 208
  parts of speech in, 78, 104, 124, 330
  pronounciation key, 16

syllabication in, 16, 180, 330–331
word origins in, 64, 256
Directions, giving and writing, 34–37, 47
Direct objects, 134–135, 138–139, 418
Direct quotations, 166–167, 399
Discussions, 8–9
Divided quotations, 168–169, 399
*Do, did, done,* 403
*Does, do,* 401

*Eat, ate, eaten,* 402
Editing. *See* Revising.
Encyclopedias
alphabetical order in, 332–333
articles in, 332–333
cross-references in, 332–333
defined, 332, 418
guide words in, 332–333, 419
index to, 332–333
volumes of, 332–333
End marks
exclamation marks, 130–131
periods, 130–131
question marks, 130–131, 140–141
Entry words
in dictionary, 332–333, 418
in encyclopedia, 332–333
Envelopes, addressing, 164–165
Exclamation marks
after exclamatory sentences, 130–131, 397
after interjections, 120–121, 420
with quotation marks, 166–167, 399
Exclamatory sentences, 130–131, 397

Fact and opinion, 40–41
Factual paragraphs
choosing topics for, 212–213, 219
defined, 210, 418
order in, 214–215
topic sentence in, 210
*Fall, fell, fallen,* 408

First draft, 224–225, 248–249, 418
Friendly letters, 164–165, 302–303
Future tense of verbs, 68–69, 419

*Give, gave, given, 410*
Glossary, 340, 419
*Go, went, gone,* 405
Guide words, 144, 332–333, 419

*Has, have, had,* 402
Helping verbs, 72–73, 419
Homophones, 316–317, 419
Hyphens, 180–181

Idioms, 208, 419
Imperative sentences, 130–131, 419
Indention, 186
Index, 340–341, 419
Indirect objects, 134–135, 138–139, 420
Information, finding
in books, 328–329
in libraries, 338–339
in newspapers, 328–329
in reference books, 316–317, 330–335
Interjections, 120–121, 420
Interrogative sentences, 130–131,
140–141, 420
Irregular verbs, 70–71, 74–75, 420
*Is, are,* 401
*Its, it's,* 402

*Know, knew, known, 406*

*Let, leave, 413*
Letters, writing
business
body, 304–305
closing, 304–305
greeting, 304–305
heading, 304–305
inside address, 304–305
signature, 304–305

capital letters in, 164–165, 396
colons in, 174, 304–305, 400
commas in, 164–165, 302–303,
    304–305, 397–398
envelope, 164–165, 302–303
friendly
    body, 164–165, 302–303
    closing, 164–165, 302–303
    greeting, 164–165, 302–303
    heading, 302–303
    signature, 164–165, 302–303
Libraries
    arrangement of, 334–335
    call numbers in, 338–339
    card catalog in, 338–339
    reference books in
        almanacs, 334–335
        atlases, 334–335
        biographical dictionaries, 334–335
        dictionaries, 330–331
        encyclopedias, 332–333
        thesauruses, 334–335
Linking verbs, 66–67, 420
Listening, 4–5, 8–9
Lyric poetry, 290–291, 292–293, 420

Metaphors, 288–289, 420
Mystery stories
    characters in, 258–259, 260–261,
        262–263
    clues in, 260–261
    defined, 258–259
    dialogue in, 262–263
    organizing, 260–261
    plot in, 260–261, 268–269
    prewriting, 258–259
    revising, 268–269, 270–271, 272–273,
        276–277
    writing, 262–263

Narrative poetry, 290–291, 420
Note-taking, 12–13, 348–349

Nouns
    articles and, 52–53
    common, 54–55, 416
    defined, 52–53, 420
    irregular forms of, 58–59
    plural, 56–59
    possessive forms of, 60–61, 172, 421
    proper, 54–55, 162, 422
    singular, 56–57

Objects
    compound, 138–139, 417
    direct, 134–135, 138–139, 418
    indirect, 134–135, 138–139, 420
Opinion and fact. See Fact and opinion.
Order in paragraphs, 198–201, 214–215
Origins of words, 64, 256, 310
Organizing, as a step in the writing
        process
    defined, 26, 237, 424
    for mystery stories, 260–261
    for stories, 246–247
Outlines, 352–353, 354–355, 420

Paragraphs
    choosing topics for, 210–211, 212–213,
        222–223, 224–225
    defined, 20, 186, 420
    descriptive, 196–203, 418
    details in, 190–191
    factual, 210–215, 418
    first drafts of, 202–203, 216–217
    indention of, 186–187
    keeping to the subject, 188–189
    main idea in, 20, 186, 188
    order in, 198–201, 214–215
    revising, 202–203, 216–217
    supporting sentences, 190–191, 193, 424
    topic sentence in, 188–189, 424
Parts of speech
    adjectives, 92–97, 415

adverbs, 102–105, 108–109, 415
conjunctions, 118–119, 417
interjections, 120-121, 420
nouns, 52–61, 420
prepositions, 114–117, 420
pronouns, 80–87, 422
verbs, 66–75, 78
Past participles, 72–73, 74–75, 421
Past tense of verbs, 68–69, 421
Periods
    after abbreviations, 162–163, 397
    to end sentences, 130–131, 166–167,
        397
Personal pronouns, 82–83, 421
Plot, 22–23, 242–243, 246–247
Plural nouns
    defined, 56
    irregular forms of, 58–59
    possessive forms of, 60–61, 172
    regular forms of, 56–57
Poems
    "Abraham Lincoln 1809–1865,"
        252–253
    "Afternoon on a Hill," 50
    "A-Ha!" 150–151
    "Brontosaurus," 184
    "Calendar," 128
    "City Rain," 290
    "A Horse is a Horse," 2
    "The Horses," 336–337
    "How to Eat a Poem," 292
    "Loneliness," 294
    "Mice," 38
    "A Narrow Fellow in the Grass,"
        106–107
    "Oh Yeah," 314
    "Raccoon," 274–275
    "Sleet Storm," 204–205
    "The Snowflake," 284
Poetry
    defined, 290
    lyric, 290–293, 420

narrative, 290–291, 420
    rhyme in, 290–291, 422
    rhythm in, 290–291, 422
    similes and metaphors in, 288, 292–293
    stanzas in, 290–291, 423
    writing, 292–293
Points of view, 8–9, 270–271
Positive form of adjectives, 94–95, 421
Positive form of adverbs, 104–105, 421
Possessive nouns, 60–61, 172, 421
Possessive pronouns, 84–85, 421
Precise words, use of, 270–271
Predicates
    before subjects in questions, 140–141
    complete, 132–133, 416
    compound, 132–133
    defined, 132
    simple, 132–133
    subjects and, 132–133
Prefixes, 298, 320–321, 326, 421
Prepositional phrases
    defined, 114, 421
    for clear description, 116–117
    prepositions in 114–115
Prepositions, 114–115
Present participles, 72–73, 74–75, 421
Present tense of verbs, 68–69, 422
Prewriting, as a step in the writing
        process
    defined, 26, 236–237, 424
    for mystery stories, 258–259
    for stories, 242–243, 244–245
Problem-solving. See Thinking skills.
Process of writing. See also Writing
        process.
    defined, 23, 236–238, 424
    organizing
        for mystery stories, 260–261
        for stories, 246–247
    prewriting
        for mystery stories, 258–259
        for stories, 242–243, 244–245

writing
for mystery stories, 262–263
for stories, 248–249
revising
for mystery stories, 268–269,
270–271, 272–273, 276–277
for stories, 250–251
Pronouns
defined, 80–81, 422
demonstrative, 86–87, 418
personal
defined, 82–83, 421
as objects, 82–83
as subjects, 82–83
possessive
defined, 84–85, 421
plural, 84–85
singular, 84–85
used alone, 84–85
used with noun, 84–85
Pronunciation key, 16
Proofreading, 228–229, 272–273, 422
Proofreading marks, 176–177, 228–229
Proper adjectives, 162–163
Proper nouns, 54–55, 162–163, 422
Punctuation marks
apostrophes, 172–173, 399–400, 415
colons, 174–175, 400, 416
commas, 170–171, 397–398, 416
exclamation marks, 130–131, 397
periods, 130–131, 397
question marks, 130–131, 140–141,
166–167, 397
quotation marks, 166–167, 168–169
Publication, revising for, 276–277

Question marks, 130–131, 166–167
Questions, word order in, 140–141
Quotation marks
defined, 422
in divided quotations, 168–169
with exact words of speaker, 166–167

other punctuation with, 166–169
Reference books
almanacs, 334–335, 415
atlases, 334–335, 415
biographical dictionaries, 334–335, 415
dictionaries, 330–331, 418
encyclopedias, 332–333, 418
thesauruses, 334–335, 424
Reports
choosing a topic, 346–347
organizing, 350–351, 352–353
outlining, 352–353
recording information, 348–349
revising, 356–357
writing, 354–355
Revising, as step in the writing process
defined, 26, 238, 424
for mystery stories, 268–269, 270–271,
272–273, 276–277
for stories, 250–251
Rhyme, 290–291, 422
Rhythm, 290–291, 422
*Ring, rang, rung,* 409
*Run, ran, run,* 404
Run-on sentences, 154–155, 422

*See, saw, seen,* 405
Senses, use of in writing, 4–5, 286–287
Sentence combining. *See* Combining
sentences.
Sentence fragments, 152–153, 422
Sentences
capitalizing first word in, 162–163,
396
combining, 148–149
of command, 130–131
complete, 18–19
complete predicates in, 132–133, 148,
416
complete subjects in, 132–133
compound, 148–149, 417
compound objects in, 138–139, 417

compound predicates in, 138–139,
 148, 417
compound subjects in, 138–139, 148,
 417
declarative, 130–131, 140–141, 417
defined, 18, 130, 422
direct objects in, 134–135
end marks in, 130–131, 397
exclamatory, 130–131, 418
fragments, 152–153, 422
imperative, 130–131, 419
indirect objects in, 134–135, 420
interrogative, 130–131, 420
objects in, 134–135
as questions, 130–131, 140–141
run-on, 154–155, 422
simple predicates in, 132–133, 148,
 423
simple subjects in, 132–133, 148, 423
as statements, 140–141
subject-verb agreement in, 136–137,
 415
Setting for stories, 22–23, 242–243, 422
Similes, 288–289, 423
Space order, 198–199, 423
Stanzas in poetry, 290–291, 423
Stories
 characters in, 22–23, 230–231
 defined, 22, 240, 255
 dialogue in, 24–25, 262–263
 mystery, 258–263, 268–273, 276–277
 plots of, 22–23, 242–243, 254
 revising, 250–251, 268–273, 276–277
 setting in, 22–23, 242–243
 writing, 248–249
Subjects
 agreement with verb, 136–137
 complete, 132–133
 compound, 138–139, 417
 defined, 132
 predicates and, 132–133
 simple, 132–133, 423

Subject-verb agreement, 136–137, 415
Suffixes, 320–321, 423
Superlative form of adjectives, 94–95,
 423
Superlative form of adverbs, 104–105,
 424
Synonyms, 316–317, 325, 424

Table of contents, 340–341, 424
Talks, giving, 10–11
Telephone messages, 306–307
Tense. *See* Verbs.
*Their, there, they're,* 413
Thesauruses, 316, 334–335, 424
Thinking skills, introduction of
 classifying, 37
 comparing and contrasting, 18
 evaluating, 8
 inferring, 4
 questioning, 29
 sequencing, 15
 synthesizing, 15
*Think, thought,* 409
*Throw, threw, thrown,* 406
Time of day, 174–175
Time order, 200–201, 214–215, 424
Title page, 340–341, 424
Titles, writing
 of books, 162–163, 396
 of people, 162–163, 396
*To, too, two,* 414
Topics
 choosing, 212–213, 222–223
 defined, 222
 developing, 224–225
Topic sentence, 20, 188–189, 210–211,
 424

Usage
 *a, an,* 411
 *between, among,* 412
 *bring, brought,* 407

*choose, chose, chosen,* 408
*come, came, come,* 403
*do, did, done,* 403
*does, do,* 401
*eat, ate, eaten,* 402
*fall, fell, fallen,* 408
*give, gave, given,* 410
*go, went, gone,* 405
*has, have, had,* 402
pronouns, 411
*is, are,* 401
*its, it's,* 412
*know, knew, known,* 406
*let, leave,* 413
*ring, rang, rung,* 409
*run, ran, run,* 404
*see, saw, seen,* 405
*their, there, they're,* 413
*think, thought,* 409
*throw, threw, thrown,* 406
*to, too, two,* 414
*was, were,* 401
*write, wrote, written,* 407
*your, you're,* 414

Verbs. *See also* Usage.
    action, 66–67, 415
    agreement with subject, 136–137
    in contractions, 318–319
    defined, 66–67
    helping, 72–73, 419
    irregular, 70–71, 74–75, 78, 420
    linking, 66–67, 420
    past participles of, 72–75, 421
    present participles of, 72–75, 421
    regular, 70–71, 72–73
    tense
        future, 68–71, 78, 419
        past, 68–71, 78, 421
        present, 68–71, 78, 422
Vocabulary
    connotation, 32, 46, 417

context, 266
denotation, 32, 418
Greek and Latin roots, 325
last names, 63–64, 90, 256
words from other languages, 63, 256,
    310

*Was, were,* 401
Wordiness in sentences, 156–157
*Write, wrote, written,* 407
Writing
    advertisements, 42–43
    book reports, 300–301
    descriptions, 146–147, 196–203,
        286–289
    directions, 34–37
    factual paragraphs, 210–215
    letters, 164–165, 302–305
    mystery stories, 258–263, 268–273,
        276–277
    notes, 12–13, 348, 349
    poetry, 290–293
    reports, 274–277, 346–355
    stories, 22–23, 240, 242–243,
        248–251, 254–255, 260–263,
        268–273, 276–277
    telephone messages, 306–307
Writing, as a step in the writing process
    defined, 26, 238, 424
    for mystery stories, 262–263
    for stories, 248–249
Writing process. *See also* Process of
        writing.
    organizing, 26–27, 237, 246–247,
        260–261
    prewriting, 26–27, 236, 242–245,
        258–259
    revising, 26–27, 238, 250–251,
        268–273, 276–277
    writing, 26–27, 28, 248–249, 262–263,
        354–355

*Your, you're,* 414